CORPORATE ADVERTISING

CORPORATE ADVERTISING

THE WHAT,
THE WHY,
AND
THE HOW

THOMAS F. GARBETT

MCGRAW-HILL BOOK COMPANY

NEW YORK   ST. LOUIS   SAN FRANCISCO   AUCKLAND   BOGOTÁ
HAMBURG   JOHANNESBURG   LONDON   MADRID   MEXICO
MONTREAL   NEW DELHI   PANAMA   PARIS   SÃO PAULO
SINGAPORE   SYDNEY   TOKYO   TORONTO

Library of Congress Cataloging in Publication Data

Garbett, Thomas F
    Corporate advertising.

    Includes index.
    1. Advertising.   2. Public relations — Corporations.
I. Title.
HF5823.G26   659.1   80-15604
ISBN 0-07-022787-X

 234567890   VHVH   8987654321

The editors for this book were William R. Newton and Beatrice E.
Eckes, the designer was Mark E. Safran, and the production super-
visor was Sally Fliess. It was set in Optima by University Graphics,
Inc.

Printed and bound by Von Hoffmann Press, Inc.

CONTENTS

7037632

PREFACE

This is a beat-a-new-path book. For years the most often asked and least satisfactorily answered question in the marketing world has been "Should we do corporate advertising?" Not one scholarly volume has been available to help shape a decision. There has been no place to turn to for the history of corporate advertising, to see its variety, its successes, its failures, what it can do, what it can't, its extravagant pretensions, its solid and economic accomplishments. Instead we have had to resort to what is worse than ignorance: vaguely conveyed experiences superficially remembered, embroidered by our imaginations, all leading to dangerous shores.

Now we have such a book. And I know of no one better equipped to write it than Tom Garbett. He has been, over the years at DDB, deeply involved in the corporate advertising of our clients. So he is not just a student of the art but an active professional, which permits him to temper theory with the hard common sense that only doing instills.

To his natural skill to organize the vast knowledge he has accumulated, he has added an invaluable ability to interpret that knowledge in terms of what must be done to bring it to effective life. He knows that facts are dead things until an original talent adds the persuasiveness of emotion. You must not underestimate that ability. It is rare among academicians who do so much of the book writing in our business.

So you will come away from Tom Garbett's book with a larger and more precise and clearer picture of corporate advertising—one that you can, at last, go to when you feel that history will be a guide. But more than that, it is one that will not delude you into thinking that this kind of advertising is a science and that all you need is a formula to do it successfully. You will get valuable information that will be a springboard for your own talents, which ultimately will be the reason for the effectiveness of how you do your corporate advertising.

WILLIAM BERNBACH
Chairman of the Executive Committee
Doyle Dane Bernbach Inc.

Acknowledgments

The nature of this book, a compilation of the activities of many people in many different departments of many companies, leaves me indebted to an awesome number of people. As far as possible, credit for all material has been attributed throughout the book. But beyond this, there are individuals who have provided support, leads, ideas, and information whom I would like to thank: Joe Belle Isle, Bill Bernbach, Henry Berry, Don Brown, Dr. John Czepiel, Mike Drexler, Peter Eder, Marie Henderson, George Huelser, John Leonard, Ed MacEwen, Joe McParland, Ed Nash, George P. Norton, Tom O'Reilly, Len Orkin, Jerry Reiner, Jack Stradel, Al Viebranz, Denise Wertz, and Dr. Ruth Ziff. And a thank you to Lester Feldman for the dust jacket design.

THOMAS F. GARBETT

INTRODUCTION

"I needed a book on this subject, so I wrote it." That old cleverism is exactly what happened. One of our largest clients, a major corporate advertiser, underwent a change of management. The new chief executive officer requested that its director of advertising prepare a white paper on corporate advertising. Exhausting the corporation's own library, he turned to the agency. We in turn discovered that the last attempt to pull the subject together had been made about 15 years ago, producing a small textbook that had long been out of print. However, a wealth of other material—speeches, articles, and research reports as well as books on peripheral aspects of the subject—was now available. A subsequent white paper was prepared from this material by us for the client. While it was written specifically for the client's needs, it became a popular piece within the agency and was used as background for account groups and client personnel as well.

This book is a somewhat expanded, more leisurely presentation of this material, but it is still written with the intent of being a source for the needy. It is undertaken on the assumption that you must have a need to understand the subject of corporate advertising or you wouldn't be reading this book. I can't imagine a reader voracious enough to pick up and browse through a book entitled *Corporate Advertising: The What, the Why, and the How* unless it was going to further his or her career as either a student, an employee of an advertising agency, or a corporate advertiser.

The subject has not been covered in any advertising courses that we're aware of and generally is a little-understood and almost never studied subspecies of advertising.

There has been surprisingly little sophistication until recently in this "seat-of-the-pants" industry. When we review the many speeches, magazine articles, and self-serving presentations by the various media, it becomes clear that the subject has not suffered from either a lack of opinion or oratory. It has, however, suffered badly from a lack of organization and disciplined thinking. This book is offered as, at least, a pointer in the direction of remedying that lack. The chapters more or less follow the natural subject breaks, which in turn are about the sequence of need that you will find in working on a corporate program. The book, therefore, has simply taken the form of the subject matter.

Staying Current

Efforts are being made to ensure that the latest available information is edited into this book, but like any book on a current subject, it will begin to age and become outdated in direct relation to the speed of change in the subject. The rapid expansion of corporate advertising and what appears to this author to be growing recognition of the need for a more disciplined approach to corporate campaigns suggest that we will see major changes in the state of the art in the next few years. Staying current professionally, therefore, should be considered a personal type of management by objectives (MBO) for corporate advertising practitioners. Here are a few suggestions, not necessarily in the order of importance (the list is not complete by any means):

- Each of the newsweeklies maintains an up-to-date presentation on corporate advertising. *Time* magazine, which refers to it as "strategic advertising," can offer a wealth of material in this area, including special effectiveness studies. It also conducts periodic corporate communication workshops. Each magazine makes an effort to acquire case histories. While these have been laundered to a high point of purity, they are nevertheless interesting and worth reading.

- The Association of National Advertisers (ANA) is another source of case histories. Again, while not of true case-study quality, the histories are worthwhile. They have been provided in the form of speeches given by invited speakers to the annual ANA Corporate Advertising Workshop presented in the fall in New York. The quality varies a good deal from speaker to speaker, but many new ideas have surfaced in the industry for the first time at these sessions. You'll have to belong to the ANA or know a member to get them.

- *Fortune* magazine conducts a highly selective seminar each year among leaders of some of America's major corporations. The highlights of these discussions are featured in a yearly booklet entitled *Crosscurrents in Corporate Communications*. It is very well done.

- *Business Week*'s principal contribution to staying current is the product itself. For a number of good reasons, this is one of the magazines of choice for virtually everyone's corporate program. As such, it is well worth following for the ads alone, but, in addition, *Business Week* occasionally has articles on the subject of corporate communications. It also maintains a list of current corporate magazine advertisers.

- The *Public Relations Journal* publishes extensive material on the subject and, in fact, devotes its November issue to corporate advertising. It conducts yearly studies on the trends in the industry, including advertising appropriations broken down by the six major media. It also monitors the changing objectives that industry expects corporate advertising to fulfill. This periodical is a must.

- *Madison Avenue*'s February and June issues are usually devoted to corporate advertising. They are very uneven, but they present good case histories.

- *The Wall Street Journal,* some large daily newspapers, and the advertising trade media such as *Advertising Age, Media Decisions,* etc., are, needless to say, essential for staying current in the advertising industry in general and not just in the corporate area. Get *The Wall Street Journal*'s corporate game called Pathfinder ©, a clever device for laying out an entire ad program. It is not much fun to play, but it is informative.

- A sourcebook on much of the material that has already been published is available for less than $20 from the Government Printing Office. It's called *Sourcebook on Corporate Image and Corporate Advocacy Advertising.* Compiled by the Subcommittee on Administrative Practice and Procedure of the Committee on the Judiciary of the U.S. Senate in 1978, it is more than 2100 pages long. While much of the material is irrelevant to a corporate advertising practitioner's daily needs, pound for pound the sourcebook is the best file drawer on the subject.

THOMAS F. GARBETT

CORPORATE ADVERTISING

SECTION 1
THE WHAT

Of course you know what corporate advertising is. Everyone knows. But the problem is that not everyone knows all the things it isn't.

CHAPTER 1 WHAT CORPORATE ADVERTISING *ISN'T*

Corporate advertising isn't product advertising. It isn't classified or mail-order advertising, and it usually isn't retail advertising. The name "corporate advertising" or one of its aliases has, at one time or another, been applied to just about every other form of advertising.

Scotty Sawyer, writing for *Industrial Marketing,* points out that corporate advertising is one of the sloppiest terms in the language of advertising. It has been misapplied to industrial advertising, which is addressed to the management of companies. It's been misapplied to public interest advertising and even to political advertising. And there's no sign that this sloppiness will be cured in the 1980s.

So, while it may seem a pedantic way to start, you will discover that it is essential to define terms when dealing with this subject. In fact, definition is a major hurdle for anyone working in the field because there is no agreed-upon term for this kind of advertising. This lack of definition affects the reliability of statistics and causes wide variations in surveys and reports. What one checking service calls corporate advertising, another calls something else. Frequently, corporate ads get erroneously placed in subcategories, creating much statistical confusion.

The very inventiveness of the advertising industry has been a contributor to this confusion with the wide variety of names that it has created. As one name, such as "institutional advertising" or "prestige advertising" (which are very much out today), would acquire poor connotations from its detractors, it would be switched to, perhaps, "identity advertising" or "strategic advertising." Some of this name changing was undoubtedly part of an effort to give a fresh look to an old or uncertain technique. And the technique is very old indeed.

The American Telephone & Telegraph Co. does not lay claim to having started corporate advertising, but the company certainly is one of the oldest users of it. With the possible exception of some "publick notice" advertising in newspapers of the 1800s, the AT&T campaign, which started in June 1908, gets the writer's vote as the real beginning of this whole form of advertising. Interestingly, that ad, which is reproduced in Chapter 2, ran in a list of ten magazines, none of which exists today. John A. Howland, assistant vice president of AT&T, in a speech before the Association of National Advertisers (ANA) Corporate Advertising Workshop in 1977 described the interesting background of this advertisement as follows:

> Why it was run can perhaps best be determined from the language of a call report written by a representative of N. W. Ayer — some 69 years ago — after he had met our people in Boston on an April afternoon in 1908, to talk about the telephone business. He was soliciting Theodore N. Vail, President of the recently-formed American Telephone & Telegraph Company — which was beginning to bring some system out of the chaos of the many small unconnected and often competing local telephone companies.
>
> That evening the Ayer man wrote these words to his home office in Philadelphia:
>
> "The word 'advertising' to the Telephone Company means something different than it does to the ordinary advertiser of commercial products. A great many people look on the telephone company as a big monopoly and they think as they have a monopoly they are going to pursue a "public be damned" policy — but this is not so. The Telephone Company is just as careful of details and wants to please the public really more than some smaller corporations would ever think of doing.
>
> "What we want to put in this advertising, if Mr. Vail should entrust us with it, is to try a series of advertisements which will sink down deep into the hearts of all classes of people who use the telephone — giving them facts and explaining all the problems which are experienced in running a big telephone company in any part of the country.
>
> "After the public has made this trip, they should have a great and more abiding faith in the good intentions of the Telephone Company.
>
> "It would be a slow process perhaps but I believe it is the only sure way."
>
> Well this turned out to be a pretty memorable call report for both the agency and the client because Ayer got AT&T's business and incidentally still has it — some 69 years later [at that date]. And the Telephone Company at that point became one of the industry's most consistent national corporate advertisers.

By the end of World War I, dozens of corporations were going to the public with nonproduct messages. An advertising business textbook of

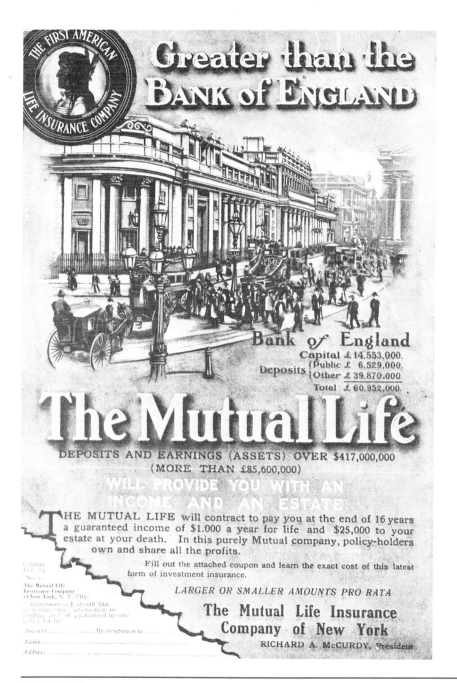

MUTUAL LIFE

"Greater than the Bank of England"

Early advertisements for banks and insurance companies frequently emphasized the solidity of the corporations rather than their products and services. To this extent, many of these early ads might be categorized as corporate. This example from 1904 by the Mutual Life Insurance Co. of New York falls into that category.

From **Door-knocker** Days   To The **Bell**

AMERICAN TELEPHONE & TELEGRAPH CO.

LOCAL AND **LONG DISTANCE TELEPHONE**

BELL SYSTEM

AND ASSOCIATED COMPANIES

THE old punched lanterns and the door-knockers savor now of romance, but only the distance of years can cast a mellow enchantment over the wet cloaks and the soggy shoes.

Amid the comforts of their own firesides, or in their offices, when men to-day pick up their telephones, they do not look down the line of the past to picture the door-knocker—but are we all very different from this door-knocking ancestor in our manifest annoyance at slight delays?

We call a number. We do not think of the *time saved* over the old method of communication. We want the connection *right off*—whether it is a block away, a furlong or a league.

So, like the old door-knocker, we knock the louder—by again ringing the bell or pounding on the transmitter—frequently in our haste undoing a portion of what has already been patiently done towards establishing the connection wanted.

Even in the face of impatience the equipoise of the operator is maintained as well as it can be. The unswerving endeavor of the management of the American Telephone and Telegraph Company and its associated Bell companies is to make its thousands of ex-change operators all measure to the same standard.

There *will* be some girls brighter than others, some with quicker perception and sweeter dispositions.

If you had to subscribe to *six* telephone systems in your locality—in order to cover the field as it is now covered by the one universal Bell system—do you imagine the girl operators would be different?

There *is* a moral to this advertisement—intended for all Bell subscribers and prospective subscribers. It is this:

Treat the girl operator as if she were both a girl and an operator and as if she were present.

It enables her to serve you more quickly—more intelligently—and consequently saves you time.

Telephoning is a mutual operation, with mutual obligations. The maintenance of the most practical, complete, *universal* telephone system that human work can accomplish involves like mutual obligations.

It is the desire of the American Telephone and Telegraph Company and the associated Bell companies to let the public know and appreciate what they are doing and how this universality of service may best be maintained.

American Telephone & Telegraph Company

AT&T

"From Door-Knocker Days to the Bell"
One of the earliest corporate advertisements, it had this objective: the education of the public to a new way of life, paving the way for the public's acceptance of a unified nationwide telecommunication system.

LIFT UP YOUR EYES !

How long ago did Orville Wright circle the drill field at Fort Myer while a few score of astonished witnesses stared open-mouthed at the sight of this first man to fly with wings for more than an hour? . . .

How long ago did the intrepid Bleriot hop in his flimsy, scorched monoplane from France to land precariously on the cliffs of Dover? . . .

How long ago did Graham-White circle the Statue of Liberty, struggling dexterously with his hands to maintain equilibrium? . . .

It seems only yesterday!

Yet in the few brief years since then man has learned a new technic in existence. He has explored the earth's atmosphere, his noble machine climbing on after human faculties had failed. . . . He has skimmed lightly over the impenetrable ice barriers of the polar regions. . . . He has taken in his flight not only the gray, fog-blanketed waters of the North Atlantic, but the empty blue seas of the South Atlantic — the Mediterranean—the Pacific—the Indian Ocean—the Gulf of Mexico. . . . He has soared confidently over the sands of Sahara and the Great Arabian Desert, where only the camel had dared venture before. . . . He has skimmed the terrible dark jungles of the Amazon, and scaled high above the silent places of Alaska. . . . He has flown in squadrons from the Cape of Good Hope to London. . . . In squadrons he has circled South America. . . . *In squadrons he has circumnavigated the globe!*

And in the ordinary routine of transportation service he travels on fixed schedules over airways that streak the skies of Europe and North America. Mail. Passengers. Express. The world is rapidly assigning special duties to this safe vehicle that cuts time in two.

Is there any epoch in all history that has been so sudden in growth from birth to universal achievement? . . . so dramatic in its nature and accomplishments? . . . so rich in promises for the future?

Perhaps the most significant thing in the great accomplishment of young Colonel Lindbergh is that in him the world sees *the first outstanding example of a generation that is born air-conscious!* Just as the past generation was born to steam, accepting railway transportation as an accomplished fact—and just as the present generation has accepted the automobile as a customary vehicle—so does the rising generation lift up its eyes to the skies! It may be hard still for many of us to accept the fact, but it is certain that the aeroplane will give as great an impetus to advancing civilization as did the automobile.

In this firm belief the Ford Motor Company is devoting its activities and resources to solving the problems that still face commercial aviation. In factory equipment, in laboratory experiment, in actual flights, the Ford Motor Company is establishing a foundation for one of the greatest industries the world has yet known. Within the last two years pilots have flown over the established Ford air routes, carrying freight, on regular daily schedules, a distance of more than 700,000 miles.

FORD MOTOR COMPANY

"Lift up your eyes!"
This corporate ad sold the concept of air transportation to the general public in 1928. Realizing that the success of the Ford Tri-Motor aircraft was largely dependent on the public's acceptance of commercial aviation, the company launched this campaign. It was credited by the magazine *Aero Digest* as being a major factor in popularizing flying among the reading public.

Birthplace of Battleships
Guns and Tanks

World's largest iron mine operated by Shell-Lubricated equipment

GREATEST SINGLE SOURCE of raw material for war production is the huge deposit of iron ore at Minnesota's Mesabi Range. More than 60,000,000 tons of ore were taken from this mammoth range in 1941, and this year's production will be even larger.

The fact that almost every shovel, tractor, truck and train on the Mesabi Range is lubricated or fueled by Shell offers unusual proof of Shell's ability to handle the toughest lubrication problems. Nevertheless, Shell oils and greases are constantly being improved to meet the ever more exacting demands of full-time production schedules. The Shell lubricants in use today are the result of constantly advancing technical research and development . . . are giving dependable service under conditions only a year ago considered impossible to solve.

Is your equipment getting this kind of up-to-the-minute lubrication? Call Shell and be sure. No matter what your lubrication problems may be, you will find Shell can be very definitely helpful in increasing the speed and quality of your production.

1941 output of iron ore at Mesabi Range totalled more than 60,000,000 tons, nearly ⅔ of all iron ore mined in the U. S. This is 11,000,000 tons more than in 1940, and the 1942 schedule calls for even greater effort. Almost all the mechanical equipment used to mine and move this huge tonnage is lubricated or fueled by Shell.

War production speeds ahead on SHELL Industrial Lubricants

SHELL OIL COMPANY

"Birthplace of Battleships"
An example of the form institutional advertising took during World War II.

1917 refers to this kind of advertising copy as "molding public opinion" copy. It describes the purpose and scope of the copy as follows:

> Advertising is intended to do three things—to make people do something, buy something, or think something. Copy that is intended to make people "think something" is termed "molding public opinion" copy. It is used for pure publicity—to direct public sentiment for political or legislative purposes, and frequently to advertise an industry.—An advertisement which aims to induce a general impression favorable to some policy, act, or product, obviously employs copy designed to influence public opinion.[1]

Armed with the knowledge of the three things that advertising was intended to do, a graduate of the Alexander Hamilton Institute School of Modern Business Advertising Principles course was prepared to change the face of corporate advertising. He got his chance in World War II. By then the term "institutional advertising" had been commonly accepted and was considered in the advertising textbooks of the period to denote a type of "future action" copy. It was virtually a catchall phrase for all advertising not selling a product or a service. This form of advertising was broadly used during the war. Although few peacetime products were available for sale to the public, some advertisers realized that if they stopped advertising for several years, it would be difficult to regain their prestige after the war. A younger generation of consumers would come into the market unfamiliar with their products. The advertising of the period frequently took the form of telling what the company was manufacturing for the Armed Forces. The graybeards among us will remember the "worthwhile waiting for" campaigns. In many cases the advertisers expressed regret that their products were not available to the public and promised improved products after the war. Some emphasized their research departments and described the better facilities they expected to have in the future.

Gradually, the term "institutional advertising" acquired a connotation of weakness and ineffectiveness as contrasted with product advertising. In fact, it became a put-down description for weak copy, as in "That product copy is too institutional."

Possibly in an effort to shake off these connotations, the inventive advertising industry found a multitude of substitutes for the word:

Identity advertising: Infrequently used by itself. It appears to have had some popularity during the psychology craze of the early 1960s. Today it

---

[1]Herbert F. de Bower, *Modern Business,* vol. 7: *Advertising Principles,* Alexander Hamilton Institute, New York, 1917.

seems to be used only with the modifier ''corporate,'' as in ''corporate identity advertising.'' This term should probably be limited to a description of a type of corporate advertising whose prime objective is one of building basic recognition, awareness, or identity and not used to designate a campaign in which changing attitudes is the paramount goal.

Public relations advertising: Archaic.

Public interest advertising: Infrequent.

Image advertising: Usually derogatory except when combined in ''corporate image advertising.''

Strategic advertising: A broad term used more often during the early 1970s. Impressive but unclear, it may be used as a euphemism as required.

Corporate advertising: Loose as this term is, it is overwhelmingly today's term of choice.

Business-to-business advertising: More correctly applied to industrial advertising.

Constituency advertising: Newly coined by *Business Week*.

The nomenclature dilemma becomes even more acute when we examine another form of advertising called ''financial advertising,'' which is sometimes confused with corporate advertising. The term usually means that an ad is from a financial institution. A bank's advertising for example, may justly be called financial advertising. With equal justification the term may be applied to any advertising addressed to a financial audience. A message by any company to the financial community is described as its financial campaign. The term may also be used when the subject matter of an ad is financial. Thus, any company's ad describing a bond offering which would customarily be called a tombstone ad might, with some justification, also be called a financial ad. But none of these types are truly corporate ads.

Current Corporate Ad Content

Today corporate advertising is being asked to serve many purposes. In fact, the research firm of Benson & Benson Inc. of Princeton, New Jersey, identified fourteen distinct major topics and more than 200 corporate ad subtopics. It made this analysis in the preparation of codes for its systematic tracking of corporate advertising by company and subject matter. This tracking service, called TRACC, was offered by the firm briefly some years ago. While the service is not now available, Benson & Benson Inc.'s president, Robert Bezilla, has indicated that the firm hopes to reinstate it if the current interest in the subject continues to grow. I am indebted to him for the following list, which is the firm's summary of code definitions but which for our purposes is a well-organized, convenient *ad subject list.*

Diversity: Mention of various products, services, or concerns incorporated in the text of the ad or in list form. Lists of subsidiaries or data on multinationality are also included.

Technology: Research, development, or application. The category also includes quality control.

Productivity: Increase in human or machine productivity.

Energy: Technology, exploration, conservation, conversion, energy shortage, or mention of a specific energy source.

Ecology: Natural-resource management, recycling, abatement of air or water pollution, or solid-waste management.

Corporate social responsibility: Grants to sponsor entertainment or educational programs; employment or training for minority-group members or women.

Consumerism: Communication with a company by the consumer; consumer-protection programs (e.g., unit pricing).

Major capital investment: Expenditures for projects, facilities, expansion, pollution controls, or energy.

Financial performance: Reference to earnings or sales; dividend announcements.

Economics and regulation: Comments on inflation, wage and price controls, legislation, government regulation, supply and demand, or the free enterprise system.

Recruiting and labor relations: Recruitment, working environment of a company, references to strikes, or employee recognition.

Acquisitions and mergers: Merger, acquisition, and incorporation announcements and statements for or against tender offers.

Name change or protection: Announcement of a name change or a new ticker symbol; trademark protection.

Corporate activity not classified elsewhere: Information about corporate activities or products (no attempt is made to sell products) not classified elsewhere.

A Special Kind of Corporate Advertising

Until rather recently there was little differentiation between what we are calling corporate advertising and what, for the moment, we will call issue advertising, advertising which is not about the corporation itself but about public issues of importance which the corporation confronts. This subdivision of corporate advertising has spawned a whole new list of labels:

Issue advertising

Cause and issue advertising

Viewpoint advertising

Opinion advertising

Advocacy advertising (if you are for the issue)

Adversary advertising (if you are against the issue)

Controversy advertising (a neat compromise)

Public interest advertising

Public affairs advertising

Public issue advertising

Currently, issue and advocacy seem to be running neck and neck in popularity. Controversy, while the most accurate designation, lost out quickly. After all, who wants to do controversial ads?

These last three variations, using the prefix word ''public,'' all conjure up the implication of public service, which, of course, applies to a very different kind of advertising indeed. Public service advertising is used specifically in the advertising industry to refer to that kind of advertising, either government- or association-sponsored, which promotes causes and activities generally accepted as desirable. By its nature, public service advertising is usually noncontroversial, whereas issue advertising almost always is controversial.

Sometimes a public service advertisement can become controversial and for a while, at least, become issue advertising. This happened to forest-fire–prevention advertising when it was discovered that forest fires frequently were natural and were not necessarily always bad; that, in fact, a certain number of forest fires was indeed part of a normal ecological process. The discovery helped put Smokey the Bear into retirement for a while. It also resulted in copy adjustments to satisfy the opposition. The survival ability of associations and government bureaus beyond their original need through adoptive measures is a fascinating phenomenon. Look at how the tuberculosis and poliomyelitis campaigns were broadened to include related problems once the basic diseases had been brought under control.

Putting public service advertising aside for a moment, we can broadly divide what we are talking about into two categories, corporate advertising and issue advertising. The first, which is the topic of most of this book, is corporate advertising, whose subject is the corporation. The second is issue or advocacy advertising, which is discussed as a separate topic in Chapter 2. It has as its subject a public, environmental, or judicial issue.

To keep the discussion simple for now, we'll just be talking about corporate advertising. Now what is it? A definition is needed. Corporate advertising is defined by the Publishers Information Bureau (PIB) about as well as by anyone else. PIB classifies advertising as corporate when it meets one or more of the following qualifications:

1. To educate, inform, or impress the public with regard to the company's policies, functions, facilities, objectives, ideals, and standards.

2. To build favorable opinion about the company by stressing the competence of the company's management, its scientific know-how, manufacturing skills, technological progress, product improvements, and contribution to social advancement and public welfare; and, on the other hand, to offset unfavorable publicity and negative attitudes.

3. To build up the investment qualities of the company's securities or to improve its financial structure.

4. To sell the company as a good place in which to work, often in a way designed to appeal to college graduates or to people with certain skills.

When we realize all the functions that corporate advertising can be asked to perform, we can readily see why it has been named and renamed over the years in attempts to describe it accurately. And perhaps we can understand management's frequent skepticism of corporate advertising when we look back at the long list of aliases.

And Now a Little Game

You should now be able to recognize a corporate ad most of the time. The ads that follow in this chapter are of different types: corporate, product, financial, industrial, advocacy, public service, etc. As you will see, they are not necessarily the best ads, but they are a reasonable cross section of much magazine advertising today.

See if you can tell which ones are corporate ads. Check yes on a tally sheet if you think that an ad is a corporate ad, or write in the kind of ad you think it is if it's your book.

How did you do? This is not really a test, and there is no passing score. But this little exercise should illustrate the often-subtle differences that separate corporate advertising from some other ad form. Nonetheless, how you categorize an ad is less important than whether the ad fulfills the objectives for which it was developed.

14

Liggett is a group of growth companies with leading brands in growth industries.

Look at them as a group and the trend is apparent.

From our earliest diversification to brands like J&B and ALPO to our most recent of Pepsi-Cola bottlers and DP/Superstar physical fitness products and sporting goods, the pattern is growth.

As it will be with those we are now actively seeking.

If growth is your investment target, look into Liggett. And, if growth is your company's pattern, by all means invite us to look into you.

LIGGETT GROUP

"Liggett groups for growth"

When Liggett Group Inc. runs a corporate ad, it's easy to recognize the ad as such. Anyone who guessed wrong on this one should consider a career change as soon as possible. Note that the ad did not include a pack of cigarettes. That omission not only eliminated the need for the Surgeon General's warning, it also helped position the corporation as having interests in a number of varied growth package-goods categories besides cigarettes.

The companies of your pleasure.

SPIRITS & WINES: J&B, WILD TURKEY, GRAND MARNIER, BOMBAY, CAMPARI, OTARD, FAZI BATTAGLIA, BERTANI, ACHAIA CLAUSS, CROFT, HENRIOT, SOTTO VOCE, VIN FOU. **PET FOODS:** ALPO, ALPO BEEF FLAVORED DINNER, ALAMO, LIV-A SNAPS. **CHEWING & PIPE TOBACCOS:** RED MAN, RED HORSE, VELVET, GRANGER, EDGEWORTH. **OTHER PRODUCTS:** DP/SUPERSTAR, PEPSI-COLA,* 3-MINUTE BRAND, SUPER POP, BLUE LUSTRE, RINSENVAC, BRITE.

*Pepsi-Cola Bottling Co. of Fresno.

29,924 a day.

That's how many domestic cars Americans bought on the average each day in 1978.

Virtually every component of the engine and drive train of those cars was produced by machine tools. Fact is, because metal parts are basic to just about every area of American life, machine tools represent a market that, even with its normal cycles, will never stop growing.

White Consolidated sold nearly $600 million of machinery and equipment to industry last year, including machine tools with such well-known names as Bullard, White-Sundstrand, Lees-Bradner, Reid and Leland-Gifford.

At White Consolidated Industries, we serve two different worlds. Besides supplying the machinery needed by industry, WCI is also the nation's third largest manufacturer of major home appliances. Together, these two broad groups have brought WCI six straight years of record sales and earnings, and annual sales of nearly $2 billion.

Our new information kit will tell you a lot more. For a copy, write Ronald Fountain, Director of Investor Relations.

That's why machine tools are one of the
White Consolidated Industries.
Cleveland, Ohio 44111 **WCI**

WHITE CONSOLIDATED INDUSTRIES

"29,924 a day"

Isn't this a straight industrial ad for machine tools? Not at all. That picture of the company's product in the lower-right-hand corner is just its way of telling you the kind of things it makes. Or perhaps the company is very proud of that particular device. But whenever you're invited to send in for information from a director of investor relations, you can be sure you're reading a corporate ad with strong underlying financial objectives.

"This is reclaimed land. The coal is out, and soon the sheep will be grazing here again."

"We need the land as much as we need the coal. We found a way to have both."

"For centuries, the Navajo have used this land for grazing their sheep," says Ben Sorrell, a Gulf Land Reclamation Supervisor. "Their whole livelihood depends on it, as it has for centuries.

Riches below

"But this land is some of the best coal-producing country in America. So the Navajo nation, which owns the land, leased part of it to Gulf's subsidiary, The Pittsburg & Midway Coal Mining Co.

"Now it's one of P&M's most productive mines. It's producing three million tons of coal a year, and it's being expanded to five million.

Riches above

"It's my job to put things back pretty much the way they were before mining started.

"As much as possible, we try to restore the character of the land, the general contours, and especially the drainage patterns.

"This is where I work: the McKinley Mine, near Gallup, New Mexico."

"When we're finished, it's as good grazing land as it ever was—sometimes better.

"It's a real challenge, getting out the coal we need, without destroying the land, which we need just as much. I'm a Navajo myself, and I'm proud of the way Gulf is meeting that challenge."

Gulf people: meeting the challenge.

Gulf Oil Corporation

GULF OIL CORPORATION

"We need the land as much as we need the coal. We found a way to have both."

It's hard for an oil company today to run any advertisement without its being immediately categorized as advocacy advertising. While this ad might be so categorized, it focuses primarily on the positive programs of the corporation, which are hardly controversial in and of themselves. Its stated objective was "to reverse negative attitudes towards Gulf by demonstrating Gulf's technical competence and its commitment to making the most efficient and socially responsible use of America's energy resources."

HUNTINGTON ALLOYS

"Electricity is a 'hot idea' for furnaces."
Could this be an issues ad promoting the use of electricity as fuel for high-temperature metal work? If you guessed that, you're wrong. It's an out-and-out industrial product ad by Huntington Alloys, Inc., for its nickel chromium alloy 601.

A few years ago, we helped her see in the dark. With this, we can help thousands.

A few years ago, thousands of people suffering with a certain kind of night blindness finally had a glimmer of hope.

All of these people—suffering from the early stages of a hereditary disease called retinitis pigmentosa—were introduced to some special binoculars that let them see in the dark.

Trouble was, these night-piercing binoculars were rather bulky. And too expensive for most family budgets.

Well now, there's a less expensive pocket-sized model.

And this too was created by the people of ITT, with the Army Night Vision Laboratory and the Retinitis Pigmentosa Foundation.

Like the binoculars, the new device contains complex electronic circuitry that amplifies the available light, so it's visible to many retinitis pigmentosa sufferers.

They can see well enough to walk at night by themselves, without anybody's help.

And as for price, we're selling this device at just what it costs to make.

Not that it's exactly cheap. But to someone who needs one, it can be priceless.

The best ideas are the ideas that help people. ITT

If you'd like to help, send your contribution to National Retinitis Pigmentosa Foundation, 8331 Mindale Circle, Baltimore, Md. 21207.

© 1978 International Telephone and Telegraph Corporation, 320 Park Avenue, New York, N.Y. 10022.

ITT

"A few years ago, we helped her see in the dark. With this, we can help thousands."

This was thought to be a public service ad by several people, particularly when they saw the last line, suggesting that contributions be sent to the National Retinitis Pigmentosa Foundation. But it's likely that nice as their gesture of including the foundation's name was, it was secondary to the International Telephone and Telegraph Company's overall objective: to appear as a corporation concerned with improving the quality of life for people in the United States through high technology. That's a classic combination for a corporate classification.

5 MILES A DAY KEEPS THE DOCTOR AWAY.

Mavis Lindgren had been subject to colds all her life. At two she had whooping cough, at 13 tuberculosis, and until middle age she was afflicted by chest colds that turned into pneumonia three times.

Then, at age 62, with her doctor's blessing, Mavis started running because she thought it would help her.

Obviously, it has. Now 71, Mavis says, "After I started running I never had another cold. I've been sick once in nine years. I had a real bad flu. I had it for three hours."

Mavis Lindgren and an estimated 10 million other joggers in America feel running keeps them healthy. It's something Blue Cross and Blue Shield Plans believe in, too. We're convinced that people who exercise and stay fit help slow down the rise in health care costs.

Of course, there are other effective ways to fight rising costs besides asking you to stay fit. To do it, we've initiated many programs with doctors and hospitals.

Second surgical opinion, medical necessity programs, home care, health maintenance organizations, same-day surgery, pre-admission testing—these and other programs are being adopted by Blue Cross and Blue Shield Plans all over the country to help keep costs in line.

We're encouraged. The average length of hospital stays for Blue Cross Plan subscribers under age 65 dropped by almost a day between 1968 and 1977. That may not sound like much. But if the length of stay were the same today as it was in 1968, we would be paying an additional $1,249,869,813 a year. In addition, the rate of hospital admissions for these subscribers dropped by 4.9%, representing $554,938,847.

But controlling health care costs without sacrificing quality is a tough problem. One we all have to work on together.

That's why Blue Cross and Blue Shield Plans are actively promoting exercise, fitness and other health programs. Naturally, we'd like you to use common sense, see your doctor and don't overdo it at first.

But if you're concerned about high health care costs, do as Mavis Lindgren and millions of other Americans are doing.

Run away from them.

For a free booklet, "Food and Fitness," or for information on how your company can view a special film, "You Can't Buy Health," write Box 8008, Chicago, IL 60680.

Blue Cross®
Blue Shield®

ALL OF US HELPING EACH OF US.

BLUE CROSS AND BLUE SHIELD

"5 miles a day keeps the doctor away."

Most people would simply call this a public service ad. It does suggest how to take care of yourself, how to live longer, and how to handle medical problems. On the other hand, you might have guessed that as the ad is coming from the Blue Cross and Blue Shield Associations it is an associations ad. But then aren't some of the things the ad is saying, such as getting a second surgical opinion and especially jogging 5 miles a day, somewhat controversial? Mightn't these statements qualify the ad as an advocacy ad, one which recommends things that are not universally accepted? Or is Blue Cross and Blue Shield really a business? Its corporate interests are best served by having people stay healthy. Wouldn't that qualify this as a corporate ad, particularly with the invitation to tune in to Public Broadcasting's coverage of the Boston Marathon?

There's one last possibility. The clue is in the offer in the last paragraph for a free booklet or "for information *on how your company can view a special film.*" That's it. This could be a product or services ad soliciting companies to sign up for the associations' insurance. The booklet is both a means of demonstrating their concern for your employees' health and also a way of securing the name of someone within the company with whom they can deal for direct solicitation.

This is a campaign with multiple objectives for Blue Cross and Blue Shield.

OUR STREETS NEED A GOOD GOING OVER.

In the past, our nation has prided itself on its road system. But things have changed. The devastating effects of severe winters, heavy usage and inadequate maintenance are now destroying our roads 50% faster than they can be maintained and upgraded.

These decaying roads cost us millions of dollars every year by slowing the flow of goods and services and by causing our cars and trucks to wear out before their time.

With increased maintenance our roads will become safer. And if we can upgrade the worst of our roads with wider lanes, easier curves and improved visibility, driving will be even less hazardous.

Improved roads don't mean increased property taxes.

Good news. Repair and modernization of our major roads do not mean raising income or property taxes. Because road maintenance is generally financed through road use taxes such as those on gasoline and tires. All we need do is make sure road user fees keep pace with inflation.

This is where you come in —by letting your lawmakers know where you stand on preserving our streets and highways. The deterioration of the nation's road system must be stopped, before it stops us.

Get all the facts. Write The Asphalt Institute, College Park, Maryland 20740.

THE ASPHALT INSTITUTE

"Our streets need a good going over."
It's unusual to see a corporate ad in less than a full page, and that's not a corporation running the ad. It's an association called the Asphalt Institute. Is it possible that anybody could argue against the need for better roads, repairing them, keeping them from falling apart, and getting rid of the potholes? This doesn't seem like controversial advertising, and yet the fact that the Asphalt Institute is paying for the ad does suggest that it may have a selfish motive. Yes, there it is: "Let your lawmakers know where you stand on preserving our streets and highways." Yes, indeed, that's an advocacy ad if I ever saw one.

The power of technology
is the power to create.
Creating the
Pratt & Whitney Aircraft engines
that are frugal with fuel
is one way
we're using ours.

UNITED TECHNOLOGIES.

Pratt & Whitney Aircraft Group • Otis Group
Essex Group • Hamilton Standard
Sikorsky Aircraft • Power Systems
Chemical Systems • Norden Systems
United Technologies Research Center
**United Technologies Corporation,
Hartford, Conn. 06101.**

UNITED TECHNOLOGIES

If you guessed that any ad that looked and sounded like this was a corporate ad, I'd have to agree with you, particularly when I found it running in *Forbes* magazine. Clearly one of its objectives is to show that the Pratt & Whitney Aircraft Group is going to compete in an energy-shortage environment with highly efficient engines. But the ad would be equally at home as a product ad to a top-management audience looking for corporate jets, except that the illustration isn't of a corporate jet and this isn't how you sell aircraft engines.

Nature is an artist of simplicity. So are we.

Government should strive to improve business conditions, not hinder them. So, Georgia has streamlined its operations for greater efficiency. We've found a way to preserve our natural resources, yet still be responsive to private enterprise. It's our one-stop environmental permitting service. Now you can go to a single state agency for all required state and federal EPA permits. Which naturally makes industrial location and expansion less complicated. And since our legislature is constitutionally prohibited from operating at a budget deficit, you won't have to pay for the fiscal irresponsibilities of others. Simply speaking, we've cut expenses as well as red tape. Creating a healthy, productive environment for everyone. For more information, including confidential site selection assistance, call or write: W. Milton Folds, Commissioner, Georgia Department of Industry & Trade, 404/656-3556, P.O. Box 1776, Atlanta, Georgia 30301, Dept. BW-971.

Georgia

GEORGIA

"Nature is an artist of simplicity. So are we."
This one won't fool you. It was not even placed by a corporation; it was placed by a state agency, the Georgia Department of Industry and Trade, to be exact. It is an example of a whole class of advertising generally referred to as industrial area development or business relocation advertising. Frequently, however, such ads carry the mood and tone of voice associated with corporate advertising.

International Paper Company

has sold its Panama City Mill
and related properties to

Southwest Forest Industries, Inc.

*The undersigned acted as financial advisor to International Paper Company
and assisted in the negotiations leading to this transaction.*

 The First Boston Corporation

March 29, 1979

THE FIRST BOSTON CORPORATION

You probably guessed just from its appearance: this is a "tombstone ad" (the common term for a financial transaction ad), placed by the First Boston Corporation, which handled the transaction. But you might also have guessed it to be a corporate ad from the First Boston Corporation, proud of its role as financial adviser in the transaction. Or you might have guessed that the Southwest Forest Industries, Inc., was announcing an acquisition.

About fifteen companies in the U.S. pay yearly dividends of a quarter of a billion dollars or more.

This year we'll be one.

The best ideas are the ideas that help people. **ITT**

ITT

"About fifteen companies in the U.S."
Is that another tombstone ad? No, that's a corporate ad by the International Telephone and Telegraph Corporation, and one specifically seeking the attention of the investment and financial community.

We've handed out another increased dividend.

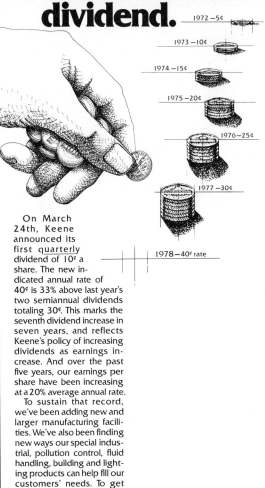

1972 – 5¢

1973 – 10¢

1974 – 15¢

1975 – 20¢

1976 – 25¢

1977 – 30¢

1978 – 40¢ rate

On March 24th, Keene announced its first quarterly dividend of 10¢ a share. The new indicated annual rate of 40¢ is 33% above last year's two semiannual dividends totaling 30¢. This marks the seventh dividend increase in seven years, and reflects Keene's policy of increasing dividends as earnings increase. And over the past five years, our earnings per share have been increasing at a 20% average annual rate.

To sustain that record, we've been adding new and larger manufacturing facilities. We've also been finding new ways our special industrial, pollution control, fluid handling, building and lighting products can help fill our customers' needs. To get the facts firsthand, write for an Annual Report to 345 Park Ave., New York 10022.

KEENE
CORPORATION

KEENE CORPORATION

"We've handed out another increased dividend."

Keene Corporation also believes in a direct approach to investors, with a straight dividend-growth story plus an invitation to write in for an annual report. Whether considered corporate advertising or viewed as a subspecies called corporate financial advertising, such ads fulfill the important role of keeping investors, potential investors, and analysts up to date on a corporation's financial health and activities.

SONG BY SONG

BY ALAN JAY LERNER: OCTOBER 22
ALMOST LIKE BEING IN LOVE
I COULD HAVE DANCED ALL NIGHT
ON A CLEAR DAY   CAMELOT

BY E. Y. HARBURG: NOVEMBER 26
OVER THE RAINBOW   APRIL IN PARIS
ITS ONLY A PAPER MOON
HOW ARE THINGS IN GLOCCA MORRA

BY LORENZ HART: DECEMBER 31
WITH A SONG IN MY HEART
THIS CAN'T BE LOVE
MANHATTAN
BLUE MOON

BY DOROTHY FIELDS: JANUARY 28
I FEEL A SONG COMING ON
ON THE SUNNY SIDE OF THE STREET
I'M IN THE MOOD FOR LOVE
I CAN'T GIVE YOU ANYTHING BUT LOVE

BY HOWARD DIETZ: FEBRUARY 25
I LOVE LOUISA   DANCING IN THE DARK
YOU AND THE NIGHT AND THE MUSIC
THAT'S ENTERTAINMENT

BY OSCAR HAMMERSTEIN II: MARCH 24
OH WHAT A BEAUTIFUL MORNING
SOME ENCHANTED EVENING
IT MIGHT AS WELL BE SPRING
THE LAST TIME I SAW PARIS

BY SHELDON HARNICK: APRIL 28
IF I WERE A RICH MAN
WHAT MAKES ME LOVE HIM
SHE LOVES ME   SUNRISE, SUNSET

A MONTHLY MUSICAL SERIES
ON GREAT AMERICAN LYRICISTS
BEGINS OCTOBER 22
9 PM CHANNEL 13 PBS
HOST: NED SHERRIN

SEYMOUR CHWAST

© 1979 Mobil Corporation

Mobil

MOBIL CORPORATION

"Song by Song"
If you said this is a "tune-in" ad, you were wrong, or at least you were half wrong. This Mobil ad and many ads like it by Alcoa, TRW, the Ford Motor Company, and other supporters of Public Broadcasting are a part of a total corporate communications program. Public Broadcasting shows which are financed by corporations as part of a public relations effort contribute a great deal to the quality of life in the United States. There is no commercial message, of course, just the company's name. But corporations are encouraged to publicize these shows to build Public Broadcasting's audience. At the same time, they strongly identify themselves as good citizens who do things in the public interest. It's a very neat way to merchandise a public relations effort. Ads such as these rightfully belong as important tools in corporate communications programs.

BLUE BELL, INC. (WRANGLER)

"Wrangler Casual Wear"
With that illustration, it's going to be hard to convince you that this ad deserves a corporate label. But if you look at the bottom (oops! . . . the last line), it says "15 years in Malta." That may give you a clue. Wrangler ran this ad to support its long-time interests in Malta in a special section promoting tourism and industrial development of that island in a magazine that it would probably never think of using for product sales.

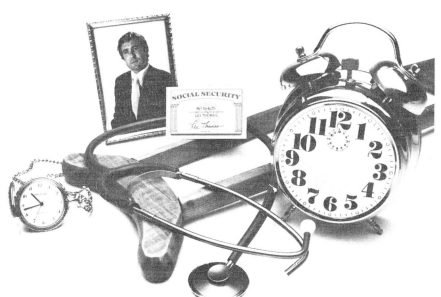

Whatever your time of life... Social Security protects you.

That's why your Social Security Card is important to you. It answers the call in case the alarm rings for four basic needs. If you are disabled, it pays disability benefits. If someone you love and depend on dies, it provides survivor benefits. When you retire, Social Security benefits help you enjoy the things you worked so hard for. And when you reach 65, or you've been getting Social Security disability checks for at least two years, Medicare helps pay the hospital and medical bills.

If you have any questions about *your* Social Security protection, call your Social Security Office. It's listed in the phone book under Social Security Administration.

**U.S. Department of
Health, Education, and Welfare**
Social Security Administration

DEPARTMENT OF HEALTH, EDUCATION, AND WELFARE: SOCIAL SECURITY ADMINISTRATION

If you said public service, I'd grudgingly have to agree with you. After all, the ad is from the U.S. Department of Health, Education, and Welfare. But it wouldn't take much to categorize this as an issue ad. Any skepticism over the Social Security Administration's long-term ability to protect the public might well make such advertising the focus for a countergroup of ads by some association out to change social security legislation. But for now, it's a public service ad, pure and simple.

"A man who drops out of recreation after an active youth is committing slow suicide."
The restorative power of recreation is AMF's ready-made "cause." How ideal for this unique conglomerate's holdings in the sports equipment field! This is a good example of a corporate program acting as an umbrella for many advertised products which might otherwise be unable to afford to reach broad-media audiences.

James A. Michener is perhaps the most gifted and prolific storyteller since Scheherazade. Among those he's told: Tales of the South Pacific, The Bridges at Toko-Ri, Sayonara, Hawaii, The Source, Iberia, Centennial. He works very hard, very long, every day. His latest book, a nonfiction analysis of our sporting life, is titled "Sports in America."

Q. Strong words. What do you mean?

A. I've reviewed every fact I could find on the subject. The statistics are clear: A man who becomes sedentary after a normally vigorous youth is shortening his life by about 18 months.

Q. But as a kid, almost everyone plays baseball, football, or basketball.

A. And they're fine for kids. But our high schools and colleges are shortchanging us in not teaching us other sports we can play as adults.

Q. And as a result, we play nothing?

A. Too often. We sit around watching younger people play our games. We drop out of body conditioning in the critical years. Career pressures, stress, tension dominate our lives and absorb our interests.

Q. Is it the same with women?

A. It doesn't seem to be. Not up until menopause, anyway. But afterward, they tend toward the male pattern.

Q. What do you recommend?

A. With your doctor's advice, easing back into recreation. It's difficult, but it's vital. For example, authorities I respect agree that even jogging can be a big help.

Q. Do you jog?

A. No, it bores me. I play tennis. Winter and summer. Even at 20°, with the snow bulldozed off the court. I need the competition, the spiritual contest, the game structure.

Q. What's the prognosis for a regenerated dropout?

A. Excellent. The body can come back awfully quickly with relatively little consequence. But the longer you wait, the more you lose.

This is one in a series of messages brought to you by AMF. We make Voit Balls, Head Skis, Tennis Rackets and Sports Wear, Skamper Trailers, Roadmaster Bicycles, AMF Bowling Products, Slickcraft Boats, Sunfish Sailboats, Hatteras Yachts, Crestliner Boats, Ben Hogan Golf Equipment, Harley-Davidson Motorcycles.

AMF
We make weekends

macy's presents the 4th of july

fireworks-on-the-hudson

you and the night and macy's fireworks . . . the city glitters, july 4th. We've been preparing for you, New York. Working throughout the year to bring you one of our town's most cherished traditions — Macy's annual Fourth-of-July-Fireworks-on-the-Hudson extravaganza.

Now we're ready. With the rat-tat-tat that, at 5 pm, starts a three-hour promenade of marching bands from 72nd to 105th Streets in Riverside Park. Ready at 9:15 to pour a blaze of light over the Soldiers' and Sailors' Monument — the beacon that officially begins the Fireworks.

Ready with a kaleidoscope of exploding shells projected from five barges in the Hudson . . . a fiery tone poem electronically choreographed and synchronized to otherworldly music . . . directed by and simultaneously broadcast over WNBC-AM Radio 66.

We're ready with a 30-minute technicolor dream that will remain in memory long after the night gives way to dawn's early light. Are you ready? To fall in love with the Glorious 4th all over again? Then come celebrate with us.

catch it in riverside park, along the waterfront, from 85th to 105th Streets. And on the Henry Hudson Parkway/West Side Highway (which will become a pedestrian mall from 8 pm) from 57th to 178th Streets. In New Jersey, see Macy's Fireworks from Edgewater, Fort Lee, Cliffside Park, Fairview and also from West New York.

MACY'S

"Macy's presents the 4th of July"
If it's Macy's, it has to be a retail ad. Not necessarily. Usually you'd be right, but in this case, no. This is Macy's version of a corporate campaign, and the ad is from a series in *The New Yorker.* In fact, one in every four of Macy's regular ads in this medium is a corporate ad.

Our whole life is but a greater
and longer childhood—*Benjamin Franklin*

From the Florence Eiseman Spring collection.
Available at I. Magnin; Junior Bazaar, St. Louis; Children's Boutique, Philadelphia;
Castle House, Cincinnati; Mignon, New Orleans; Marjorie Speakman, Wilmington; and other fine stores.

A beautiful 16 x 20 poster of the above thought and illustration is available from Florence Eiseman, 301 N. Water St., Milwaukee, Wisconsin 53202.

FLORENCE EISEMAN

"Our whole life is but a greater and longer childhood."
Could an ad with that quotation from **Benjamin Franklin** be a corporate ad? No, and it's
not a retail ad either, even though it lists specialty stores where the children's dresses
are available. It's simply an imaginative fashion products ad.

Simulated television picture.

The story of the   cat and the

(Or how to remember how real   the picture can look

The photograph above is a dramatization of something that actually happened.

We wanted to tell you how real we think the picture is on Sylvania color television.

Of course, GTE Sylvania engineers would be happy to do so. Likewise our dealers. And set owners too.

But they could be biased. Besides, we wanted to do it in a way you'd remember.

We did. In a dramatization that's on the air now.

It's a commercial (if you haven't seen it) that starts with a cat at an open window.

He's looking into a room in which a film of a canary

is being shown on a Sylva

The cat stands there moving with the moveme

Silently he drops to th his prey, he starts towar

As the cat nears the s

730 Third Ave., New York 10017

"The story of the cat and the canary."
By its outward appearance you would have to say this is a product ad, but, in fact, when it ran in 1971, it was classified by the advertiser as a corporate ad. It was produced and run out of General Telephone and Electronics Corporation's corporate ad budget. A TV commercial featuring the same cat and canary and telling the same story was run by the Sylvania TV set division as regular product advertising. To tie in its activity with the corporation's, this ad was prepared as part of the corporate program. The point? No matter how sure you think you are, you'll never be absolutely certain of whether an ad is corporate or not unless you know its objectives.

ary.

or television.)

set.

the film...his head
icture on the screen.
owly, as if stalking

s. Snarls. And then

...springs.
We hope you'll remember this little dramatization when you're shopping for a color television set.
Especially if you want a really real-looking picture.

GTE SYLVANIA
a part of General Telephone & Electronics

"A telephone cable fiber as thin as

GTE

**"A telephone cable fiber as thin as a human hair? Gee!
(No, GTE!)"**
Today's General Telephone & Electronics Corporation's corporate advertising clearly
has corporate objectives, specifically to raise the level of awareness of this otherwise
nearly invisible giant corporation. Operating as the local telephone company to less
than 10 percent of the population and selling almost all its consumer products under
other brand names such as Sylvania and Philco, the corporation has very limited identity
through products and services. Its reputation among the general United States
population, therefore, is largely dependent on its corporate advertising. The short,
memorable message "Gee! No, GTE!" is flexible enough to act as the punch line of a
great variety of ad subjects, including this one on fiber optics telecommunications
transmission.

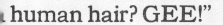

human hair? GEE!"

(No, GTE!)

It's truly a miracle of modern science. A hair-thin fiber, made out of glass, that transmits your voice with light impulses.

Just six of these fibers are used to form a telephone cable. And it can handle just as many calls as conventional copper cable which is sixteen times the size.

The big benefit being that as telephone traffic gets greater and greater (which it certainly will), these cables will be able to handle it without taking up much space under the ground.

"Fiber Optics" (as it's called) isn't just theory anymore. It's actually serving thousands of our customers in California.

Because we at GTE finally took it out of the labs. And put it under the streets.

GTE

Communications/Electronics/Lighting/Precision Materials

CHAPTER 2 CORPORATE ADVERTISING VERSUS ISSUE ADVERTISING

While advocacy, or issue, advertising is not the subject of this book, it is the subject of other current books, and it is also closely related to corporate advertising. Moreover, advocacy advertising can be extremely controversial and may become even more so in the course of the 1980s. It's essential, therefore, before going on to the basic corporate subject, to put advocacy advertising into some kind of perspective relative to the field.

Advocacy advertising is by no means a new kind of advertising. Even the AT&T ad of 1908 reproduced on page 40 had advocacy overtones. The stage was being set for a regulated, but monopolistic, nationwide telephone network. AT&T made certain that people would realize the chaos that multiple phone networks could cause in a city.

But advocacy advertising showed little growth until the mid-1970s, not only in the United States but in countries around the world. A combination of many social forces account for the upsurge in its use. Because it is controversial by nature and because it is subject to misuse, much more will be written on the subject in the future (probably more will be written than is really known). Opinions on advocacy advertising are rampant. Facts are very scanty. But this circumstance won't inhibit most writers: the sociological and psychological implications of advocacy advertising are far too attractive to be ignored.

Telephone service, a public trust

An Advertisement of the
American Telephone and Telegraph Company

THE widespread ownership of the Bell Telephone System places an obligation on its management to guard the savings of its hundreds of thousands of stockholders.

Its responsibility for so large a part of the country's telephone service imposes an obligation that the service shall always be adequate, dependable and satisfactory to the user.

The only sound policy that will meet these obligations is to continue to furnish the best possible service at the lowest cost consistent with financial safety.

There is then in the Bell System no incentive to earn speculative or large profits. Earnings must be sufficient to assure the best possible service and the financial integrity of the business. Anything in excess of these requirements goes toward extending the service or keeping down the rates.

This is fundamental in the policy of the company.

The Bell System's ideal is the same as that of the public it serves—the most telephone service and the best, at the least cost to the user. It accepts its responsibility for a nation-wide telephone service as a public trust.

AT&T

"Telephone service, a public trust"
This ad from 1908 would be categorized as issue, advocacy, or controversy advertising. Back then it was considered simply an ad explaining the American Telephone & Telegraph Co.'s point of view. The Bell System was probably the first corporate advertiser and has certainly been one of the most consistent users of this technique.

One Last Definition

In the many attempts to define this form of advertising, whether it is called advocacy, adversary, issue, or even propaganda advertising, the key words are ``controversial issue.'' The element of controversy seems to be worthy, in fact, of use as the base for the definition. This element of controversy is also the reason that this type of advertising is receiving widespread attention from various groups, that it is being suggested as a subject for further government regulation, and that it should be given great consideration before it is made a part of any corporate communications program.

Albert Stridsberg, associate professor at the New York University Graduate School of Business Administration, editor of the quarterly *Advertising World* and the new *Corporate Advertising Newsletter,* suggested a very workable definition in his book *Controversy Advertising:*

> Controversy Advertising: Any kind of paid public communication or message, from an identified source and in a conventional medium of public advertising, which presents information or a point of view bearing on a publicly recognized controversial issue.[1]

While the professor's definition is excellent, his term ``controversy advertising'' is unfortunate. As pointed out in Chapter 1, this is not a term that either an advertiser or an agency would like to attach to its efforts. Stirring up much controversy at the moment is S. Prakash Sethi, who prefers to use the term ``advocacy advertising.'' Dr. Sethi is director of the Center for Research in Business and Social Policy at the University of Texas in Dallas. His book *Advocacy Advertising and Large Corporations* was released within weeks of Stridsberg's book. He describes advocacy as

> part of a genre of advertising known as corporate image, or institutional, advertising. It is concerned with the propagation of ideas and a lucidation of controversial social issues of public importance in a manner that supports the position and interests of the sponsor while expressly denying the accuracy of facts and down-grading the sponsor's opponents.[2]

If anything, his definition seems more controversial for what he calls advocacy advertising than Stridsberg's definition is for what he calls controversy advertising.

The fact is that the controversial aspects of this type of advertising are accepted by sponsors as unfortunate but necessary because of the importance of the issue to their company. Corporate sponsors of this type of ad

---

[1]Albert Stridsberg, *Controversy Advertising,* based on a worldwide study sponsored by the International Advertising Association and published by Hastings House, Publishers, Inc., New York, 1977, p. 18.

[2]Lexington Books, Lexington, Mass., 1977, p. 7.

The winner of World War III

A nuclear war, if it comes, will not be won by the Americans. It will not be won by the Russians. And although it has been so ordained by Mao Tse-tung, it will not be won by the Chinese.

The winner of World War III will be the cockroach.

"Let a man absorb 600 roentgens [of radiation] and he perishes soon and miserably," says Dr. H. Bentley Glass, a leading biologist, "but 100,000 roentgens may not discomfort an insect in the least."

"The cockroach, a venerable and hardy species, will take over the habitations of the foolish humans, and compete only with other insects or bacteria."

If the cockroaches knew what was going on in Vietnam, if they realized how close to nuclear war the foolish humans have got themselves, they would be descending on the better neighborhoods to choose from the homes that may soon become available. In the United States. In the Soviet Union. In China. In Europe.

A few observations about Vietnam:

1. It has become a war that nobody can win.

2. The South Vietnamese, whom everybody is so anxious to save, are being destroyed in the process. (With friends like that, they don't need enemies.)

3. It has become quite apparent, in Santo Domingo as well as in South Vietnam, that the United States cannot be the world's self-appointed policeman. It just doesn't work.

There is no easy way out of the mess in Vietnam. But we think there is still time to take constructive steps:

We ask the President to stop the bombing of North Vietnam, and to negotiate with all the parties concerned, *including the people we are fighting—the Vietcong.* The negotiations must provide that the people of Vietnam be free to determine their own future.

We realize of course that the United States cannot just talk to itself in Vietnam. We have urged, and will continue to urge the Vietcong and North Vietnam to show a willingness to negotiate under neutral auspices.

If you think this makes sense, if you think this is closer to what you voted for in the last election, then do something about it.

Write or wire the President today, and send copies to your Senators. (Many of them are more worried than they are admitting in public.)

And if you can't stand the thought of the cockroach taking over the world, send a contribution to SANE so that we can afford to run this advertisement in other cities.

Nat'l. Committee for a SANE Nuclear Policy
17 East 45th Street, New York, N.Y. 10017
__ Here is $ ___ for your work.
__ Please send me more information on SANE.
Name _____
Address _____
City _____ State _____

SANE

"The Winner of World War III"

Controversial ads are frequently run by citizen groups, unions, and politicians. They are by no means a corporation's exclusive tool. This ad appeared in 1962 for the National Committee for a SANE Nuclear Policy. Prophetic in its early warning, it not only attacked the war in Vietnam but also advocated a nuclear policy that would confine the radiation dangers to their then-limited levels. The copywriter was Dave Reider; the art director, Lenny Sirowitz.

"Everybody's organized but the people."

John Gardner asks you to join him in forming a mighty "Citizen's Lobby," concerned not with the advancement of special interests but with the well-being of the nation.

I know that many of you share my concern over what is happening to our country.

That is why I am coming to you; to ask you to join me in forming a new, independent, non-partisan organization that could be an effective force in rebuilding America.

It will be known as Common Cause.

It will not be a third party, but a third force in American life, deriving its strength from a common desire to solve the nation's problems and revitalize its institutions of government.

Wherever you touch the public process in this country today, almost without exception, you will find a failure of performance.

The air we breathe is foul. The water we drink is impure. Our public schools are in crisis. Our courts cry out for reform. Race conflict is deepening. Unemployment is rising. The housing shortage has driven rents through the roof.

The things that government is supposed to do, it is not doing. The things it is not supposed to do—interfering with the lives and liberties of its citizens—it is doing.

How we can work together in Common Cause.

The first thing Common Cause will do is to assist you to speak and act in behalf of legislation designed to solve the nation's problems. We will keep you up to date on crucial issues before Congress. We will suggest where and where to bring pressure to bear.

Common Cause is an outgrowth of the Urban Coalition Action Council. Operating under a governing board of extraordinary diversity (mayors, leaders from business, labor, minority and religious groups), the Action Council proved to be astonishingly effective in influencing major legislation.

So we know from first hand experience that citizen action can get results.

I shall not attempt to list here all the issues with which Common Cause will be concerned.

We believe there is great urgency in ending the Vietnam war now. We believe there must be a major reordering of national priorities, and that the Government cannot go on spending $200,000,000 a day for "national defense". We believe the problems of poverty and race must be among our first concerns. We will call for new solutions in housing, employment, education, health, consumer protection, environment, family planning, law enforcement and the administration of justice.

We intend to take the phrase "Common Cause" seriously. The things that unite us as a people are more important than the things that divide us. No particular interest group can prosper for long if the nation is disintegrating. Every group must have an overriding interest in the well-being of the whole society.

One of our aims will be to revitalize politics and

After spending the last 5 years in Washington as Secretary of Health, Education & Welfare and as Chairman of the Urban Coalition, John Gardner is convinced that only an aroused and organized citizenry can revitalize "The System" and change the nation's disastrous course.

government. The need is great. State governments are mostly feeble. City government is archaic. The Congress of the United States is in grave need of overhaul. The parties are virtually useless as instruments of the popular will. We can no longer accept such obsolescence.

Most parts of the system have grown so rigid that they cannot respond to impending disaster. They are so ill-designed for contemporary purposes that they waste taxpayers' money, mangle good programs and frustrate every good man who enters the system.

The solutions are not mysterious. Any capable city councilman, state legislator, party official, or Member of Congress could tell you highly practical steps that might be taken tomorrow to make the system more responsive. But there has been no active, powerful, hard-hitting constituency to fight for such steps. We can provide that kind of constituency.

Skeptics say "But you can't really change such things." Nonsense. The Congress of the United

States has changed in dramatic ways since its founding. Why should we assume it has lost the capacity to change further?

The political parties have changed even more dramatically since the birth of the Republic. They can change again.

Many of you share my anger at institutions and individuals that have behaved irresponsibly. But, if we're going to focus our anger, a good place to begin is with ourselves.

We have not behaved like a great people.

We are not being the people we set out to be. We have not lived by the values we profess to honor. And we will never get back on course until we take some tough, realistic steps to revitalize our institutions. We had better get on with it.

In recent years we have seen too much complacency, narrow self-interest, meanness of mind and spirit, irrational hatred and fear. But as I travel around the country, I see something else. I see great remaining strength in this nation. I see deeper reserves of devotion and community concern than are being tapped by present leadership. I see many, many Americans who would like to help rebuild this nation but don't know where to begin.

I invite you to be among the first to join us in Common Cause.

We cannot and should not depend on big contributors. The money to support our work must come from the members themselves.

We therefore ask you to enclose a check for $15 with your membership application.

If you can afford more, send an additional contribution.

With a large and active membership, we can begin to remake America.

—*John W. Gardner*

COMMON CAUSE

"Everybody's organized but the people."
This ad, which ran in the early 1970s, launched Common Cause. It ran in *The New York Times* and brought in $117,000, which started this citizens' committee group. The copywriters were Dave Reider and John Gardner; the art director was Lester Feldman.

think of it as issue advertising whether they call it that or not. They consider and then initiate this advertising in spite of the fact that, not because, it is controversial.

The Origin of Issue Advertising

Issue advertising, as I prefer to call it, has probably been placed by as many special-interest groups and governments as by corporations. Its origins, in fact, seem more deeply rooted in radical causes in the form of outdoor posters and political-issue campaigns than in advertising conducted by companies. Stridsberg points out that during the 1930s issue advertising was used to express the points of view of labor unions and associations of small businessmen. Organizations like the International Ladies' Garment Workers Union (ILGWU) produced a complete stage review called *Pins and Needles,* which toured the country to promote the cause of the union and the purchase of United States goods against cheaper foreign competition. The ILGWU's present campaign on both television and radio uses this musical-show format.

During this early period it was unusual for a corporation to risk making enemies with controversial public statements. A rare exception was Warner & Swasey, which in 1936 began a series in business magazines, in a campaign that the company continues to this day. Its ads represent a conservative and consistent viewpoint on American economic values and the free enterprise system.

World War II saw a heavy use of government public information in ad form. This was really issue advertising on subjects relating to the war, whether it concerned the planting of victory gardens or reminded people that a slip of the lip could sink a ship. The nearly universal acceptance of the justice of our cause kept it from being viewed as controversy advertising. By contrast, in later years, during the less popular war in Vietnam, the controversy generated by public information issued by the government and by the war itself would spark numerous antiwar efforts, including many paid antiwar advocacy campaigns.

Stridsberg presents an interesting view of the development of the phenomenon of activist advertising which grew through the 1960s and then, under the stimulation of the war, blossomed. He attributes the development in part to the growing number of young creative people who entered the advertising industry from blue-collar environments following World War II. This new talent pool of commercial artists and copywriters and television producers related strongly to the activists and dabbled in the counterculture. These concerned and talented people produced advertising for such causes as the Peace Corps and equal rights legislation. Individual aggressive campaigns, including those on the antirat bill by Burt Steinhauser and Chuck Kollewe and Common Cause by David Reider and Lester Feldman, fought for and against many issues. By the time the war in Vietnam began, this pattern of assembling concerned volunteers and creating gutsy controversial advertising was well established. Many volunteer groups sprang up, such as one led by Yale undergraduate Ira Nurkin and David McCall, chairman of the McCaffrey & McCall, Inc., advertising agency, who assembled the campaign to "unsell" the war in Vietnam. This campaign produced the now-famous poster of a battered and bandaged Uncle Sam with the heading "I Want Out."

Other organizations such as Public Interest Communications, the Public Media Center, the Public Advertising Council in the Public Interest, Projects for Peace, and the People's Bicentennial Commission were formed. They produced high-quality, professional advertising in opposition to legislation which they viewed as detrimental to the environment. Examples included legislation concerning high electricity rates, nuclear electric power, E. & J. Gallo Winery labor practices, and the Sierra Club's efforts to save the redwood.

Willingness to use this form of advertising was rare among United States corporations prior to the mid-1970s. The turning point appears to have been reached just before the outbreak of Israeli-Arab hostilities in 1973. *Media Decisions* magazine[3] observed that the Near East hostilities marked the turning point for the oil companies toward advocacy advertising and a heightened trend among industries toward a new spirit of social accountability. It was decided to explain policies and actions to the public via paid advertisements. The companies started telling what was being done with the plants producing the goods and why. They became more articulate about environmental problems. The corporations found that they had to communicate more openly not only with their customers but also with government regulators, investors, and workers.

As Stridsberg continues to point out:

> This change of direction occurred simultaneously with the eruption of hostilities in the East and the subsequent oil embargo and the onset of a severe recession in the U.S. which had actually been triggered before the petroleum crisis. Also the return of the youth generation, older and more subdued, to the Establishment seems to have coincided with an opportunity to employ their creative approaches in the service of business advocacy.[4]

He sums up the basic causes for the sudden increase in controversy adver-

[3]February 1975, p. 50.
[4]Stridsberg, op. cit., p. 46.

Wonder what a Frenchman thinks about

Two years ago a Frenchman was as free as you are. Today what does he think—

—as he humbly steps into the gutter to let his conquerors swagger past,

—as he works 53 hours a week for 30 hours' pay,

—as he sees all trade unions outlawed and all the "rights" for which he sacrificed his country trampled by his foreign masters,

—as he sees his wife go hungry and his children face a lifetime of serfdom.

What does that Frenchman—soldier, workman, politician or business man—think today? Probably it's something like this—"I wish I had been less greedy for myself and more anxious for my country; I wish I had realized you can't beat off a determined invader by a quarreling, disunited people at home; I wish I had been willing to give in on some of my rights to other Frenchmen instead of giving up all of them to a foreigner; I wish I had realized other Frenchmen had rights, too; I wish I had known that patriotism is *work,* not talk, *giving,* not getting."

And if that Frenchman could read our newspapers today, showing pressure groups each demanding things be done for them instead of for our country, wouldn't he say to American business men, politicians, soldiers and workmen —"If you knew the horrible penalty your action is bound to bring, you'd bury your differences now before they bury you; you'd work for your country as you never worked before, and wait for your private ambitions until your country is safe. Look at me . . . I worked too little and too late."

WARNER & SWASEY
Turret Lathes
Cleveland

You Can Turn it Better, Faster, for Less . . . With a Warner & Swasey

1941

WARNER & SWASEY

Since the late 1930s the Warner & Swasey Company has been calling them the way they see them to American business. This ad from 1941 warns the American public of the dangers in not uniting against the common enemy. They use the fate of the French worker in World War II as an example of the fate of the disunited. Warner & Swasey has run more than 1000 ads on a variety of public issues of concern at different times during this 40-year period. Subjects range from the rights of a corporation to a legitimate profit, overgrown government, the free enterprise system, and concern about rising crime to excess government spending. A look at some of their advertising headlines over the years reflects not only the subject matter but the fierce independent spirit of a company that believes in speaking out, but, incidentally, usually only to other business people, judging by its media list.

- Where do your wages come from? (1944)
- To cure a headache, you don't cut off your head. (1947)
- If you own a hammer, you are a capitalist. (1948)
- They don't keep feeding you cheese after the trap is sprung [on the dangers of the welfare state]. (1950)
- There's no such thing as profit before taxes. (1952)

Business men are like the bashful boy
who sent his girl a valentine but didn't sign it

— and then wondered why she didn't smile on him, next time they met.

It is business whose taxes support America's schools 1½ days every week.

It is business men whose companies and private gifts largely assure the success of hospital and charity drives and pay for the research seeking to cure disease and poverty.

It is business that is pouring money into cleaning up slums, and training the hard-core unemployed.

It is business whose research (and, yes, search for legitimate profit) has so improved home appliances and factory machines that work on them is done better and easier in 7 hours that used to take 12, and used to make us old men and women at 40.

But do you ever see these dramatic facts on TV? Or featured in your newspaper?

Business men say they're too busy to talk about such things. So they "hide their light under a bushel" — and wonder why it smothers there.

Specialized control system development and manufacturing is now commercially available from the Warner & Swasey Electronic Products Division.

THE WARNER & SWASEY COMPANY
Corporate Offices
11000 Cedar Avenue
Cleveland, Ohio 44106

PRODUCTIVITY EQUIPMENT AND SYSTEMS IN MACHINE TOOLS, TEXTILE AND CONSTRUCTION MACHINERY

This Advertisement appears in U.S. News, September 13, 1971; Forbes, September 15, 1971

- But what if father charged for the lemons [with an illustration of a child with a lemonade stand]? (1957)
- How much federal aid did the pilgrims get? (1959)
- The bigger the government, the smaller the people. (1960)
- When they say it's free, look out. (1961)
- The greatest war on poverty is a successful corporation. (1964)
- Wonderful things happen when you let Americans alone. (1968)
- What's right with America? (1970)
- Soft judges make hardened criminals. (1972)
- Sure it cost a lot to live, but look what you're getting. (1974)

In 1971 Warner & Swasey ran an ad not only defending its position in running a strong company-point-of-view type of advertising but warning other businesses that it was time for them to speak up as well. Its headline: "Business men are like the bashful boy who sent his girl a valentine but didn't sign it."

Whether you agree or disagree with Warner & Swasey's ad program (maybe its graphics disturb you), this machine-tool company has carved a very distinctive niche for itself in corporate images with its spirit of American do-it-yourself independence.

A Hog Can Cross the Country Without Changing Trains—But YOU Can't!

The Chesapeake & Ohio Railway and the Nickel Plate Road are again proposing to give human beings a break!

It's hard to believe, but it's true.

If you want to ship a hog from coast to coast, he can make the entire trip without changing cars. You can't. It is impossible for you to pass through Chicago, St. Louis, or New Orleans without breaking your trip!

There is an invisible barrier down the middle of the United States which you cannot cross without inconvenience, lost time, and trouble.

560,000 Victims in 1945!

If you want to board a sleeper on one coast and ride through to the other, you must make double Pullman reservations, pack and transfer your baggage, often change stations, and wait around for connections.

It's the same sad story if you make a relatively short trip. You can't cross that mysterious line! To go from Fort Wayne to Milwaukee or from Cleveland to Des Moines, you must also stop and change trains.

Last year alone, more than 560,000 people were forced to make annoying, time-wasting stopovers at the phantom Chinese wall which splits America in half!

End the Secrecy!

Why should travel be less convenient for people than it is for pigs? Why should Americans be denied the benefits of through train service? No one has yet been able to explain it.

Canada has this service ... with a choice of two routes. Canada isn't split down the middle. Why should we be? No reasonable answer has yet been given. Passengers still have to stop off at Chicago, St. Louis, and New Orleans—although they can ride right through other important rail centers.

It's time to pry the lid off this mystery. It's time for action to end this inconvenience to the travelling public ... NOW!

Many railroads could cooperate to provide this needed through service. To date, the Chesapeake & Ohio and the Nickel Plate ALONE have made a public offer to do so.

How about it!

Once more we would like to go on record with this specific proposal:

The Chesapeake & Ohio, whose western passenger terminus is Cincinnati, stands ready now to join with any combination of other railroads to set up connecting transcontinental and intermediate service through Chicago and St. Louis, on practical schedules and routes.

The Nickel Plate Road, which runs to Chicago and St. Louis, also stands ready now to join with any combination of roads to set up the same kind of connecting service through these two cities.

Through railroad service can't be blocked forever. The public wants it. It's bound to come. Again, we invite the support of the public, of railroad people and railroad investors—for this vitally needed improvement in rail transportation!

Chesapeake & Ohio Railway · Nickel Plate Road

Terminal Tower, Cleveland 1, Ohio

CHESAPEAKE & OHIO RAILWAY

"A hog can cross the country without changing trains—but YOU can't!"

The transcontinental railroads in the mid-1940s had just announced that through service was impractical. This ad and the resultant heavy press publicity brought about a reversal of their position within weeks. In this case, an advocacy position was taken by one business against the policies of other companies. The ad was applauded and viewed by the press as very much in the public interest.

Starch 1979 Profile of Activists*

Total, United States; index	100	Total, United States; index	100
Sex		**Locality type**	
Male	115	Metro central city	95
Female	87	Metro suburb	108
		Nonmetro	92
Age			
18–34	87	**TV viewing**	
35–54	149	Heavy	66
55+	66	Medium	86
		Light	150
Education			
Attended or graduated from college	218	**Newspaper reading**	
		Heavy	166
Graduated from high school	68	Medium	100
Less than high school graduation	27	Light	74
Occupation		**Radio listening**	
Professional or managerial	229	Heavy	103
Clerical or sales	112	Medium	100
Other employed	66	Light	97
Not employed	69		
		Primary readership	
Household income		Average for all 17 publications studied	144
$20,000 or more	155		
$10,000–$19,999	75		
Under $10,000	52		

SOURCE: This profile of activists is from the 1979 Starch study of primary readership, which included a measure of sociopolitical activity. The study found that 1 out of 10 adults (9.2 percent) falls into the activist category as Starch defines it. This profile is reproduced with the permission of Starch/INRA/Hooper, Inc.

*Activists have done two or more of the following within the past 12 months:

1. Written a letter to a state or federal official about a political issue.
2. Contributed time or money to a political or social action group.
3. Alone or with others visited a public or private organization to make known feelings on a political or social issue.

tising within the past decade as having been a combination of the following:

- Penetration of education and communications training downward into a much broader level of the postwar generation, creating a large pool of talent.

- A sustained period of economic expansion, which encouraged independence, development of adversary opinion, and strong social motivation among youth.

- Emergence of a series of controversial questions (environment, energy, population increase) upon which the new generation of advertising people focus their attention and sharpen their skills.

- A subsequent shift in political and economic fortunes motivating young advertising people to place their skills at the disposition of the Establishment, at the moment that corporate society perceived a significant need to use commercial advertising for expression of its policies.[5]

Why Corporations Use It

Indeed this is how it happened — how, in broad terms, the stage was set for the social phenomenon of activist advertising. But is this explanation sufficient to answer the question of why corporations became so deeply involved? Why did corporations begin to take on the tools used largely by pressure and radical groups up to that time? Why did they decide to leave the relatively safe anonymity of most corporate communication programs, which avoid making enemies at all costs, for this new, highly visible posture and knowingly invite attacks from many publics?

Make no mistake about it. Entering into an advocacy campaign is a risky business for any corporation. The advantages must be weighed against:

- Mixed public reaction, including that of some customers.
- Possible legislative backlash.
- Possible regulatory backlash.
- Mixed and possibly strong reaction from college-age and other young people who are the company's source of future employees.
- Possible loss of loyalties among existing employees.
- Mixed reaction from stockholders. (The company can expect to lose a few.)
- Major debates at the conference-board level.

There can be only one valid reason for risking all these negatives. The level of pain that the corporation is experiencing from some particular public issue warrants the risk and the expense, an expense which it knows in advance will probably not be allowed as a business tax deduction.

Campaigns of a size and scope to reach and motivate any major portion of the United States public are expensive. They can cost in the millions, not thousands, of dollars. To justify such an expenditure a corporation must have a deep need and a deep conviction that "this is the only way." Any company which doesn't weigh this situation carefully or enters into a true public controversy just to gain attention, feeling that the notoriety itself will be beneficial, is standing on very swampy ground.

It is true that many pseudo issues that can be handled with relative safety are available. Who would argue over the need to conserve energy?

[5]Ibid.

If the ad is confined to that single aspect of the energy controversy, you're probably on safe ground. But when you leave this issue and move into related issues, as the American Electric Power Company (AEP) did some years ago in its famous "Arabs" campaign, the action can get very exciting. American Electric Power's position in favor of using coal more extensively by modifying pollution regulations and strip-mining codes quickly escalated the issue of saving energy into a full controversy, with the Environmental Protection Agency (EPA) on one side and the company on the other. The company's then chairman, Donald C. Cook, was well aware of this possibility and entered into the campaign fully accepting controversy as the price necessary to fight antipollution standards, which were particularly hard and expensive for AEP to meet with its equipment. Today the corporation continues to feel that overall the campaign and the reaction to it were worth the high expenditure and the notoriety.

It must be anticipated that even a relatively mild issue can, with certain interpretations, be turned into a controversy. Conceivably, even motherhood would not be safe from an attack by a planned-parenthood organization or perhaps by advocates of the equal rights amendment. The fact remains, however, that there is a vast difference in the amount of controversy to be expected from different issues. The important point is to recognize this difference, know who your opposition will be, and anticipate the intensity of the opposition before entering into the program.

There's another reason why so many corporations seem to be willing to endure the adverse reactions that they know will result from strong controversial communications programs. It is their indignation over what they perceive as the lack of recognition of their businesses' contribution to the continuing overall high American standard of living. This view developed from the growing awareness in the mid-1970s of the rapidly declining status of American business in the eyes of the American public. Eric A. Weiss, the public issues consultant for the Sun Company, Inc., traced the decline of public confidence in business in his speech before the ANA Corporate Advertising Workshop in November 1977. Using various polls, he showed a precipitous drop in confidence. In reply to the Yankelovich, Skelly and White poll question "Which of these statements best describes your opinion about business in general?" steadily declining percentages agreed with the statement. "Business tries to strike a fair balance between profits and the interests of the public":

Year	Percent agree
1968	70
1969	58
1970	33
1971	Unavailable

Year	Percent agree
1972	32
1973	34
1974	19
1975	19
1976	15
1977	15
1978	17
1979	19

Similar studies by other research companies produced similar findings throughout the mid-1970s and into 1978. Only now do these attitudes appear to be bottoming out. Recognition of this fact by business executives who saw themselves confronted with an increasingly hostile environment, executives who felt that they were on the side of the angels but were faced with a public that "just didn't understand them," contributed to their willingness to spend substantial sums and take sizable risks in speaking out on subjects of concern to their corporations.

Other factors have contributed to the more aggressive posture:

- A growing frustration resulting from the often-simplistic answers to many complex issues provided by consumer groups, groups which themselves use paid media to explain their side of the story or which are capable of gaining wide media coverage through demonstrations or "happenings" calculated to attract press attention.

- A defensive response to the all-too-frequent exposures of the questionable activities of various businesses. Watergate resulted in improved ethical standards throughout business as well as the political community. Successive exposures of what are euphemistically called "questionable payments" have been galling to many businesses, particularly those with extensive activities overseas, where such payments are viewed as "normal" business custom. Again, this development created a defensive posture in many corporations, which felt that they were being unfairly judged on past activities under the new morality and that the vast number of positive contributions by business were being overlooked.

- A press perceived to be hostile. This view is probably not a fair appraisal, but it is an accepted tenet not only of many business executives but of politicians, movie stars, and others who attract press attention. The fact that good news is dull and bad news is good copy may account for much of this so-called press bias. The business community is correct, however, in thinking that publicity releases and press conferences will not usually give it the kind of exposure it would like to receive in order to express fully its side of the story.

THE ECONOMICS OF RECYCLING.

A major growth industry that grew out of the used aluminum beverage can.

Recycled cans have become an economic source of metal. That reduces Alcoa's consumption of bauxite and coal — both valuable natural resources. Recycling also reduces our dependence on foreign imports, making a positive contribution to the nation's balance of trade.

Environmental Economics

Recycling is making our country a more pleasant place to live. Through the efforts of an estimated 750,000 aluminum can collectors, litter is being reduced and our environment is being improved. In just nine years, the number of aluminum cans

Recycling is vital to our industrial economy. It saves energy, creates jobs, provides a supplemental source of raw material for production, and helps turn the problems of litter and waste into economic opportunities.

Energy Economics

Problems of energy availability loom large for industry as we gear production schedules to the future. Energy requirements for aluminum production are decreasing, and aluminum can recycling is one reason. In 1972, the aluminum industry made a commitment to reduce energy use by 10 percent per pound of production by 1980. With the help of aluminum can recycling, the industry has already achieved 85 percent of that goal.

Producing new aluminum from used aluminum beverage cans saves 95 percent of the energy required to produce molten aluminum from ore. Recycling not

recycled annually has risen from 184 million to more than 7 billion; from 8 million pounds in 1970 to over 330 million in 1978.

With municipal resource recovery facilities, it is now possible to remove and recycle aluminum from the solid waste stream. And recycling reduces the amount of solid waste, thereby relieving already over-burdened landfill facilities.

Social Economics

The aluminum can has become a popular consumer convenience. Today, through the recycling efforts of hundreds of thousands of concerned citizens, it has become an attractive economic incentive to individuals, schools, civic and church groups and municipalities.

Discarded aluminum cans can be turned in for cash at any one of the growing number of recycling centers nationwide — currently over 2500. Full-scale collection programs for aluminum beverage cans were initiated by the aluminum industry in 1970. Since then, collectors have earned over $180 million for their efforts — dollars that have strengthened our economy.

Besides providing extra income incentive and earning opportunities for citizens, recycling has resulted in numerous economic benefits for communities. It has created up to 15,000 new jobs — people to weigh and process cans, drivers to transport them, workers who recycle used cans into new metal.

The economics of recycling means more dollars in the mainstream of the U.S. economy. More jobs. Cleaner living. More freedom from import requirements, and a dependable source of raw material.

only conserves energy, but also much-needed capital and precious raw materials. A facility to remelt recycled aluminum can be built for one-tenth of the cost, and in half the time, of new aluminum refining and smelting equipment.

These benefits, and more, are making the aluminum can an energy-efficient, long-term, cost-effective container.

We can't wait for tomorrow.

▲ALCOA

Can Reclamation. CR-9023

ALCOA

Are recycling programs a public issue? Yes, but it's hard to categorize the Aluminum Co. of America's handling of the subject as controversy advertising. The corporate and commercial interests of a corporation can frequently be surprisingly compatible. When a creative philosophy which does both jobs at once can be developed, the company has a highly efficient program.

In Alcoa's case, the company isolated three major objectives for its corporate ad program:

1. Remind people of the essential role that aluminum products play in their lives.
2. Convince people that aluminum products conserve energy.
3. Increase awareness of the success of recycling aluminum beverage cans.

When the basic story is enlarged to include the economics of recycling, it becomes a strong message to the business and financial community in *The Wall Street Journal* (the ad shown here), illustrating the work of a company aggressively trying to shape its future.

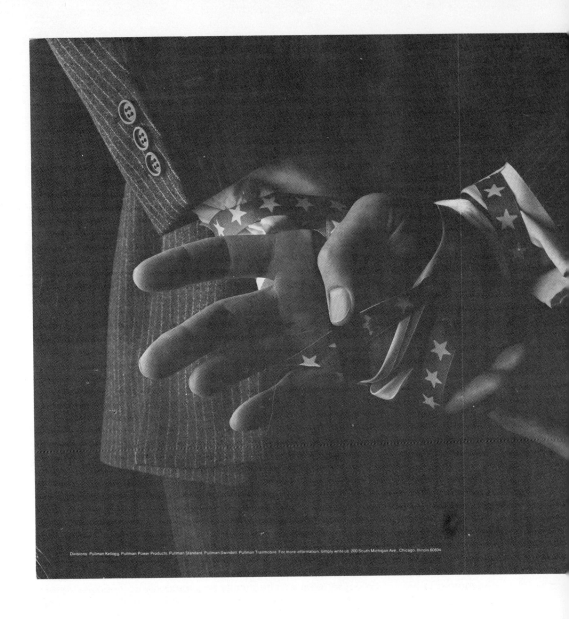

Divisions: Pullman Kellogg, Pullman Power Products, Pullman Standard, Pullman Swindell, Pullman Trailmobile. For more information, simply write us, 200 South Michigan Ave., Chicago, Illinois 60604.

What U.S. business is wearing overseas today.

If you think it's easy to do business overseas today, chances are you aren't carrying an American passport.

The whole world of international business has to fight against competition, distance, language and cultural awkwardness, currency problems and other generalized obstacles to success.

But with an American passport, you also get to struggle against restrictions of your own government. While your counterparts in other countries are encouraged, supported, funded, and actively facilitated by theirs.

Despite it all, the capital-producing creativity of American business has never been equalled by any other system or society on earth.

Pullman's engineering and construction operations, for example, have taken U.S. plant technology to places that you just can't get to from here, with everything from blueprints to bridges to transportation to financing.

Even with both hands tied behind our backs, U.S. business has the strength to prevail.

Cut us loose and who knows what wonders you might see?

Pullman Incorporated

Pullman began this corporate-identity advertising program in 1975. It elected to speak out on issues of concern to business executives, thereby using the advocacy approach but with deep underlying identity objectives. In other words, this might be viewed as a pseudo advocacy campaign. As described by Samuel B. Casey, Jr., chairman of Pullman, Incorporated, Pullman was fairly well known as a name to the investment community for the wrong reasons. More than six out of ten potential investors believed that its main business was still the manufacture of railroad passenger cars, although it had ceased that operation in 1949. In reality, Pullman is a holding company with many different worldwide activities along with a large-scale need for capital formation to finance its plans. It recognized its problem as being one of communications more than anything else.

Instead of addressing this directly with ads about the corporation, Pullman elected to take certain key subjects related to American business, the free enterprise system, and, specifically, the problem of capital formation under today's tax structure and center an ad campaign on these issues. Addressed to the financial and business community, each ad points out Pullman's view on these major issues. In addition, each communicates something about the company's capabilities in the areas of energy, transportation, plant engineering, and construction. The ads relate the need of capital formation and international understanding to the company's business. Pullman's chairman cites a pride in this program and a successful track record in improving awareness of the company among the target audience as well as in generating improved attitudes.

Such advertising is very hard to categorize as controversial although on the surface it would appear to be so. As long as it's addressed to the financial and business community, it is largely business executive talking to business executive, and the message is falling on sympathetic ears. The so-called issues are really devices utilized for their associative and attention-getting values and incur a low level of controversial risk and backlash.

- Escalating world problems that frequently put into conflict the aims and objectives of society's many components. This situation has produced a constantly shifting collection of trade-off decisions confronting the public, the government, and business. Again, the American Electric Power campaign is a good example of this kind of trade-off: environmental concerns versus energy needs. Another example would be the antinuclear debates by power companies that feel they must have nuclear power versus environmental groups that are frankly scared. It is hard for a corporation to sit back and say nothing when it sees strong public sentiments which could result in, let's say, curtailing its nuclear planning. There may well be sound ecological reasons for such curtailment, but isn't the public owed the other side of the story? The company's own figures and studies probably show more clearly than anyone else's the cost consequences of such a curtailment decision. If the company comes out and states what will happen to rates, its ads will appear to many to be threatening. The company could be accused of blackmailing the public. But if it doesn't speak out, it likely will be accused of not fulfilling its utility franchise, which calls for providing adequate facilities to produce required amounts of energy at reasonable costs. There is no easy answer.

- There has been a growing clamor for business executives to ''speak out on your own behalf'' from a number of sectors including the press and some government officials, not to mention many business and trade associations. Even regulators of utilities have on occasion quietly suggested to companies that they take their legitimate story to the public, their constituents. While elected officials may well recognize the complex technical and economic facts in a rate case, they are often unable to stand up against public opinion. Public commissions have suggested to business executives that they have to get out and tell the public the whole story — get out and give the public the facts that it has not been getting from consumer or environmental or activist groups.

- Lastly, there are major changes in the way American society is functioning today. A succession of raised expectations has been followed by disappointments in recent years. This situation was described very well by Gene Pokorny, executive vice president of Cambridge Reports, Inc., who also spoke at the November 1977 ANA Corporate Advertising Workshop. He pointed out the phenomena which are summarized here. In 30 postwar years American society had experienced the largest economic expansion in the history of the world; nothing comparable to this kind of advancement had ever occurred. As a result, through this period the average American perceived the American economy as the best there was. It was not an altogether unrealistic expectation by most of the population that its vastly improved lifestyle would continue and possibly would get better and better. A portion of this prosperity was based on low energy costs. The rapid increase in energy rates and the escalating inflation have done much to shake the public's confidence in the American system. So too have the upheavals in the political environment. From the early 1960s on there have been the civil rights movement, a myriad of protests, campus demonstrations, the Berkeley unrest, and then the war in Vietnam, the urban riots of 1967 and 1968, Watergate, Central Intelligence Agency disclosures, and Federal Bureau of Investigation disclosures. The combined effect of these events in both economic and political areas has caused people to call into question their long-held expectations. The result has been a massive increase in alienation, disbelief, cynicism, distrust, mistrust, and doubt.

The bottom line is that a great many people believe that the economy is not working. Why? Who's to blame? Answer: Somebody . . . business . . . "them."

The loss of faith in our system has recently been extended to the shaking of confidence in the scientific community, once viewed as providing near-Godlike answers to all problems. Debates go on between scientists today as to the safety, practicality, and advisability of many products. Topics range from aerosol sprays and their effect on the ozone layer to the long-range, human side effects of chemicals, drugs, and medical procedures. The public, the average consumer, doesn't know whom to believe or where to turn, whether in science, business, labor, or government. Losing faith in the various levels of authority, people have, in a sense, fallen back to rely on themselves. The result, Pokorny believes, is an increased desire for participation in what's going on around them — not necessarily just voter participation, because that too is declining, but participation in the decision process that people think affects their own lives. Pokorny refers to this development as politicalization or democratization of the policy process. In other words, more and more people want to be heard from in the decisions that affect their lives. Among those who want to be heard and want to speak out are business executives, speaking for the corporations that have become integral parts of their lives.

Recent Opinion Research Corporation and Yankelovich studies indicate that there is some hope that business's overall reputation with the public has stopped declining. In fact, some studies indicate that it may be getting slightly better. It's too early to tell whether in reality this is happening. The apparent improvement may simply be a reflection of the decline of the public's trust in other public sectors below the level of its trust in business.

Some people say we must reach "zero" pollution.

But at what cost? And how fast?

At Bethlehem Steel, we work hard—every day—to control pollution. But the cost is high. We've already spent approximately $400 million to clean up a major portion of the pollutants from the air and water we use. We consider this money well spent.

$600 million more

In an effort to meet existing pollution control laws and regulations, we have many more projects under way or anticipated in the near future. These projects are expected to cost us some $600 million over the next five years.

Where does that leave us?

Depending upon how far regulatory agencies go in stringent interpretation of the present laws and regulations, we may be faced with spending hundreds of millions more to try to remove the last traces of pollution. We do not think that this would be money well spent.

Attempting to remove the last increment of pollution involves new and uncertain technology. The attempt will consume a considerable amount of scarce energy and natural resources. And, in many cases, it will merely transfer pollution problems to the power companies or chemical manufacturers.

Is it time for a rearrangement of priorities?

We are faced as a nation with troublesome alternatives. Do we continue our headlong rush to implement some of the air and water clean-up standards that have yet to be proved necessary—or even sound—or shall we give equal consideration to jobs, our energy requirements, capital needs, and other demands for social priorities?

We believe the national interest now requires that we face up to the dual necessity of preserving our environment while at the same time assuring our economic progress.

Our booklet, "Steelmaking and the Environment," tells more about the problems of pollution and what we're doing to help solve them. For a free copy, write: Public Affairs Dept., Room 476-WSJ, Bethlehem Steel Corp., Bethlehem, PA 18016.

Bethlehem

BETHLEHEM STEEL

Bethlehem Steel Corp. is another company which believes in the value of issue advertising. William A. Latshaw, its manager of advertising, pointed out that only paid advertising permits the company to say what it wants to say in the way it wants to say it. This quotation is from Bethlehem's stated objectives:

1. American corporations are less and less controlled by decisions made in the boardrooms and more and more controlled by decisions made in the halls of Congress and in the conference rooms of the myriad Federal and State agencies; and

2. Unless business and industry speak up and speak out in their own self-interest and encourage others to join them, present and emerging legislative and administrative restraints will continue to have a negative impact on the viability of our corporation and on the free enterprise system.

Bethlehem's advertising division develops and produces this ongoing program, which has covered not only the practical limitations that pollution control has reached in certain areas but the need for better earnings and plant expansion to maintain high employment.

The Growing Storm of Controversy

There is no doubt that issue advertising is currently in an unstable state. Changes in its use will, of course, occur as public issues change, but the direction it will take is uncertain.

There are a number of scenarios that issue advertising might follow in the 1980s:

Scenario 1:   Start by assuming that the energy crisis worsens. This will be followed by a number of resultant and related problems. Each problem in turn will produce a proliferation of factions, each of which will have a solution that it is convinced is the only way to go. Many energy-related problems are apt not to be susceptible of any total solution but will involve trade-off and compromise proposals that swap long-range for short-range goals or trade energy for environmental safety. Under such conditions, debates will arise between groups, committees, political forces, and business. The debates will become heated as conditions worsen in different segments of society. The energy crisis will hit different industries differently, be they hotels, airlines, automobile manufacturers, or what have you. Each industry will respond to the crisis by an effort to seek social support for the system which seems best to ease its own brand of economic distress. If business ads become particularly effective and/or offensive and happen to be at odds with political solutions, the quick response will probably be some form of restrictive public reaction. Possibly this restriction will be as mild as more stringent tax interpretation, but there may be legislation that will strain or break the intent of the First Amendment.

Scenario 2:   This scenario assumes that conditions will continue pretty much as they are. First, one or another major corporation becomes a leader in advocacy advertising in its own particular area and then drops back as it finds that the economics of the program are not particularly attractive. The cost effectiveness of most advocacy advertising is very much open to question. Continuing problems in the economy are almost certain to bring about cuts in this form of advertising. In the meantime, debates on advocacy advertising continue, in general following one of two lines of thought. One position is currently being expressed quite vocally by S. Prakash Sethi. Although he claims that "corporations should have the right to express their views on controversial social issues, using any communications channels available including paid advertising," he advocates introducing controlling legislation now. He describes this step in a letter to *Madison Avenue* magazine:

My proposals would deal with maintaining the integrity of political process by requiring corporations to label their ads as "political" when they seek the First Amendment protection, that such ads not be tax-deductible, thereby keeping them on an equal basis with individual citizens, and that management be required to seek stockholders' approval for such campaigns since it purports to speak on political issues on behalf of stockholders. This is not a call for government regulation but is a healthy approach towards self-regulation within the framework of democratic principles and free enterprise system.[6]

The other side of the picture is well represented by Barry Biederman, senior vice president of Needham, Harper & Steers's Corporate Futures. Also in a letter to *Madison Avenue,* appearing with and in answer to that of Dr. Sethi, who had previously voiced his views at an ANA workshop, Biederman said:

> The only trouble is, his definition of ''political'' includes a lot of corporate advertising that most of us would not ordinarily consider political. And all such advertising would lose its tax-deductibility.
>
> The example that comes to mind is one that I raised during the A.N.A. discussion: Corporate campaigns that feature a company's workers. This approach has often been used and it seemed a good test case. Yes, said the professor, ''people'' campaigns are definitely political. The audience at the Workshop, as I am sure anyone there will remember, greeted Professor Sethi's answer with as much derision as I did.
>
> In the last analysis, Professor Sethi's proposals are impractical, would be costly to shareholders and customers alike, and ultimately would severely restrict the ability of corporate advertisers to conduct their business in an orderly or economic fashion. But perhaps that's what Professor Sethi is really after.[7]

I have omitted the mud and zingers from both letters, but the remaining quotations are indicative of the direction that the controversy is likely to take.

Legislative action in this area would be a long process and would be apt to abort before resolution. It would not take too long for politicians to recognize that, in defining a corporation's advocacy program, they would also be setting rules which would affect advocacy advertising by consumer groups, unions, and voter groups as well as industry. Possibly such rules would limit their own political campaigns as well.

The problem of definition in this field must be apparent to anyone reading this far. To be successful legislation would need to define what is nearly undefinable.

Scenario 3: The last scenario is optimistic and probable, but it does depend on business executives' restraint in the use of this advertising tool. If they avoid blatant abuse and unnecessarily provocative sticks in the regulatory eye, the current controversy will subside. The ad technique is likely

[6]*Madison Avenue,* April 1979, p. 8.
[7]Ibid.

to lose its present fascination to business for natural economic reasons. A number of factors suggest this as the most likely scenario. The recession is reducing the volume of this kind of advertising. It is also refocusing corporations' attention on their priorities in communication. When budgets are reexamined, cost effectiveness will be restudied and some programs reduced. Corporate advertising, in its short history, has shown some tendency to decline more quickly during recession periods, and advocacy advertising seems even more vulnerable. As this kind of advertising becomes less noticeable, less newsworthy, and of less concern to various pressure groups, the controversy will die.

Needless to say, I am rooting for the third scenario. There is a real need and place in our society for good issue advertising. When injustices occur or when an issue which needs airing is lying fallow, a corporation or a group should be able to stand up and tell it the way it sees it. It should not have to move mountains to run an issue ad. Nor should it be expected to list all the pros and cons on both sides of the argument, as Professor Sethi once proposed. Rather, it should be allowed to give the issue its best shot. There will be plenty of people on the other side ready to give theirs. The debate will be healthy. Even the EPA admitted that in the American Electric Power controversy.

Remember that the risk to the advertiser is a powerful control. If the advertising misfires, the advertiser loses credibility. The truth will ultimately surface. The more powerful and attention-getting the ad campaign, the more quickly the truth will surface. The fact that advertising, really great advertising, can kill a bad product more quickly than no advertising isn't just a nice-sounding phrase. It really happens. The same principle works equally for corporate and advocacy advertising. A really bad point of view dramatically and successfully presented will result in sufficient discussion and airing of the subject to kill it more quickly than letting it lie dormant for years and years.

"It is truly enough said that a corporation has no conscience; but a corporation of conscientious men is a corporation with a conscience." — Henry David Thoreau

Time is running out.

Tell President Carter what you think he should do about energy.

We've paid for the page opposite. It contains no message. We leave that for you. Because a message from thousands of voters carries more clout in Washington than a message from us.

It's that simple. We hope thousands of you will write. We hope your messages will help spur action on a national energy policy.

Speak out, America

There's a new administration in Washington. New directions. New ideas. New ears. Let them hear what you have to say.

The cost of energy keeps going up. (That's no surprise to you if you've paid a fuel bill lately.) Domestic oil and gas resources dwindle. Each year America grows *more* dependent on foreign oil, not less.

The Mid-east oil embargo in 1973-74 meant higher prices, gas lines, more unemployment, more inflation. At that time, our country imported 38% of the oil we consumed. Today America imports 42%! And the OPEC nations just raised the price of oil again.

Tell it to the President

America needs a sane and sensible energy policy. And we need it now. The one thing we can't do is wait. Our scarcest resource—time —is running out.

Use the page at right to tell the President you want action now on an energy policy. In your own words and for your own reasons. Then tear it out and send it to President Carter.

What's in it for you?

The same thing that's in it for us. More abundant

supplies of energy. Less waste. Increased development of domestic resources. And decreased dependence on foreign fuels.

Take it to the top.

Bethlehem

Bethlehem Steel Corp. also ran this provocative and innovative spread, headlined "Time is running out. Tell President Carter what you think he should do about energy." This spread included a right-hand page already addressed to the President with plenty of blank space to express one's views.

The President
The White House
Washington, D.C. 20500

Dear Mr. President:

Respectfully,

Bethlehem Steel

Over the years Bethlehem has attacked foreign steel dumpings, the need for deregulation to allow the free marketplace to work, and pleas for recognition that environmental restrictions which inhibit plant expansion result in lost jobs and a weaker United States steel industry. It is a classic legitimate user of issue advertising.

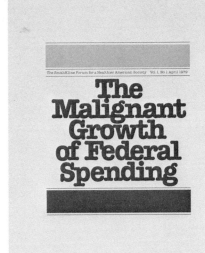

SMITH KLINE CORPORATION

In 1979 Smith Kline Corporation began its unusual series of corporate advertisements with this four-page insertion in the news weeklies and *The Wall Street Journal.* It stated its advertising aim as providing a forum for social, political, and economic issues which are covered by leaders in a variety of fields. This one is by former Secretary of the Treasury William E. Simon on the subject of inflation. Robert F. Dee, chairman of the board and chief executive officer of Smith Kline Corporation, stated that this type of ad is its way of taking action:

"It is our contribution to the social well-being of America. Its purpose is to put before you positive ideas about social, political, and economic issues that all Americans are now confronting. . . . Our commitment of resources for the purpose is a matter of social conscience, and we believe it is in the interest of our shareholders, employees, customers, and suppliers, all of whom are profoundly affected by the health of our nation and its economy."

While this technique would certainly be classified as issue advertising, it avoids many of the pitfalls and the embroilment of a corporation in a hot issue by utilizing eminent persons who are more or less responsible for their own views. The corporation simply provides the space for publication. Underlying these seemingly altruistic objectives is the recognition that the corporation must work in a society which could provide a better business environment if certain conditions were corrected. Below that objective is undoubtedly the image of good citizenship, which fits very nicely with the high ethical standards and reputation that a drug concern is naturally anxious to attain.

Commentary:

William E. Simon examines the true cause of the inflation that can put an end to our way of life.

"The best way to destroy the capitalist system is to debase the currency."
—Nikolai Lenin

"By a process of inflation, governments can confiscate, secretly and unobserved, an important part of the wealth of their citizens. By this method they not only confiscate, but they confiscate arbitrarily; and while the process impoverishes many, it actually enriches some... There is no subtler, no surer means of overturning the existing basis of society than to debauch the currency. The process engages all the hidden forces of economic law on the side of destruction and does it in a manner that not one man in a million is able to diagnose."
—John Maynard Keynes

The fight to restore fiscal responsibility to our national government and over-economic inflation is, above all, a fight for the freedom, dignity and prosperity of all Americans—a fight that compels the sincerest support of anyone who cherishes those values.

Americans are a practical and compassionate people. It is vital, therefore, to broaden understanding of the misguided policies that hobble American productivity, and to demonstrate that the poor, the elderly, the sick and the disadvantaged have everything to gain from an elderly move away from big spending and big government. For this aspect of the fight, we must arm ourselves with the facts.

If the poor did not exist, the collectivists would have to invent them.

Despite a quintupling of the Federal budget (from under $100 billion to over $500 billion in just eighteen years, rationalized as the cure for a host of social ills), the record of accomplishment is dismal.

The fleecing of America.

Greenbacks, greenbacks everywhere.

We cannot spend ourselves rich.

Tyrants without jackboots.

It's later than we think.

The ultimate choice.

—W. E. Simon

CHAPTER 3 THE SIZE AND SCOPE OF CORPORATE ADVERTISING

Going into the 1980s, corporate advertising represents an industry worth more than $500 million. That figure is considerably less than most estimates given by agency and media executives talking or writing on the subject. High-side estimates go up to $1 billion with virtually no backup substantiation. The problem, of course, is again one of definition. It is often difficult to determine accurately which advertisements are truly corporate.

Overall Growth

Perhaps one of the most reliable although conservative estimates comes from the magazine *Public Relations Journal.* Its current estimate, which as of early 1980 is for 1979 expenditures, is $330,716,300. This figure covers corporate advertising in six major media and does not include production costs. This periodical has provided comparable figures since 1971 and, it is hoped, will continue to do so in the future. The data customarily appear in the November issue.

The fact that the estimate may be somewhat conservative is of little importance when compared with its availability for tracking purposes over a period of time. The data are compiled exclusively for the *Public Relations Journal* by LNA Multi-Media Services, published by Leading National Advertisers, Inc., New York. The information is collected by LNA from Publishers Information Bureau magazines and supplements, *Broadcast Advertisers Reports,* and the Institute of Outdoor Advertising. Spot TV expenditures are determined by monitoring 260 stations and 75 top markets. Outdoor expenditures represent national poster and paint advertising in plant operator markets of more than 100,000 population. The figures in the table on page 69 are reproduced with the periodical's permission.

Public Relations Journal also studies and shows separately expenditures for association advertising (see table on page 70). This includes advertising by such associations as the Florida Citrus Commission, the General Motors Corporation Dealer Association, and the American Dairy Association, which clearly would seem to be outside the definition of corporate advertising that we are using in this book. However, association advertising includes the advertising of the American Gas Association and the Blue Cross and Blue Shield Associations, which might be judged to be forms of corporate advertising. You can decide for yourself.

The trend shown in these tables is that through 1977 corporate advertising and association advertising were both increasing more rapidly than the rate of inflation and more rapidly than product advertising. The year 1978 showed a slowing down, which was the result of a sharp drop in spot television (48.1 percent) and radio (58.2 percent). This was largely, if not totally, a reflection of a change in reporting methods. Some spot TV expenditures previously included were reclassified by LNA. (This is one more example of corporate advertising's perpetual fact-gathering problems.) Not unexpectedly, corporate advertising also appears to be more subject to cutbacks during recession periods than product advertising.

The tables also include a six-media breakdown. Although they reveal no clear trend for any one medium over a long period of time, they do show the vitality of television and magazines. There is even less of a long-term pattern when corporate advertising figures are compared with association advertising figures. Neither appears to be following the media trends of the other. In turn, their pattern of buying is dissimilar to total advertising expenditures for the entire advertising industry. While I can offer no direct explanation of the difference, this situation may not be surprising when one considers that corporate advertising accounts, at most, for only from 0.8 to 2.3 percent of total advertising media expenditures in the United States and that its needs are uniquely different from those of other advertising.

Size and Types of Advertisers

While the corporate share of advertising expenditures is low, the number of participants is high. More than half of the major corporations in the United States engage in national corporate advertising. Of *Fortune*'s 500 largest industrials 277 were national corporate advertisers in 1978, according to a special analysis of the *Fortune* 500 list conducted for us by the

Six-Media Advertising Expenditures, 1972–1978

Company corporate advertising (in millions of dollars)

	1971	1972	Percent change	1973	Percent change	1974	Percent change
Consumer magazines	$64,711.9	$68,258.6	5	$87,905.4	29	$102,231.0	16
Sunday magazines	587.1	735.6	25	1,158.2	57	719.4	−38
Network television	50,055.0	64,074.7	27	84,517.9	32	78,903.8	−7
Spot television	39,505.8	41,788.8	6	48,697.3	17	40,708.0	−16
Radio	1,860.5	4,828.9	159	3,294.8	−32	611.2	−81
Outdoor	855.5	2,124.1	148	1,403.9	−34	1,162.8	−17
Six-media totals	$157,575.8	$181,810.7	15	$226,977.5	25	$224,336.2	−1

	1975	Percent change	1976	Percent change	1977	Percent change	1978	Percent change
Consumer magazines	$88,961.0	−13	$115,750.4	30.1	$133,362.6	15.2	$155,025.4	16.2
Sunday magazines	735.7	2	6,256.7	750.4	5,750.6	−8.1	3,908.7	−32.0
Network television	72,485.1	−8	104,971.7	44.8	125,157.8	19.2	138,214.0	10.4
Spot television	46,337.4	14	63,697.9	37.5	61,420.4	−3.6	31,903.3	−48.1
Radio	900.5	47	1,236.6	37.3	2,897.5	134.3	1,210.9	−58.2
Outdoor	710.9	−39	811.6	14.2	679.1	−16.3	454.0	−33.1
Six-media totals	$210,130.6	−6	$292,724.9	39.3	$329,268.0	12.5	$330,716.3	0.4

Six-Media Advertising Expenditures, 1972–1978

Association advertising (in millions of dollars)

	1971	1972	Percent change	1973	Percent change	1974	Percent change
Consumer magazines	$23,515.1	$22,579.2	−3	$21,967.4	3	$21,174.7	−4
Sunday magazines	407.1	713.5	75	996.7	40	2,060.8	7
Network television	20,731.6	24,109.4	16	23,686.0	−2	20,441.3	−14
Spot television	23,441.0	31,785.1	36	37,681.0	19	37,236.5	−1
Radio	1,029.5	1,219.3	18	1,126.5	−8	1,899.5	69
Outdoor	3,511.2	5,273.3	50	4,874.0	−8	4,670.1	−4
Six-media totals	**$72,635.5**	**$85,859.8**	**18**	**$90,331.6**	**5**	**$87,482.9**	**−3**

	1975	1976	Percent change	1977	Percent change	1978	Percent change
Consumer magazines	$22,110.4	$22,490.9	1.7	$25,561.3	13.7	$32,575.8	27.4
Sunday magazines	1,579.7	729.0	−53.9	1,292.0	77.2	913.3	−29.3
Network television	26,320.8	33,763.2	28.3	36,886.1	9.2	33,951.6	−7.9
Spot television	40,474.3	56,427.7	39.4	75,702.2	34.2	86,280.1	13.9
Radio	1,740.1	1,171.4	−32.7	1,129.9	−3.5	1,409.4	24.7
Outdoor	2,996.6	3,135.3	4.6	4,514.6	43.9	4,960.5	9.9
Six-media totals	**$95,221.9**	**$117,717.5**	**23.6**	**$145,086.1**	**23.2**	**$160,090.7**	**10.3**

Research Library of the *Reader's Digest* and reproduced here with the permission of both periodicals. A similar study using 1975 figures showed fairly similar results: 238 of the top 500. Of the 500 companies in the accompanying list, those marked with an asterisk were corporate advertisers in 1978.

It is clear from an analysis of the list that the larger the company the more apt it is to engage in corporate advertising. Using the *Fortune* 500 ranking, we find the following:

- 49 of the top 50 were corporate advertisers.
- 96 of the top 100 were corporate advertisers.
- 129 of the top 150 were corporate advertisers.
- 171 of the top 200 were corporate advertisers.
- 202 of the top 250 were corporate advertisers.
- 225 of the top 300 were corporate advertisers.
- 240 of the top 350 were corporate advertisers.
- 252 of the top 400 were corporate advertisers.
- 265 of the top 450 were corporate advertisers.
- 277 of the top 500 were corporate advertisers.

When we examine some of the larger companies which did not employ corporate advertising, frequently we find that they have well-known consumer products or that they are companies which have taken a sabbatical for a year or two and were corporate advertisers in the past and perhaps will again be in the future.

Among the fifty largest utilities ranked by *Fortune* magazine, we find a lesser use of national corporate advertising (twelve of the fifty), as shown in the accompanying table. Once again we find that the larger companies appear to be more frequent users of national corporate advertising. It is important to note that many of these utilities are regional and may have regional corporate programs, which are beyond the scope of this analysis.

The fact that the larger the company, the more apt it is to engage in corporate advertising is also noted in a 1977 survey conducted by Dr. Joseph Chasen and Dr. William S. Sachs of the College of Business Administration, St. John's University, New York. The cost of sponsorship was borne by *National Geographic* magazine, but the analysis, interpretation, and conclusions are those of the authors. They concluded that the major determinator in whether corporate advertising was used was not just the size of the company but the nature of the business. Companies whose mainstay is industrial products or service functions (financial, transportation, and utilities) are more likely to engage incorporate advertising. Some 66 percent of industrial firms and 61 percent of service companies covered in the survey had had a corporate advertising program during the preceding 5 years. Only 35 percent of the companies manufacturing consumer

Corporate Advertisers* among the 500 Largest Industrial Corporations in 1977   (Ranked by Sales)[1]

Rank	Company[2]	Rank	Company[2]
1	*General Motors (Detroit)	23	*Sun (Radnor, Pa.)
2	*Exxon (New York)	24	*Phillips Petroleum (Bartlesville, Okla.)
3	*Ford Motor (Dearborn, Mich.)	25	*Dow Chemical (Midland, Mich.)
4	*Mobil (New York)		
5	*Texaco (White Plains, N.Y.)	26	*Westinghouse Electric (Pittsburgh)
		27	*Occidental Petroleum (Los Angeles)
6	*Standard Oil of California (San Francisco)	28	*International Harvester (Chicago)
7	*International Business Machines (Armonk, N.Y.)	29	*Eastman Kodak (Rochester, N.Y.)
8	*Gulf Oil (Pittsburgh)	30	*RCA (New York)
9	*General Electric (Fairfield, Conn.)	31	*Rockwell International (Pittsburgh)
10	*Chrysler (Highland Park, Mich.)	32	*Caterpillar Tractor (Peoria, Ill.)
11	*International Tel. & Tel. (New York)	33	*Union Oil of California (Los Angeles)
12	*Standard Oil (Ind.) (Chicago)	34	*United Technologies (Hartford)
13	*Atlantic Richfield (Los Angeles)	35	*Bethlchem Steel (Bethlehem, Pa.)
14	*Shell Oil (Houston)		
15	*U.S. Steel (Pittsburgh)	36	*Beatrice Foods (Chicago)
		37	*Esmark (Chicago)
16	*E. I. du Pont de Nemours (Wilmington, Del.)	38	*Kraft (Glenview, Ill.)
		39	*Xerox (Stamford, Conn.)
17	*Continental Oil (Stamford, Conn.)	40	*General Foods (White Plains, N.Y.)
18	*Western Electric (New York)	41	*R. J. Reynolds Industries (Winston-Salem, N.C.)
19	*Tenneco (Houston)	42	*Ashland Oil (Russell, Ky.)
20	*Procter & Gamble (Cincinnati)	43	*LTV (Dallas)
		44	*Monsanto (St. Louis)
21	*Union Carbide (New York)	45	*Amerada Hess (New York)
22	*Goodyear Tire & Rubber (Akron, Ohio)	46	*Firestone Tire & Rubber (Akron, Ohio)
		47	*Cities Service (Tulsa)

[1]SOURCE: *Fortune Double 500 Directory,* 1978.

[2]NOTE: Of the 500 largest industrials, 277 companies (marked with asterisks) used some form of corporate advertising in 1978.

Rank	Company[2]	Rank	Company[2]
48	Marathon Oil (Findlay, Ohio)	76	*TRW (Cleveland)
49	*Boeing (Seattle)	77	*National Steel (Pittsburgh)
50	*Minnesota Mining & Manufacturing (St. Paul.)	78	Farmland Industries (Kansas City, Mo.)
		79	*Signal Companies (Beverly Hills, Calif)
51	*W. R. Grace (New York)	80	*Allied Chemical (Morristown, N.J.)
52	*Philip Morris (New York)		
53	*Greyhound (Phoenix)		
54	*Colgate-Palmolive (New York)	81	*Johnson & Johnson (New Brunswick, N.J.)
55	*Ralston Purina (St. Louis.)	82	*Honeywell (Minneapolis)
56	*Georgia-Pacific (Portland, Oreg.)	83	*General Mills (Minneapolis)
57	*International Paper (New York)	84	*Republic Steel (Cleveland)
58	*Continental Group (New York)	85	*General Dynamics (St. Louis)
59	*Gulf & Western Industries (New York)	86	*American Brands (New York)
60	*Deere (Moline, Ill.)	87	*Consolidated Foods (Chicago)
61	*Coca-Cola (Atlanta)	88	*CPC International (Englewood Cliffs, N.J.)
62	*Armco Steel (Middletown, Ohio)	89	*Raytheon (Lexington, Mass.)
63	*PepsiCo (Purchase, N.Y.)	90	*Textron (Providence)
64	*McDonnell Douglas (St. Louis)		
65	*American Can (Greenwich, Conn.)	91	*CBS (New York)
		92	*Owens-Illinois (Toledo)
66	*Standard Oil (Ohio) (Cleveland)	93	American Home Products (New York)
67	*Borden (New York)	94	*Inland Steel (Chicago)
68	*Champion International (Stamford, Conn.)	95	*Uniroyal (Middlebury, Conn.)
69	*Litton Industries (Beverly Hills, Calif.)	96	*Warner-Lambert (Morris Plains, N.J.)
70	*Aluminum Co. of America (Pittsburgh)	97	*Dresser Industries (Dallas)
71	*Lockheed (Burbank, Calif.)	98	*NCR (Dayton, Ohio)
72	*Getty Oil (Los Angeles)	99	*PPG Industries (Pittsburgh)
73	*Bendix (Southfield, Mich.)	100	United Brands (New York)
74	*Weyerhaeuser (Tacoma, Wash.)		
75	*Sperry Rand (New York)	101	American Cyanamid (Wayne, N.J.)

Rank	Company[2]	Rank	Company[2]
102	*Burlington Industries (Greensboro, N.C.)	129	*St. Regis Paper (New York)
103	*FMC (Chicago)	130	*Whirlpool (Benton Harbor, Mich.)
104	*Reynolds Metals (Richmond, Va.)		
105	Carnation (Los Angeles)	131	*North American Phillips (New York)
106	*Celanese (New York)	132	*Babcock & Wilcox (New York)
107	*Boise Cascade (Boise, Idaho)	133	*Northwest Industries (Chicago)
108	Crown Zellerbach (San Francisco)	134	*IC Industries (Chicago)
109	*Singer (New York)	135	*H. J. Heinz (Pittsburgh)
110	*American Motors (Southfield, Mich.)	136	*Anheuser-Busch (St. Louis)
111	*B. F. Goodrich (Akron, Ohio)	137	*Motorola (Schaumburg, Ill.)
112	Teledyne (Los Angeles)	138	Mead (Dayton, Ohio)
113	*Bristol-Myers (New York)	139	Emerson Electric (St. Louis)
114	*Kaiser Aluminum & Chemical (Oakland, Calif.)	140	*Fruehauf (Detroit)
115	Central Soya (Fort Wayne, Ind.)	141	*Dana (Toledo)
		142	American Standard (New York)
116	*Kerr-McGee (Oklahoma City)	143	Campbell Soup (Camden, N.J.)
117	*Standard Brands (New York)	144	Lykes (New Orleans)
118	Nabisco (East Hanover, N.J.)	145	*Norton Simon (New York)
119	Archer-Daniels-Midland (Decatur, Ill.)	146	Kimberly-Clark (Neenah, Wis.)
120	*Ingersoll-Rand (Woodcliff Lake, N.J.)	147	Merck (Rahway, N.J.)
		148	*Hercules (Wilmington, Del.)
121	*Eaton (Cleveland)	149	*Avon Products (New York)
122	*General Tire & Rubber (Akron, Ohio)	150	Associated Milk Producers (San Antonio)
123	Burroughs (Detroit)		
124	*Texas Instruments (Dallas)	151	*Gould (Rolling Meadows, Ill.)
125	*Combustion Engineering (Stamford, Conn.)	152	American Broadcasting (New York)
126	*Pfizer (New York)	153	*Northrop (Los Angeles)
127	*Borg-Warner (Chicago)	154	*Dart Industries (Los Angeles)
128	Iowa Beef Processors (Dakota City, Neb.)	155	*Agway (Dewitt, N.Y.)

Rank	Company[2]	Rank	Company[2]
156	Ogden (New York)	185	White Motor (Eastlake, Ohio)
157	*Gillette (Boston)		
158	*NL Industries (New York)	186	*Koppers (Pittsburgh)
159	Interco (St. Louis)	187	Squibb (New York)
160	*Levi Strauss (San Francisco)	188	*Studebaker-Worthington (New York)
161	*Grumman (Bethpage, N.Y.)	189	*AMAX (Greenwich, Conn.)
162	*Quaker Oats (Chicago)	190	*U.S. Industries (New York)
163	*J. P. Stevens (New York)		
164	*Allis-Chalmers (West Allis, Wis.)	191	*Carrier (Syracuse, N.Y.)
165	*Kellogg (Battle Creek, Mich.)	192	*Clark Equipment (Buchanan, Mich.)
		193	*Budd (Troy, Mich.)
166	*Diamond Shamrock (Cleveland)	194	Ethyl (Richmond, Va.)
167	*Colt Industries (New York)	195	International Minerals & Chemical (Libertyville, Ill.)
168	*Scott Paper (Philadelphia)		
169	*Eli Lilly (Indianapolis)	196	*Cummins Engine (Columbus, Ind.)
170	*Control Data (Minneapolis)	197	*National Distillers & Chemical (New York)
		198	*Time Inc. (New York)
171	*Del Monte (San Francisco)	199	*Pennzoil (Houston)
172	*Owens-Corning Fiberglas (Toledo)	200	*Abbott Laboratories (North Chicago, Ill.)
173	*Walter Kidde (Clifton, N.J.)	201	*Williams Companies (Tulsa)
174	*Olin (Stamford, Conn.)	202	*Stauffer Chemical (Westport, Conn.)
175	*Johns-Manville (Denver)	203	*Rohm & Haas (Philadelphia)
176	*Pillsbury (Minneapolis)		
177	*Martin Marietta (Bethesda, Md.)	204	*AMF (White Plains, N.Y.)
178	*Charter (Jacksonville, Fla.)	205	Marmon Group, Inc. (Chicago)
179	*Jim Walter (Tampa, Fla.)		
180	*Paccar (Bellevue, Wash.)	206	*Emhart (Farmington, Conn.)
181	Land O'Lakes (Minneapolis)	207	Foster Wheeler (Livingston, N.J.)
182	*White Consolidated Industries (Cleveland)	208	*Oscar Mayer (Madison, Wis.)
183	*SCM (New York)	209	Genesco (Nashville)
184	*Hewlett-Packard (Palo Alto, Calif.)	210	Sterling Drug (New York)

Rank	Company[2]	Rank	Company[2]
211	*Heublein (Farmington, Conn.)	237	*Sherwin-Williams (Cleveland)
212	*U.S. Gypsum (Chicago)	238	*Joseph E. Seagram & Sons (New York)
213	Tesoro Petroleum (San Antonio)	239	*Castle & Cooke (Honolulu)
214	*Warner Communications (New York)	240	*Allegheny Ludlum Industries (Pittsburgh)
215	*Revlon (New York)		
		241	Westvaco (New York)
216	*Chromalloy American (St. Louis)	242	*Brunswick (Skokie, Ill.)
217	*Upjohn (Kalamazoo, Mich.)	243	*Zenith Radio (Glenview, Ill.)
218	*Crane (New York)	244	MBPXL (Wichita)
219	Times Mirror (Los Angeles)	245	*Diamond International (New York)
220	*Murphy Oil (El Dorado, Ark.)	246	*Libbey-Owens-Ford (Toledo)
		247	National Can (Chicago)
221	*Corning Glass Works (Corning, N.Y.)	248	*Timken (Canton, Ohio)
222	A. E. Staley Manufacturing (Decatur, Ill.)	249	Wheeling-Pittsburgh Steel (Pittsburgh)
223	Geo. A. Hormel (Austin, Minn.)	250	*Phelps Dodge (New York)
224	*Armstrong Cork (Lancaster, Pa.)	251	Amstar (New York)
225	*Union Camp (Wayne, N.J.)	252	*Anderson, Clayton (Houston)
		253	Air Products & Chemicals (Allentown, Pa.)
226	American Petrofina (Dallas)	254	Schering-Plough (Kenilworth, N.J.)
227	Tosco (Los Angeles)	255	United Merchants & Manufacturers (New York)
228	Pet (St. Louis)		
229	*GAF (New York)		
230	*Polaroid (Cambridge, Mass.)		
231	*Digital Equipment (Maynard, Mass.)	256	*Jos. Schlitz Brewing (Milwaukee)
232	Gold Kist (Atlanta)	257	Commonwealth Oil Refining (San Antonio)
233	Crown Cork & Seal (Philadelphia)	258	*Kennecott Copper (New York)
234	Sunbeam (Chicago)	259	*Great Northern Nekoosa (Stamford, Conn.)
235	*Asarco (New York)	260	Eltra (New York)
236	McGraw-Edison (Elgin, Ill.)	261	Airco (Montvale, N.J.)

Rank	Company[2]	Rank	Company[2]
262	*Lear Siegler (Santa Monica, Calif.)	286	*Louisiana-Pacific (Portland, Oreg.)
263	Evans Products (Portland, Oreg.)	287	*St. Joe Minerals (New York)
264	Kane-Miller (Tarrytown, N.Y.)	288	Campbell Taggart (Dallas)
265	Brown Group (St. Louis)	289	*Hammermill Paper (Erie, Pa.)
		290	Lever Brothers (New York)
266	*MCA (Universal City, Calif.)		
267	Blue Bell (Greensboro, N.C.)	291	*Smith Kline (Philadelphia)
268	Clark Oil & Refining (Milwaukee)	292	*Interlake (Oak Brook, Ill.)
269	*General Signal (Stamford, Conn.)	293	Knight-Ridder Newspapers (Miami)
270	Clorox (Oakland,, Calif.)	294	*National Gypsum (Dallas)
		295	*Rexnord (Milwaukee)
271	*Lone Star Industries (Greenwich, Conn.)	296	Universal Leaf Tobacco (Richmond, Va.)
272	Norton (Worcester, Mass.)	297	A. O. Smith (Milwaukee)
273	International Multifoods (Minneapolis)	298	Whittaker (Los Angeles)
274	*G. D. Searle (Skokie, Ill.)	299	Avnet (New York)
275	*Baxter Travenol Laboratories (Deerfield, Ill.)	300	Carborundum (Niagara Falls, N.Y.)
		301	Baker International (Orange, Calif.)
276	*Richardson-Merrell (Wilton, Conn.)	302	*ACF Industries (New York)
277	*Pennwalt (Philadelphia)	303	Sperry & Hutchinson (New York)
278	*Reliance Electric (Cleveland)	304	Eastern Gas & Fuel Associates (Boston)
279	*Certain-teed (Valley Forge, Pa.)	305	*Potlatch (San Francisco)
280	*Liggett Group (Durham, N.C.)	306	Harsco (Camp Hill, Pa.)
		307	*Cooper Industries (Houston)
281	West Point-Pepperell (West Point, Ga.)	308	*Joy Manufacturing (Pittsburgh)
282	Peabody Holding (St. Louis)	309	*Reichhold Chemicals (White Plains, N.Y.)
283	Black & Decker Manufacturing (Towson, Md.)	310	*Scovill Manufacturing (Waterbury, Conn.)
284	Akzona (Asheville, N.C.)	311	Hershey Foods (Hershey, Pa.)
285	*Chesebrough-Pond's (Greenwich, Conn.)	312	General Host (Stamford, Conn.)

Rank	Company[2]	Rank	Company[2]
313	R. R. Donnelley & Sons (Chicago)	338	Morton-Norwich Products (Chicago)
314	*McGraw-Hill (New York)	339	*Consolidated Aluminum (St. Louis)
315	*Kaiser Steel (Oakland, Calif.)	340	Pitney-Bowes (Stamford, Conn.)
316	Springs Mills (Fort Mill, S.C.)	341	Indian Head (New York)
317	Cone Mills (Greensboro, N.C.)	342	Crown Central Petroleum (Baltimore)
318	Mohasco (Amsterdam, N.Y.)	343	Inmont (New York)
319	Willamette Industries (Portland, Oreg.)	344	Revere Copper & Brass (New York)
320	Tecumseh Products (Tecumseh, Mich.)	345	Addressograph-Multigraph (Cleveland)
321	Cyclops (Pittsburgh)	346	Becton, Dickinson (Rutherford, N.J.)
322	*Sundstrand (Rockford, Ill.)	347	*Adolph Coors (Golden, Colo.)
323	*Harris (Cleveland)	348	Hoover (North Canton, Ohio)
324	Outboard Marine (Waukegan, Ill.)	349	Cluett, Peabody (New York)
325	Anchor Hocking (Lancaster, Ohio)	350	Federal Co. (Memphis)
326	*Stanley Works (New Britain, Conn.)	351	*Flintkote (Stamford, Conn.)
327	Alumax (San Mateo, Calif.)	352	Sybron (Rochester, N.Y.)
328	*Bemis (Minneapolis)	353	*GATX (Chicago)
329	*AMP (Harrisburg, Pa.)	354	*Pabst Brewing (Milwaukee)
330	CF Industries (Long Grove, Ill.)	355	Newmont Mining (New York)
331	Witco Chemical (New York)	356	Norin (North Miami, Fla.)
332	Spencer Foods (Spencer, Iowa)	357	UV Industries (New York)
333	*General Cable (Greenwich, Conn.)	358	Cabot (Boston)
334	Cessna Aircraft (Wichita)	359	Thomas J. Lipton (Englewood Cliffs, N.J.)
335	Square D (Park Ridge, Ill.)	360	*Dayco (Dayton, Ohio)
336	Southwest Forest Industries (Phoenix)	361	Norris Industries (Long Beach, Calif.)
337	*Chicago Bridge & Iron (Oak Brook, Ill.)	362	*Champion Spark Plug (Toledo)
		363	A-T-O (Willoughby, Ohio)

Rank	Company[2]	Rank	Company[2]
364	Hart Schaffner & Marx (Chicago)	391	Twentieth Century-Fox Film (Los Angeles)
365	*Bangor Punta (Greenwich, Conn.)	392	Signode (Glenview, Ill.)
		393	Cannon Mills (Kannapolis, N.C.)
366	Fleetwood Enterprises (Riverside, Calif.)	394	Peavey (Minneapolis)
367	Natomas (San Francisco)	395	Brockway Glass (Brockway, Pa.)
368	*Gannett (Rochester, N.Y.)	396	Bell & Howell (Chicago)
369	M. Lowenstein & Sons (New York)	397	Purex (Lakewood, Calif.)
		398	Federal Mogul (Detroit)
370	*Bucyrus-Erie (South Milwaukee, Wis.)	399	Trane (La Crosse, Wis.)
		400	Texasgulf (Stamford, Conn.)
371	Amsted Industries (Chicago)		
372	Superior Oil (Houston)	401	*Wheelabrator-Frye (Hampton, N.H.)
373	*Saxon Industries (New York)	402	Miles Laboratories (Elkhart, Ind.)
374	Fairmont Foods (Houston)	403	Green Giant (Chaska, Minn.)
375	Sheller-Globe (Toledo)	404	American Bakeries (Chicago)
376	McLouth Steel (Detroit)	405	H. K. Porter (Pittsburgh)
377	ConAgra (Omaha)		
378	Cincinnati Milacron (Cincinnati)	406	*Hobart (Troy, Ohio)
379	National Service Industries (Atlanta)	407	Wallace Murray (New York)
380	*MAPCO (Tulsa)	408	Eagle-Picher Industries (Cincinnati)
		409	*Midland-Ross (Cleveland)
381	Cutler-Hammer (Milwaukee)	410	VF (Wyomissing, Pa.)
382	Great Western United (Dallas)		
383	Macmillan (New York)	411	Questor (Toledo)
384	Vulcan Materials (Birmingham, Ala.)	412	Simmons (Atlanta)
		413	Envirotech (Menlo Park, Calif.)
385	New York Times (New York)	414	Harnischfeger (Brookfield, Wis.)
386	Lubrizol (Wickliffe, Ohio)	415	General Instrument (New York)
387	*NVF (Yorklyn, Del.)		
388	Parker-Hannifin (Cleveland)	16	*Collins & Aikman (New York)
389	Gardner-Denver (Dallas)	417	General Cinema (Chestnut Hill, Mass.)
390	Dan River (Greenville, S.C.)	418	*DPF (Hartsdale, N.Y.)

Rank	Company[2]	Rank	Company[2]
419	Arvin Industries (Columbus, Ind.)	446	Hanes (Winston-Salem, N.C.)
420	*Fairchild Camera & Instrument (Mount View, Calif.)	447	Bluebird (Philadelphia)
		448	Dover (New York)
		449	Nashua (Nashua, N.H.)
421	Kellwood (St. Louis)	450	Dow Corning (Midland, Mich.)
422	*Stokely-Van Camp (Indianapolis)	451	Jonathan Logan (Secaucus, N.J.)
423	*Tektronix (Beaverton, Oreg.)	452	Gerber Products (Freemont, Mich.)
424	*Masco (Taylor, Mich.)	453	*Congoleum (Milwaukee)
425	*Hughes Tool (Houston)	454	Insilco (Meriden, Conn.)
426	Memorex (Santa Clara, Calif.)	455	Fairchild Industries (Germantown, Md.)
427	Ball (Muncie, Ind.)	456	Wm. Wrigley Jr. (Chicago)
428	Quaker State Oil Refining (Oil City, Pa.)	457	Federal Paper Board (Montvale, N.J.)
429	Ex-Cell-O (Troy, Mich.)	458	Inland Container (Indianapolis)
430	Thiokol (Newton, Pa.)	459	Pacific Resources (Honolulu)
431	Nalco Chemical (Oak Brook, Ill.)	460	*Scott & Fetzer (Lakewood, Ohio)
432	Masonite (Chicago)	461	Globe-Union (Milwaukee)
433	Ward Foods (New York)	462	*Peabody International (Stamford, Conn.)
434	H. P. Hood (Boston)	463	*Columbia Pictures Industries (New York)
435	Washington Post (Washington)	464	Briggs & Stratton (Wauwatosa, Wis.)
436	Cameron Iron Works (Houston)	465	Cook Industries (Memphis)
437	Perkin-Elmer (Norwalk, Conn.)	466	Belco Petroleum (New York)
438	Louisiana Land & Exploration (New Orleans)	467	*National Semiconductor (Santa Clara, Calif.)
439	U.S. Filter (New York)	468	Mattel (Hawthorne, Calif.)
440	Avery International (San Marino, Calif.)	469	Houdaille Industries (Fort Lauderdale, Fla.)
441	*Ferro (Cleveland)	470	Warnaco (Bridgeport, Conn.)
442	*Beech Aircraft (Wichita)		
443	Fieldcrest Mills (Eden, N.C.)		
444	Amtel (Providence)		
445	Hoover Ball & Bearing (Saline, Mich.)		

Rank	Company[2]	Rank	Company[2]
471	Roper (Kankakee, Ill.)	486	Arcata National (Menlo Park, Calif.)
472	*Handy & Harman (New York)	487	*Foxboro (Foxboro, Mass.)
473	*Olinkraft (West Monroe, La.)	488	Dairylea Cooperative (Pearl River, N.Y.)
474	Westmoreland Coal (Philadelphia)	489	*Armstrong Rubber (New Haven, Conn.)
475	*Bausch & Lomb (Rochester, N.Y.)	490	P. R. Mallory (Indianapolis)
476	EG & G (Wellesley, Mass.)	491	American Hoist & Derrick (St. Paul)
477	Varian Associates (Palo Alto, Calif.)	492	Rath Packing (Waterloo, Iowa)
478	Maryland Cup (Owings Mills, Md.)	493	Tyler (Dallas)
479	American Chain & Cable (Bridgeport, Conn.)	494	Monfort of Colorado (Greeley, Colo.)
480	Johnson Controls (Milwaukee)	495	Idle Wild Foods (Worcester, Mass.)
481	Midland Cooperatives (Minneapolis)	496	Koehring (Brookfield, Wis.)
482	Harcourt Brace Jovanovich (New York)	497	Butler Manufacturing (Kansas City, Mo.)
483	National Starch & Chemical (Bridgewater, N.J.)	498	Economics Laboratory (St. Paul)
484	Talley Industries (Mesa, Ariz.)	499	Dennison Manufacturing (Framingham, Mass.)
485	Hyster (Portland, Oreg.)	500	McCormick (Hunt Valley, Md.)

goods had had such a program. This study concluded that, despite popular belief to the contrary, most corporations do practice continuity: 54 percent reported having run programs *every* year in the preceding 5 years. Subjectively, this is a surprising finding: perhaps many companies are consistently doing something but are not doing something consistently.

A similar analysis of *Fortune*'s other company rankings reveals similar patterns. The larger the company, the more apt it is to engage in national corporate advertising. Of *Fortune*'s fifty largest life insurance companies, twenty-two were national corporate advertisers, and twenty-one of the largest diversified financial companies were national corporate advertisers. Naturally, those companies whose businesses are confined to specific regions are far less apt to have programs that are national in scope.

Corporate Advertisers* among the Fifty Largest Utilities (Ranked by Assets) in 1977

Rank	Company
1	*American Telephone & Telegraph (New York)
2	*General Telephone & Electronics (Stamford, Conn.)
3	*Southern Company (Atlanta)
4	Pacific Gas & Electric (San Francisco)
5	*American Electric Power (New York)
6	*Commonwealth Edison (Chicago)
7	Consolidated Edison (New York)
8	Southern California Edison (Rosemead, Calif.)
9	*Public Service Electric & Gas (Newark, N.J.)
10	Virginia Electric & Power (Richmond, Va.)
11	Middle South Utilities (New Orleans)
12	Duke Power (Charlotte, N.C.)
13	*Texas Utilities (Dallas)
14	Philadelphia Electric (Philadelphia)
15	Consumers Power (Jackson, Mich.)
16	General Public Utilities (Parsippany, N.J.)
17	Detroit Edison (Detroit)
18	Florida Power & Light (Miami)
19	Columbia Gas System (Wilmington, Del.)
20	Pennsylvania Power & Light (Allentown, Pa.)
21	Niagara Mohawk Power (Syracuse, N.Y.)
22	Northeast Utilities (Berlin, Conn.)
23	United Telecommunications (Westwood, Kan.)
24	El Paso (Houston)
25	American Natural Resources (Detroit)
26	Texas Eastern Corp. (Houston)
27	Carolina Power & Light (Raleigh, N.C.)
28	Houston Industries (Houston)
29	Ohio Edison (Akron, Ohio)
30	*Central & South West (Dallas)
31	Long Island Lighting (Mineola, N.Y.)
32	Baltimore Gas & Electric (Baltimore)
33	Union Electric (St. Louis)
34	*Peoples Gas (Chicago)
35	Pacific Power & Light (Portland, Oreg.)
36	Northern States Power (Minneapolis)
37	Allegheny Power System (New York)
38	Continental Telephone (Atlanta)
39	*Northern Natural Gas (Omaha)
40	*Consolidated Natural Gas (Pittsburgh)

Rank	Company
41	Transco Companies (Houston)
42	Cleveland Electric Illuminating (Cleveland)
43	Potomac Electric Power (Washington, D.C.)
44	Pacific Lighting (Los Angeles)
45	*Panhandle Eastern Pipe Line (Houston)
46	Northern Indiana Public Service (Hammond, Ind.)
47	Duquesne Light (Pittsburgh)
48	Illinois Power (Decatur, Ill.)
49	New England Electric System (Westborough, Mass.)
50	Gulf States Utilities (Beaumont, Tex.)

SOURCE: *Fortane Double 500 Directory,* 1978.

NOTE: Twelve of the fifty largest utilities, marked with asterisks, used some form of corporate advertising in 1978.

SECTION 2
THE WHY

Should you or shouldn't you? There will be debates, and that's healthy; and there will be times when corporate advertising is not needed. But that's more unusual than usual. This section explores the conditions in which corporate advertising is cost-productive and efficient and provides argumentation for those debates.

CHAPTER 4 CORPORATE ADVERTISING: THE PROS AND CONS

You won't work long in corporate advertising before you realize that not everyone is on your side. In fact, you'll probably find enough detractors of corporate advertising to make you wonder if you're not in some unclean part of the business. Relax; it's a great business, but snipers do come with the territory.

To hear some of the arguments raised against corporate advertising, you might think that there is something intrinsically bad about the activity itself. That's foolish. Corporate advertising is simply a tool. It may be used at inappropriate times, or it may just be poorly done, but in and of itself it is not wrong. To say that it is wrong is like a carpenter saying that he doesn't believe in a ripsaw. Admittedly, a ripsaw may not always be the most appropriate tool to use, but there are instances when it is exactly right.

Arguments against corporate advertising seem to fall into a limited number of familiar categories. One of them is, "*A low profile is better for the corporation at this time.*" Under certain conditions this can be a valid position, even though it's hard to find a time when a low silhouette is the best posture.

A particularly bad press on some product or company action may require a hiatus in a corporate program, but even then problems of this sort frequently are better met with a well-conceived corporate campaign presenting the positive sides of the company's case. Such a program can offset the negative news.

No better example exists than the successful campaign by the International Telephone and Telegraph Company following the massively adverse publicity that it received in the early 1970s. Today ITT's positive reputation ranks with those of other major corporations in national surveys.

The response to the ITT corporate program which began in 1974 was rapid. To quote from a speech by John L. Lowden, then the company's director of advertising and sales promotion:

> Awareness and familiarity with ITT increased substantially — from 34% in January, 1974 to 56% in December, 1974. . . .
>
> The ITT corporate advertising campaign has been a significant contribution to offsetting negative publicity factors and in shaping favorable attitudes towards ITT. . . .
>
> The most dramatic increases are with those corporate characteristics stressed in our new corporate advertising. That is, a percentage point change of 65% in LEADER IN TECHNOLOGY . . . 57% in RELIABLE . . . 44% in DEVELOPS MANY NEW PRODUCTS . . . 41% in MAKES QUALITY PRODUCTS . . . 37% in LEADS IN R&D TO IMPROVE PRODUCTS.
>
> Other interesting increments were these: 23% in CARES ABOUT GENERAL PUBLIC . . . 20% in PROTECTS JOBS OF U.S. WORKERS . . . 9% in GOOD STOCK TO BUY OR OWN . . . and 8% in GOOD BALANCE BETWEEN PROFITS AND THE PUBLIC INTEREST.[1]

On the subject of adverse publicity, a device used occasionally by some of the more daring local utilities is worth mentioning. If such a utility is faced with an unpopular announcement such as a rate hike or a major delay in a long-awaited service, it will run an ad on the subject in the local paper *before* sending out the news release. The ad presents fully the utility's side of the issue, and since the announcement is voluntary, the company benefits from a posture of forthrightness and candor. Far more important is the dampening effect of the ad on the newspaper's handling of the press release, which by now has become old news. No paper is going to consider the release "front page" anymore. If the utility is lucky, the issue may end right there. The device doesn't always work, but it's worth considering.

While keeping a low profile is assumed to be a safe course of action, there is some evidence that it can actually be a very dangerous course. Witness a study by advertising researchers Katherine Martan and J. J. Boddewyn, reported in the *Journal of Advertising Research.* The conclusion is:

> Since an increasing number of companies are thrown in a high-profile position through incidental public exposure, the question of a more developed profile-management arises. Incidental exposure to high visibility leaves the company ill-prepared to counter public argumentation, and to be on the defensive places the company in unfavorable arguing posi-

---

[1]ANA Corporate Advertising Workshop, Hotel Plaza, New York, Mar. 26, 1975.

tion, compared with an offensive strategy. . . . Thus in the future a shift away from low profile can be predicted.[2]

The researchers explain that there will always be an image of some sort if there is any awareness of the existence of the company at all:

> The missing information about the company is substituted by generalizations and can be distorted by the frame of reference of the individual (Bartlett 1916; Boldon 1961). People tend to react to this image more than to the object itself; hence, the less formed and filled-out the image is of a given company, the more subject it is to wild distortion through incidental, unplanned public exposure of an adverse sort.[3]

This analysis, which includes a survey of public affairs company officials, chief executive officers, and advertising directors, further suggests that associations about a company which assumes a low profile are not nearly as positive as associations about companies which seek a high profile:

> The low profile most usually associated such companies with words such as avoidant, uninvolved, passive, yielding and uninfluential. The high profile attributes were largely opposite, positive labels: visible, active, leader, pushy, vulnerable.[4]

The last two labels suggest that there is a counterrisk as well.

Less scientifically based but probably more persuasive is the classic and often-quoted argument against the low profile by Bruce Barton, the second *B* in BBD&O (Batten, Barton, Durstine & Osborn). It was written in 1947, but it could have been written for the 1980s.

> But the overwhelming fact is that, today, neither you nor any other big corporation can really halt its advertising. You can suspend the small part over which you have control.
> The part you do not control will roll on in ever-increasing volume. It is the advertising given you by politicians with axes to grind . . . by demagogues who may point you out as typical of all that is bad in business . . . by newspapers that hope to build circulation by distorting your acts . . . by labor leaders misrepresenting your profits . . . by all other operators in the field of public opinion, some unfriendly and many merely misinformed.
> Thus, you are going to have national advertising whether you want it or not!
> The only question you have to decide is whether it is worth a little money, a fractional percentage of your annual sales, for advertising of your company that will be factual, informative, and constructive. Or whether in the present state of world politics, where the electorate is the court of final appeal in ALL business decisions, you can afford to take the

---

[2]Issue of August 1978. Reprinted by permission of the *Journal of Advertising Research*.
[3]Ibid.
[4]Ibid.

risk of having all your advertising emanate from sources beyond your control.[5]

Today, more than 30 years later, that statement holds more truth than ever before. There are many more publics to be reached; there are many more issues to be faced.

Another argument against corporate advertising goes like this: *"It's an added cost we just can't afford at this time."* Capital demands are so great that the money must be put into _____ [you can fill in the blank]. Usually there's no counterargument. Management is constantly faced with making decisions on budget priorities, and there will be times when achieving even the best corporate communications objectives will be outweighed by more pressing demands. The important point here is to evaluate very carefully just what achieving communications objectives will accomplish in all areas of the company. For instance, an improved reputation may make securing capital easier and thereby eliminate the immediate problem, or the right campaign may improve the price-earnings ratio and reduce a cash need for acquisition purposes. The possibilities are immense and should not be overlooked. A full appraisal of the possibilities of capital enhancement should be explored under these conditions.

This next argument will probably come from someone with direct line responsibility for sales: *"We already spend millions on product advertising. That is the best representation this corporation can have. Why should we siphon money away from product support, where we can trace a direct dollar return, just to put it in something as far removed and vague as a corporate communications program?"* This seems to be a view held by many of the large package-goods corporations, which engage in corporate advertising less frequently than do other large industrial corporations.

In the ANA's 1979 survey of current trends in corporate advertising, which reported on the practice of 302 major United States corporations, industry categories were divided into eight classifications. Of the 129 non-users of corporate advertising, 80 fell into the consumer-goods category, and the majority of the companies which received the questionnaires but did not respond were also in consumer goods.

Similar results were revealed in the *National Geographic* study conducted in 1977 (see Chapter 3), which showed that of companies whose major products were consumer goods only 1 in 3 had corporate campaigns. In contrast, for companies whose major efforts were in industry or in services the ratio was 2 in 3.

It is entirely possible that some consumer-goods corporations are in positions in which they would gain little from a separate corporate effort, particularly if large-volume successful products bear household names which either are the same as or are highly associated with the name of the parent corporation. Remember, however, that regardless of how well

[5]*Strategic Advertising Case Book,* Time, Inc., New York, 1976.

Product and service classification	Corporate advertising users	Corporate advertising nonusers	Total
Consumer package goods	16	56	72
Consumer durable goods	11	24	35
Consumer services (travel, hospitality, insurance, financial)	37	15	52
Diversified consumer, business, and industrial	24	10	34
Diversified business and industrial	35	5	40
Basic materials (metal, paper, fiber, chemical, etc.)	32	14	46
Petroleum	15	2	17
Limited-line business and industrial	3	3	6
	173	129	302

known a product is, corporate association with it is usually far less strong than management suspects. More important, products and their advertising may not be conveying as accurate a picture of the corporation as it would like. This can be particularly true of the corporation's posture before the financial community. The kind of picture that may sell a cigarette, a cold cream, or a cold cereal to the general public can actually detract from the image that a company would like to have on Wall Street.

Management tends to think of advertising in terms of sales. John E. Kennedy said it first in 1905: "Advertising is salesmanship in print." In companies where this statement is a fact of life, proved anew every day as it is in package-goods companies, management seems to see advertising only in its relation to sales. But this A/S ratio is not the only ratio that may be considered. There are many other things that advertising can do which can form their own valuable business ratios. You might consider the A/P, or advertising-personnel ratio, the relationship of a good corporate program to better morale, reduced turnover, easier recruitment, etc. Each of these items is an important factor in a company's profit picture, and each is subject to improvement through the right corporate ad program.

To cite another example, there might be an A/F ratio, presenting advertising's relation to finances, the profits that might accrue from an improved reputation in the financial community. So, as product advertising can enhance profits by its effect on sales, corporate advertising can enhance profits by its effect on other items of the corporate balance sheet.

One of the most difficult attitudes to contend with is simple, blind negativism: "*I just don't think corporate advertising does anything for a company.*" You will notice that no substantial, specific reason is given for this feeling; there is just a vague distrust. Dealing with this attitude successfully depends on the person in the corporation who holds this view and where he or she stands in the corporation's hierarchy. Obviously, the farther up the ladder, the greater the problem. Lower down, it may be best to ignore the problem until the program is under way and then let the results speak for themselves.

If the attitude is that of a ranking decision maker, the ad department is likely to find itself scrambling for research data that bear on the subject. (Possibly, that's how you found this book, and we hope that you'll find some answers you're looking for by pursuing the many sources we have cited throughout the chapters.) A study completed for *Time* magazine by Yankelovich, Skelly and White, Inc., in 1979 may be the most helpful you can find. Certainly, it is the most ambitious attempt yet made to prove that corporate advertising is effective. In fact, the study goes even further. It gives good evidence that corporate advertising is more effective than product advertising in terms of enhancing a corporation's reputation.

Entitled *Corporate Advertising/Phase II: An Expanded Study of Corporate Advertising Effectiveness,* the study is a much enlarged version of a similar one conducted by Yankelovich, Skelly and White in 1977 that evaluated awareness levels of five companies which were active corporate advertisers compared with five companies which were not. The earlier study provided paired corporate and noncorporate advertisers by industry and product line. Seven hundred interviews were conducted among executives and managers with personal incomes of $25,000 or more in corporations and financial institutions. In this earlier study, which now assumes the role of a pilot, the results highlighted were as follows:

- Corporate advertisers have 13% higher awareness than non-corporate advertisers. Corporate advertisers have a 22% higher familiarity than non-corporate advertisers.
- Overall impression for corporate advertisers is 34% higher.

In addition, specific favorable attitudes are more often associated with corporate advertisers than non-corporate advertisers such as

- The quality of their product.
- The competence of their management.
- The attractiveness of their stock and the soundness of their financial condition.
- Their performance in the area of social responsibility such as planning of natural resources, concern about waste disposal, and truth in advertising.[6]

The 1977 study was subject to minor attacks by critics who thought that it was limited and that it included certain corporations which dominated the results. These corporations were International Business Machines and General Foods, which because of their size might have been expected to distort the relatively small sample. When the results were tallied without these two corporations, however, the analysis proved to be about the same.

[6]Yankelovich, Skelly and White, Inc., 1979.

The new study, which was carried out among sixty-four companies in nine industries, supports the validity of the first. Personal in-home interviews were conducted in twenty-five major markets among 1533 male and female respondents, all college graduates, in households with incomes of $30,000 or more (this was a thoughtful approach to maintaining a broader demographic base in our present economy). Fieldwork was conducted in the fall of 1979.

The sixty-four major companies were first arranged on a scatter chart that showed the range in advertising expenditures, with one side of the chart measuring product advertising and the other corporate advertising. In this way the companies were arranged into four groupings along their median expenditures. The quadrants were as follows:

- High-corporate–high-product advertising expenditures
- High-corporate–low-product advertising expenditures
- Low-corporate–high-product advertising expenditures
- Low-corporate–low-product advertising expenditures.

Sales revenues and advertising expenditures covered the first 9 months of 1979. The ad revenue information was obtained from Leading National Advertisers, Inc. (LNA).

The questioning was based on a fundamental theory of advertising communications, namely, that high ad expenditures will result in high advertising recall, which in turn will lead to high familiarity with good association with a company's specific traits and produce a favorable overall impression. All this leads to high potential supportive behavior. The positive effects of corporate advertising were evident for every critical measurement:

	Corporate advertising expenditures (64 companies)		Net percentage differential of high expenditures	Advantage in percent of high expenditures
	High (33); $500,000 or more (percent)	Low (31); under $500,000 (percent)		
Total recall	51	36	+15	+42
High recall	30	19	+11	+58
High familiarity	31	21	+10	+48
High association with specific traits	22	17	+ 5	+29
High favorable overall impression	35	27	+ 8	+30
High potential supportive behavior	16	12	+ 4	+33

NOTE: Average company scores.

Corporate advertisers did better on specific traits used to evaluate a corporation:

Association with specific traits	Corporate advertising expenditures (64 companies)		Net percentage differential of high expenditures	Advantage in percent of high expenditures
	High (33); $500,000 or more (percent)	Low (31); under $500,000 (percent)		
Quality products	39	32	+7	+22
Innovative R&D	34	26	+8	+31
Good financial record	28	21	+7	+33
Competent management	24	18	+6	+33
Responsive to consumers	23	18	+5	+28
Concerned − resources	20	14	+6	+43
Honest company	19	16	+3	+19
Responsive to employees	15	10	+5	+50
Truth in advertising	13	12	+1	+ 8
Helps control inflation	6	4	+2	+50
Average, all traits	22	17	+5	+29

NOTE: Average company scores.

And corporate advertisers benefit from more personal supportive behavior:

Respondents say they are likely to	Corporate advertising expenditures (64 companies)		Net percentage differential of high expenditures	Advantage in percent of high expenditures
	High (33); $500,000 or more (percent)	Low (31); under $500,000 (percent)		
Recommend employment	27	21	+6	+29
Buy stock	26	18	+8	+44
Buy product without comparison shopping	25	18	+7	+39
Read annual report	22	16	+6	+38
Procorporate position vis-à-vis consumerism, government, labor, merger or acquisition*	11	9	+2†	+22
Average potential supportive behavior	16	12	+4	+33

NOTE: Average company scores.
* Average.
† Significant in 4 of 5 cases; all other figures significant in 95 of 100 cases.

It is the dimension that corporate advertising appears to add to product advertising which most executives will find startling. By arranging the highs and lows of corporate and product advertisers into quadrants, cross examination revealed the following:

- In advertising recall, high-corporate advertisers had a significant advantage versus product advertisers with the same or even higher expenditures.

- High-corporate–low-product advertisers achieved total advertising-recall scores almost equal to those of low-corporate–high-product companies with a substantially smaller budget.

- Corporate advertisers achieved higher familiarity with the same or substantially lower product advertising budgets.

- Corporate advertisers achieved higher association with specific desirable traits with the same or substantially lower product advertising budgets.

- Corporate advertisers achieved higher favorable overall impressions with the same or substantially lower product advertising budgets.

- Corporate advertisers achieved higher potential supportive behavior with the same or substantially lower product advertising budgets.

In summary, corporate advertisers achieved higher scores on all five key measurements of effectiveness studies with the same or lower advertising expenditures regardless of product advertising expenditures, sales revenues, or price-earnings ratios. Altogether, these are remarkable findings which will almost certainly stimulate greater use of corporate advertising in the 1980s.

The Opinion Research Corporation has been able to demonstrate that a corporate communications program designed to strengthen a company's reputation in one area also strengthens it in areas not covered by the program. It has found that the planned enhancement of one dimension of a company's image usually has the bonus effect of reinforcing other dimensions as well. What seems to happen is that if people have reason to regard a company favorably in one respect, they will be predisposed to think well of it in some other respects even though they have little or no specific evidence for doing so.

People's knowledge of a corporation is generally limited. There's far more about a company that they don't know than the little they do know. Being somewhat lazy, people are willing to accept this knowledge and generalize about a company on the basis of very few hard facts. This willingness to generalize and categorize on very little evidence provides corporate advertising with the means to reach the public effectively well beyond the actual content of an ad. It can relate something to the public that it wants to hear and talk about the positive aspects of a corporation's program and its activities in the community. When the public is convinced of these things, it is willing to generalize that other things about the company also are worthwhile.

Stop and recall the impassioned arguments at a club or a bar advanced by people on subjects they know little about. Most of the arguments are couched in black or white terms, all good or all bad. Given one or two facts to which to relate their arguments, people will say, "And that Yankee pitcher became the greatest thing that ever happened to baseball," or "This politician is not only crooked, but his whole family is crooked." That same bias and willingness to overgeneralize can also apply to business reputations, and it can apply well above the barroom level even when supposedly sober judgments are involved. Corporate advertising can provide the few but vital nuggets of corporate excellence upon which the public can base positive generalizations about a company.

Perhaps the size and complexity of a corporation seem too great to be conveyed in a corporate advertising campaign. You may hear the argument *"Our businesses are far too complicated to explain in advertising."* You don't have to explain everything; in fact, you shouldn't try. Just treat the positive, interesting, and memorable company activities.

A very frequent line of attack on corporate advertising generally includes zingers like these: *"People buy products not companies."* *"Give me that corporate advertising money, let me put it into product advertising, and I'll show you how to get a return on your money."* *"The best corporate advertising is good product advertising."* If you work in the field long enough, you'll hear such comments. They may come from anyone in an organization, but most often they are made by divisional company managers who in some way contribute (either above or below their bottom lines) to the corporate advertising coffers. There is usually little support for corporate advertising below the level of the chief executive officer and the CEO's immediate staff executives. Those in line positions, with bottom-line responsibilities, have an often-understandable, if short-range, tendency to view corporate advertising as "soft" and less productive in their own sales-oriented sphere of activity.

Any company officials who engage in discussions that try to evaluate whether it's better to spend money on product advertising or on longer-range corporate advertising might as well devote themselves to deciding whether it's better to buy a new packaging machine or replace the lights in the hallways. The expenditures are needed for two entirely different jobs.

That there is confusion between product and corporate advertising is undoubted. This confusion arises out of the fact that there is a relationship between them. Good corporate advertising can make product selling easier, and good product advertising can enhance a corporation's image, especially if product and corporation carry the same name. While that last point would appear obvious, there is a tendency for product executives in line management to assume that the public always knows which product comes from which corporation. This is far from the case.

The effect which corporate advertising can have on product sales undoubtedly varies with the product class. Specifically, the effect of corporate advertising on lower-priced consumer products, particularly package goods, is minimal compared with the effect that it may have on high-ticket, considered purchases, whether of consumer or industrial products. The effect of corporate advertising can be seen to increase in a continuum with the change in several factors:

Low-priced ⟶ high-priced
Frequent purchases ⟶ infrequent purchases
Impulse ⟶ considered purchase
package goods ⟶ industrial
Heavy product advertising ⟶ no product advertising
Low technology ⟶ high technology
Individual product sale ⟶ long line of products

Corporate advertising's effect on industrial products is particularly evident since these products are often purchased for delivery and quality characteristics based upon the reputation of the company. This is especially important for smaller-volume items which could never be expected to support advertising of their own. To quote Willard Salter, who is with *Time* magazine in Boston:

> The right corporate posture can benefit product sales beyond the conventional divisional advertising. Why? Because, not all products are equally advertised or promoted. To have a well known, respected name behind an unadvertised product often translates into easier additional sales. A company that makes or distributes two thousand products can usually promote no more than two hundred adequately by divisional advertising. To a degree, corporate advertising can influence the other 1,800 creating additional profits.

Or as Lynn Townsend has said:

> Customers buy more than a product. Customers tend to buy the company that makes the product. They buy its size, its sincerity, the confidence it inspires.

Many executives from major corporations share this point of view, and the academic world concurs:

McGRAW·HILL AD A

The original McGraw·Hill ad appeared in the mid-1950s. It featured the stern visage of Gil Morris, a vice president and account supervisor at Fuller and Smith and Ross, McGraw-Hill's advertising agency and the originator of the ad. Prepared as a product ad promoting the need of industrial advertising, it has since become virtually the corporate identity of McGraw·Hill itself.

"I don't know who you are.

I don't know your company.

I don't know your company's product.

I don't know what your company stands for.

I don't know your company's customers.

I don't know your company's record.

I don't know your company's reputation.

Now—what was it you wanted to sell me?"

MORAL: Sales start <u>before</u> your salesman calls
—with business publication advertising

McGRAW-HILL PUBLISHING COMPANY, INC., 330 WEST 42nd STREET, NEW YORK 36, N. Y.

"*I don't know who you are.*
I don't know your company.
I don't know your company's product.
I don't know what your company stands for.
I don't know your company's customers.
I don't know your company's record.
I don't know your company's reputation.
Now—what was it you wanted to sell me?"

MORAL: Sales start **before** your salesman calls—with business publication advertising.

McGRAW-HILL MAGAZINES
BUSINESS•PROFESSIONAL•TECHNICAL

McGRAW-HILL AD B

Following Gil Morris's death and in deference to his memory, the ad was revised and updated with a professional model.

"I don't know who you are.
I don't know your company.
I don't know your company's product.
I don't know what your company stands for.
I don't know your company's customers.
I don't know your company's record.
I don't know your company's reputation.
Now—what was it you wanted to sell me?"

MORAL: Sales start **before** your salesman calls—with business publication advertising.

McGRAW-HILL MAGAZINES
BUSINESS • PROFESSIONAL • TECHNICAL

McGRAW-HILL AD C

In 1972 with further updating the McGraw-Hill ad, now with a modern buyer type every bit as tough and skeptical, rolls on.

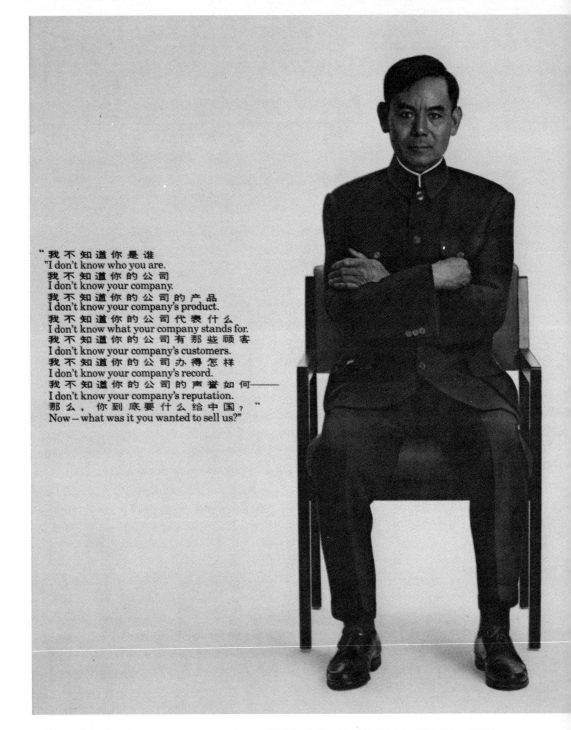

"我 不 知 道 你 是 谁
"I don't know who you are.
我 不 知 道 你 的 公 司
I don't know your company.
我 不 知 道 你 的 公 司 的 产 品
I don't know your company's product.
我 不 知 道 你 的 公 司 代 表 什 么
I don't know what your company stands for.
我 不 知 道 你 的 公 司 有 那 些 顾 客
I don't know your company's customers.
我 不 知 道 你 的 公 司 办 得 怎 样
I don't know your company's record.
我 不 知 道 你 的 公 司 的 声 誉 如 何——
I don't know your company's reputation.
那 么 ，你 到 底 要 什 么 给 中 国？"
Now—what was it you wanted to sell us?"

McGRAW·HILL AD D

More recently, this most adaptable of ads was used by McGraw-Hill to promote its People's Republic of China *American Industrial Report* circulation. Again the buyer is every bit as inscrutable.

McGraw-Hill helps you do business in the People's Republic of China.

You know how advertising in McGraw-Hill magazines helps your company contact prospects, arouse interest in products, overcome sales resistance, and create preference when you're selling to businesses here in America.

But you may not know that McGraw-Hill's *American Industrial Report* can do the very same things to help you sell to your toughest prospects in the People's Republic of China. And you also may not know that *American Industrial Report*, as the first U.S. technical magazine accepted into modern China, has more than five years of experience and marketing expertise.

During the early 1980's, the People's Republic of China will spend an estimated $30 billion-plus for foreign technology and capital goods. By 1985, they'll be buying a projected total of $12-15 billion worth from companies in the United States.

Obviously, the People's Republic of China is an important new market for American manufacturers.

But it's one thing to identify an important new market. And quite another to successfully

capture a share of it.

Selling industrial products in the P.R.C. involves the same problems as selling them in the United States.

Plus the problems of a different language and culture. And a different political, economic and foreign trade system.

There are almost 1 billion Chinese. McGraw-Hill's American Industrial Report reaches the .1% you need to do business with.

Every month, *American Industrial Report* reaches 35,000 end-users, engineers, managers, Foreign Trade Corporation and ministry officials. With an estimated pass-along of 50 readers per copy, that gives you exposure to 1 million Chinese—the .1% of the population who, as key decision-makers, are your key prospects.

American Industrial Report also helps you reach them in their own language. With free translation of your advertising copy into modern Chinese characters—the kind used in technical journals in the P.R.C., not Hong Kong or Singapore. We also give you free, expert advice on how to avoid the kind

of political and cultural errors that could alienate or confuse the very people you're trying to sell to.

A free guide to selling in the P.R.C. and to the magazine that helps you do it.

American Industrial Report would like to share what it's learned over more than five years of serving end-users in the People's Republic of China—and serving American advertisers who want to sell to them.

We've put it all into a free 84-page guidebook, which you can get by writing *American Industrial Report*, 1221 Avenue of the Americas, New York, New York 10020. Or calling Robert Christie at 212-997-6730.

Write or call for your copy today.

Now that the People's Republic of China has opened the door, see how *American Industrial Report* can help you get a foot in it.

McGraw-Hill Magazines

[A] company's generalized reputation has an important bearing on how its sales prospects make buying decisions. Generally speaking, the better a company's reputation, the better are its chances (1) of getting a favorable first hearing for a new product among customer prospects and (2) of getting an early adoption of that product.[7]

One last argument: *"We tried it once, and it didn't seem to do us much good."* Somehow that kind of statement, usually delivered with an air of great experience, always reminds me of an old joke, a kind of explanation for celibacy.

Many campaigns of the past, judging by appearances, probably did not produce the kind of results hoped for. But campaigns seem to be getting better, and judging by the increased use of corporate advertising and by the growing number of companies that stay at it year after year, it must be doing something for somebody. The fact that more and more people are applying measurements of performance against their programs adds weight to the belief that they are succeeding as never before.

If, in fact, a company once ran a corporate campaign that was judged to be unsuccessful, the old program should be dug up, the records reread, and a proper postmortem performed. Reexamining the project in light of the better disciplines that are being applied to corporate communications today (see Chapter 10) may be enlightening. There may have been dozens of reasons why the old campaign failed, but you can be sure that one reason was almost certainly a lack of continuity. You have to stay with a program, build it, and develop it. A short in-an-out effort is usually a large disappointment.

[7]Theodore Levitt, Harvard Graduate School of Business Administration, Boston, 1965, p. 25.

CHAPTER 5 CORPORATE ADVERTISING TO THE FINANCIAL COMMUNITY

Corporate advertising to the financial community is so important to many companies that it might be considered a separate category or, at least, a subspecies of corporate advertising. Too often there's confusion when we talk about "financial" advertising because it's assumed that we're dealing with the tombstone type of ad, which sets forth stock and bond offerings and other public financial announcements. The term "financial advertising" is also applied to the advertising that banks and financial institutions run. In the context of this book we are referring to corporate advertising addressed to the financial community.

There is a lot of this kind of advertising, but few companies will admit in public surveys that the reason for their corporate advertising is to affect the financial community. In an ANA study citing the objectives given by major corporations for their corporate advertising, none of the companies included financial objectives per se. It could be said, however, that financial objectives were implicit in the corporations' broad responses, e.g., "improving the level of awareness of the company, the nature of its business interests, profitability, etc."

Perhaps the reason that financial objectives do not surface in surveys is that implications of an improved perception of the corporation by stockholders, financial sources, investors, stock analysts, and money managers are so clearly accepted that they are not spelled out in the objectives. If such an assumption is the case, it is unfortunate because a clear spelling out of what a corporation is trying to accomplish in the financial world would sharpen the effectiveness of most corporate advertising. It is more likely that the reluctance to pin down the financial implications of a corporate campaign is a fear of appearing to be touting the stock. It is as though there were something illegal or immoral in running ads whose purpose is to improve the financial perception of a corporation (see Chapter 13, ``Corporate Advertising and the Law'').

The law is vague in this area, thanks to the reluctance of the Securities and Exchange Commission (SEC) to clarify the principles involved in self-promotion of a corporation's stocks. And, in fact, many company lawyers are wary of giving advice in this area. But neither lack of clarity in the law on the self-promotion of stock movement nor unwillingness to step up and clearly state improved financial perceptions as an advertising objective has in any way inhibited the amount of advertising addressed to this purpose. It is one of the major growth areas in the growing corporate advertising industry. This growth is not at all surprising, for there are a number of sound reasons for interest in this kind of campaign.

Why Corporate Advertising to the Financial Community?

First, the financial implications of an improved perception of a corporation by stockholders, financial sources, investors, stock analysts, and money managers can be quite dramatic and exciting. A 1-point increase in a widely held stock can easily mean many millions of dollars ($1 multiplied by the number of shares of stock outstanding). In the case of a giant corporation such as the American Telephone & Telegraph Co., whose stock is the most widely held, a 1-point increase is about $650 million. For Westinghouse Electric Corp., to cite another example, the figure would exceed $200 million.

An improvement in stock prices which betters the price-earnings ratio can have, in addition to its obvious acquisition advantages, opportunities for stock options and dividends for employees. It also provides easier and more advantageous equity offerings. Consider its effect on bonds. Even a slightly improved rating can mean a great deal on a large bond offering. To cite an example from the past, in 1968 AT&T sought to raise $250 million with a 28-year corporate bond issue. At the time, the amount required was considered too large for any one house. Two syndicates were formed, by Halsey, Stuart & Co. and Morgan Stanley & Co. Both syndicates researched their bids completely, and when the sealed bids were opened, they were very, very close. The difference on the surface would seem inconsequential: just $13/10,000$ of 1 percent. But that tiny fraction of 1 percent would have cost AT&T more than $1.5 million. So don't take bond costs lightly.

NL Industries Reports...

Record income for third quarter and nine months

> This report is a part of our program to keep you informed of what is happening at NL Industries.
> If you would like additional information, please contact us.
>
> *Ray C. Adam*
> Ray C. Adam
> Chairman and
> Chief Executive Officer

NL Industries, Inc. reported record earnings for the third quarter and first nine months of 1979.

Commenting on the record results, Ray C. Adam, chairman and chief executive officer of NL Industries, said, "The third quarter earnings reflected the improved performance of all NL operating groups. We fully expect the gains in earnings to continue, with fourth quarter and year end results reaching record levels."

Earnings up 38% for third quarter and 28% for nine months

Net income for the third quarter was $30,671,000, or 90 cents per common share, up 38% from earnings of $22,233,000, or 65 cents per common share, for the third quarter of 1978. Third quarter sales amounted to $531,131,000, which were 13% above sales of $470,946,000 for the same period last year.

Earnings for the first nine months of 1979 totaled $77,418,000, or $2.26 per common share, and were 28% higher than the net income of $60,452,000, or $1.76 per common share, for the first nine months of 1978. Nine months sales reached $1,610,686,000 in 1979, 17% above the nine months sales of $1,382,255,000 last year.

Petroleum Services, Chemicals and Metals show strong gains

NL Petroleum Services operations continued to report excellent results in the third quarter. The greatest earnings gains were achieved by drilling fluids and services in the foreign market, oilfield downhole services, and blowout preventers for oil and gas well drilling operations.

NL Chemicals earnings and sales benefited from the markedly improved results achieved by titanium pigments in the European market. Specialty chemicals' sales and earnings also improved worldwide.

NL Metals earnings, overall, were ahead of the year ago quarter, with automotive prototype engineering, metal fasteners, and recycled lead reporting increases. NL's 50%-owned subsidiary, Titanium Metals Corporation of America, which serves the aerospace market, again recorded strong gains in earnings and sales. Magnesium continued to show moderate monthly losses as high energy costs offset continuing technical and production improvements.

NL Industries, Inc. is a leading worldwide manufacturer and supplier of petroleum services and equipment, specialty chemicals, and fabricated metal products with sales of approximately $2 billion.

Sales and Earnings (Unaudited) (In Thousands, except per share amounts)	For the three months ended September 30		For the nine months ended September 30	
	1979	1978	1979	1978
Sales	$531,131	$470,946	$1,610,686	$1,382,255
Income before taxes on income	$ 54,540	$ 42,978	$ 138,912	$ 113,615
Provision for taxes on income	23,869	20,745	61,494	53,163
Net Income	$ 30,671	$ 22,233	$ 77,418	$ 60,452
Income per Share of Common Stock:	$.90	$.65	$2.26	$1.76

Note: Income per Share of Common Stock has been calculated after deduction for preferred stock dividend requirements ($.03 and $.10 per Share of Common Stock for the three months and nine months ended September 30, respectively).

NL Industries, Inc.
1230 Avenue of the Americas
New York, N.Y. 10020

NL INDUSTRIES

"Record income for third quarter and nine months"
A straightforward presentation of the financial performance of the corporation, in language as might be found in an annual report. In addition, it includes simple statements about the performance of the various company product lines.

Bunker Ramo tops previous third quarter and nine month results as earnings momentum continues.

In a business climate of growing uncertainty, Bunker Ramo has achieved significantly higher results for both the third quarter and first nine months of 1979. Compared to the similar periods in 1978, third quarter earnings increased 41% on a 6% sales gain, while earnings for the first nine months rose 47% on a 15% increase in sales.

Financial Highlights (in millions, except per share data)				
	Third Quarter ended Sept. 30 1979	Third Quarter ended Oct. 1 1978	Nine Months ended Sept. 30 1979	Nine Months ended Oct. 1 1978
Sales	$102.8	$96.6	$316.8	$257.7
Net Income	$ 6.5	$ 4.6	$ 17.2	$ 11.7
Earnings Per Share	$ 1.02	$ 0.73	$ 2.69	$ 1.86

The good news behind the good numbers.

Despite conflicting economic signals, the company's backlog climbed still further from its all-time high at the end of 1979's second quarter. Much of this strength is due to sales of our Amphenol®

electrical/electronic connectors to military, aerospace, telephone, business equipment, and instrument markets. As well as to aggressive marketing of our electronic information systems to banks, thrift institutions, insurance companies and brokerage houses.

A streetcar named Vienna.

In Austria's capitol, the city's streetcars are being equipped with Amphenol® connectors that utilize Bunker Ramo's leading position in fiber optics technology. In this particular application, one fiber optics cable does the job of 110 conventional copper cables — transmitting all necessary control and signal

information at lightwave frequencies, and providing the added benefit of three redundant channels in the same small space.

Your credit is good.

If you've ever stood in line at a retail outlet waiting to have a check approved, you'll certainly approve of our Financial Transaction Terminal and the variety of services it provides the consumer. Included are check verification and guarantee for approval of personal, payroll and government checks; authorization to verify credit card legitimacy and purchasing power; deposits, withdrawals, transfers and inquiries to and from checking, savings and card accounts; and payments to card and club accounts, utilities and loans.

Find out what Bunker Ramo's up to now.

For our latest financial reports, write William Van Dyke, V.P., Bunker Ramo Corporation, 900 Commerce Drive, Oak Brook, Illinois 60521.

Ticker symbol: BR

BUNKER RAMO CORPORATION

"Bunker Ramo tops previous third quarter."
A simple statement of earnings achievement and an explanation of some of the company's major activities throughout the world. The reader is given an invitation to secure its latest financial report. Note the interesting addition of the ticker symbol, BR, a helpful touch for the financial reader.

Keep in mind that both the syndicates that competed had access to the same information. Both were privy to all the research, all the forecasts, and all the census data; yet their bids came out differently. The reason for the difference was a question of opinion, of the syndicates' attitude toward the corporation — a perceived value to which advertising may be able to add. Gustave L. Levy, once a senior partner of Goldman, Sachs & Co., summed it up very well when he said, "P/E ratios are a state of mind and not a science."

If that statement was true when it was made in the 1960s, it is even more valid today. Investors are being asked to make market decisions on more and more companies that are inadequately followed by a diminished number of security analysts. Mark J. Appleman, a consultant on corporate communications, investor relations, and the marketing of corporate securities, states that "approximately 3,000 investment-worthy companies are not currently followed by security analysts. This widespread research deficiency is expected to worsen with the continuing contraction of the securities industry and concomitant reduction of the number of research departments and sell-side analysts." He goes on to account for the boom in financial corporate advertising in the late 1970s by observing:

> Having been ignored by traditional financial marketing channels, hundreds of companies are buying space and time to tell their story. For the most part, they hope to prevent further market attrition, exclusion from the equity capital markets, and possibly involuntary merger or takeover.
>
> Although some of these companies may be indulging in image polishing, most are accepting the cost and risk of paid promotion reluctantly and only as a last resort.
>
> In short, the current boom in corporate financial advertising reflects a pressing need to improve market recognition rather than a clear record of repeated success in reaching specific management objectives.

While Appleman decries the lack of hard data and of proper disciplines in much of current corporate advertising, he does point out four potential advantages that he feels are substantial for the use of corporate ads.

The ads can be:

1. Cancelled, repeated, and varied at the discretion of the company, independent of news editors.

2. Coordinated with other communication efforts to highlight specific corporate or product developments.

3. Used to generate requests for either extensive or specialized corporate information.

4. Designed to meet management objectives and produce measurable results, such as:

    a. encouraging shareowners to add to their holdings;

    b. attracting the attention of potential new investors;

    c. engaging the interest of financial analysts, market makers, and registered representatives;

    d. increasing or sometimes decreasing trading volume;

    e. lowering the cost of improving the prospects of obtaining equity financing;

    f. improving the price earnings multiple.[1]

Does Corporate Advertising to the Financial Community Work?

The question is whether corporate advertising can actually have any effect on these aspects of the financial sector. Logic suggests that individual stockholders will be reassured that they are investing wisely when they perceive that a corporation is on the move. There is evidence from the product advertising side that basic familiarity is necessary before people will buy. By extrapolation the stockbroker's job, therefore, is easier when he or she deals with a customer who is already familiar with the corporation and its business.

This need for presold familiarity with an issue becomes more obvious when you consider that according to an SEC study only about 1 investment decision in 5 is influenced by a broker's recommendation. (Other studies suggest that the ratio may possibly be 1 in 10.) Moreover, as previously mentioned, the number of stock analysts upon whom a broker can rely has diminished. If you add to all that the brokerage firms' need to tighten internal restrictions because of legal liabilities for unsuitable recommendations, you have an overwhelming argument for reaching the investor on a more direct basis such as corporate advertising and not relying solely on the older-line financial channels.

Institutional investors, money managers, and financial analysts themselves, as parts of the financial community, are a different matter. We may seriously question the impact of general corporate advertising on members of this more sophisticated professional group, which accounts for well over 60 percent of trading activity. They most likely view corporate advertising objectively, less for its content and more for a sign that a company is aggressively engaged in doing business and enhancing its reputation. In and of itself that is not a bad message for a company to convey to this important group.

We come back again to the partially answered question: Can a corporate campaign actually affect these financial areas? Are there any hard

[1]*The Corporate Shareholder,* Corporate Shareholder Press, New York.

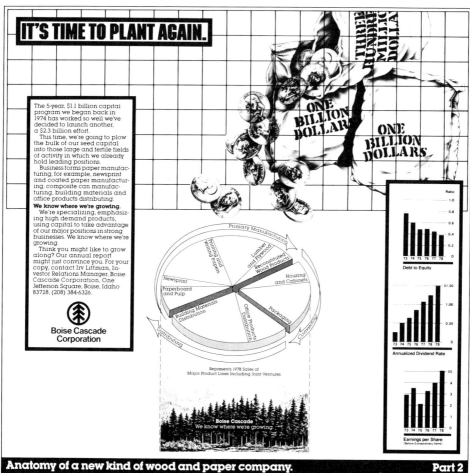

IT'S TIME TO PLANT AGAIN.

The 5-year, $1.1 billion capital program we began back in 1974 has worked so well we've decided to launch another, a $2.3 billion effort.

This time, we're going to plow the bulk of our seed capital into those large and fertile fields of activity in which we already hold leading positions.

Business forms paper manufacturing, for example, newsprint and coated paper manufacturing, composite can manufacturing, building materials and office products distributing.

We know where we're growing.

We're specializing, emphasizing high demand products, using capital to take advantage of our major positions in strong businesses. We know where we're growing.

Think you might like to grow along? Our annual report might just convince you. For your copy, contact Irv Littman, Investor Relations Manager, Boise Cascade Corporation, One Jefferson Square, Boise, Idaho 83728, (208) 384-6326.

Boise Cascade Corporation

ONE BILLION DOLLARS

ONE BILLION DOLLARS

THREE HUNDRED MILLION DOLLARS

Ratio
1.0
0.8
0.6
0.4
0.2
0
73 74 75 76 77 78
Debt to Equity

$1.50
1.00
0.50
0
73 74 75 76 77 78 79
Annualized Dividend Rate

$5
4
3
2
1
0
73 74 75 76 77 78
Earnings per Share
(Before Extraordinary Items)

Primary Manufacturing
Printing and writing papers
Lumber and Plywood
Reconstituted Wood Products
Newsprint
Housing and Cabinets
Paperboard and Pulp
Packaging
Building Materials Distribution
Other Products Distribution
Distributing
Converting

Represents 1978 Sales of Major Product Lines Including Joint Ventures

Boise Cascade
We know where we're growing

Anatomy of a new kind of wood and paper company. **Part 2**

BOISE CASCADE CORPORATION

"It's time to plant again."
Boise Cascade uses an imaginative space unit, a full page plus an adjoining inside column, to tell its financial story.

facts to deal with, any proven campaigns? We believe that there are, but we also know that corporations almost universally consider this information proprietary. They don't share their stock-market success stories.

In 1976 two Northwestern University professors, Eugene P. Schonfeld and John H. Boyd, made public the results of a large-scale econometric analysis of the relationship between stock prices and corporate advertising. In brief, their research indicated that corporate advertising can have a positive, statistically significant impact on the stock price of a company. However, the impact of corporate advertising on stock prices was found to vary with the overall direction of the stock market. Moreover, the effect of corporate advertising seemed to vary from company to company.

The basic approach of the Boyd and Schonfeld research was to fit a nonlinear model to cross-sectional data in which the closing stock price at the end of the year was the dependent variable and six financial variables and corporate advertising expenditures were independent variables. The independent financial variables were defined as earnings per share, total assets, the gross profit margin on sales, the ratio of total liabilities to common equity, and two dichotomous variables representing the continuity of earnings and dividend growth over the preceding 5 years. Corporate advertising was defined as total media expenditures in eleven business publications that could be traced to corporate ad budgets as opposed to product-line or divisional spending.

The data, which were adjusted for splits and stock dividends, covered 721 companies with sales greater than $200 million during the years 1971, 1972, and 1973. These years were specifically selected for study because they included a strong bull market, a strong bear market, and a mixed market.

Schonfeld and Boyd found that there was a classic diminishing response relationship between corporate advertising expenditures and stock price once the effects of the financial variables had been taken into account. The influence of corporate advertising was greatest when the stock market was trending up but was not significant when the market was trending down. However, some advertisers with especially effective campaigns seemed to get significant positive benefits from corporate advertising expenditures even in a down market.

After their research, Professor Schonfeld formed Schonfeld & Associates, a Chicago-based general management consulting firm. One of its first assignments was a turnkey project on corporate advertising and stock prices for Bozell & Jacobs International, Inc., a major advertising agency. The result of this project was a detailed analysis of corporate advertising strategies and tactics and their impact on quarterly stock prices and trading volume.

United Telecom.
A different breed of telephone system.

For many years, telephone systems have been thought of as steady, but slow-growing, companies.

Then we changed all that. We're United Telecom, operators of United Telephone, America's third largest telephone system.

While we have the stability that all telephone systems have, we also have the dramatic growth that most of them don't. Just since 1972, our revenues from United Telephone have more than doubled—from less than $480 million to more than $1 billion.

But today, we're more than a telephone company. We also operate two other fast growing telecommunications companies. One is United Computing Systems (UCS), a computer services company. The other is North Supply Company, which distributes the telecommunications products of more than 300 manufacturers.

While our telephone revenues were more than doubling in the last 6 years, UCS and North were growing even faster. Since 1972, UCS has zoomed from $8.2 million in sales to over $75 million. During this same period, North's sales grew from $86.7 million to more than $270 million.

All told, our overall growth at United Telecom has been astonishing—from about $650 million in 1972 to over $1.4 billion today.

Which just goes to show steady doesn't have to mean slow.

For our complete growth and earnings story, write for our latest annual report to: D.G. Forsythe, United Telecommunications, Inc., Box 11315, Kansas City, Missouri 64112.

New York Stock Exchange symbol: UT. Newspaper listing: UniTel.

An affirmative action employer.

United Telecom
United Telecommunications, Inc.

More than a telephone company.

UNITED TELECOM

United Telecom operates the third-largest telephone system in the United States. There are, in fact, almost 1600 independent telephone companies, many of them in rural and smaller suburban areas, which are also areas of great potential growth. This growth and the stability-utility story are important developments for telecommunication companies to present to the financial community.

Schonfeld & Associates constructed a data base of financial and advertising information for 460 companies for the period from 1974 through 1976. This data base consisted of quarterly financial and stock-market performance, corporate advertising expenditures in network TV, spot TV, newspapers, magazines, network radio, and outdoor advertising. It also included data on advertising content obtained by clipping and coding more than 16,000 corporate advertising insertions from seventeen publications.

A two-stage nonlinear model was fitted to this data base by multiple regression analysis. The first stage represented the relationship between stock price and financial performance, including corporate advertising expenditures. The second stage represented advertising campaign characteristics after the influence of first-stage variables had been taken into account. Two types of variables were included in the second stage: strategic variables (media class used and ad themes) and tactical variables (media vehicles used and execution treatments, such as a photographic illustration).

The research has been widely disseminated by Bozell & Jacobs through speeches, articles, and new-business presentations. The work is, of course, proprietary and not publicly available, unlike the earlier work of Boyd and Schonfeld. However, several facts are known about this B&J-sponsored research:

1. The statistical findings of B&J closely match the earlier work of Boyd and Schonfeld, replicating and confirming the earlier effort. (Publication of this replication by Schonfeld and Boyd has been approved by Bozell & Jacobs and should be available soon.)

2. B&J claims to have isolated the effectiveness of different media in influencing the impact of corporate ad campaigns on stock prices. However, Bozell & Jacobs and Schonfeld & Associates have agreed not to disseminate this aspect of the research in order to avoid controversy and to avoid disrupting the media relations of B&J.

3. The most effective message strategy for corporate advertising seems to be new information about the company and its products and information which enables investors to interpret the company's financial performance and prospects. Messages which concentrate on earnings growth, dividend growth, and the like seem to be less effective than informational messages. The reason may be that corporate advertising carrying information on financial performance such as earnings growth rates or increased dividends appears long after the information has been carried by investor wire services and similar electronic systems.

I present no brief for this more complex aspect of this study. Although its conclusions are quite compatible with conventional advertising principles, its attempts to examine ad components such as illustrations, placement of headlines, etc., as separate matters and then to relate these components to stock prices seems extremely ambitious. However, the fundamental conclusions about stocks' reaction to corporate advertising in general certainly seem soundly based.

Studies made by the *American Business Press* quite separately from the foregoing indicate that advertisers who maintain budgets during down years recover more quickly in up periods. Just how conclusive these few studies are may be debated by some, but in all the material studied we have never found anyone who seriously questioned corporate advertising's potential ability to affect positively a corporation's standing in the financial community. Individual campaigns may fail, but the basic technique is sound.

What Constitutes the Financial Community?

Just what do we mean when we say "the financial community"? It's essential to have a very clear idea of this term before any planning work can begin. If you talk about the approximately 25 million stockholders in the United States, you must consider broad-based media and recognize that you are embarking on an advertising program of more than $1 million. If, on the other hand, you look at the financial community in its narrower sense, to include only those who are actually involved in transactions on the various exchanges, you're talking about a total of approximately 50,-000 people.

Between these two extremes, the financial community can be thought of as a composite of elements. It consists of the New York Stock Exchange member firms and registered representatives. Similarly, the American, NASDAQ, Chicago, Midwest, and Pacific exchanges are component parts. Of course, there are the individual shareholders themselves, but beyond them is an equally segmented group, the so-called institutional market, which consists of the purchasers of large blocks of stock, such as mutual funds, life insurance companies, non-life insurance companies, nonmember brokers, commercial banks and trust companies, pension funds, and savings and loan associations.

The research department of *The Wall Street Journal* has done an excellent job of categorizing and quantifying these various target groups:[2]

[2]The figures, which are reprinted with the permission of *The Wall Street Journal*, are from its study *The Supershoppers: A Census of Corporate Finance Professionals*, published in 1977.

UOP—a leader in reverse osmosis systems

THE SIGNAL COMPANIES

"Signal Strategy"
The ad uses size, color, and illustration in the growing battle to reach and impress the financial community. The conventional earnings statement is there, but the ad offers the reader much, much more.

SIGNAL STRATEGY:

Position UOP to quench the thirst for new technology.

As water shortages threaten around the world, the need for purification through new desalination technology is growing rapidly. UOP, a major part of Signal, is a leader in reverse osmosis systems, which use half the energy of distillation methods and also greatly reduce lead time and capital requirements. UOP's current desalination projects range from the Colorado River to the Red Sea.

UOP is positioned to serve other major areas of growing technological need. The oil shortage has made the upgrading of refining and petrochemical processes of vital importance and UOP's leadership in these fields is long-established. Concern about pollution is growing rapidly in the U.S. and around the world—UOP's leadership ranges from catalytic conversion for auto exhausts to flue gas cleanup and waste water treatment.

To maintain its technological advantage in these and other fields, UOP spent $36 million in research and development in 1978. With 187 U.S. patents issued in 1978, UOP ranked 23rd among all U.S. companies.

Extending Garrett's fuel-saving technology from aircraft to automobiles. The Garrett Corporation's fuel-saving engines have captured 50% of the market for turbine propulsion engines in general aviation. Economical Garrett gas turbines are finding new markets in industry. Garrett's world leadership in turbochargers for trucks, aircraft, and other applications has been extended into automobiles to meet the need for more economical engines. Turbochargers reduce fuel con-

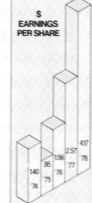

$ EARNINGS PER SHARE

sumption 20% by making small engines do the work of larger ones. To maintain leadership in all these areas, Garrett invested $161 million in research and development in 1978.

Expand Mack product line to include medium-duty diesel trucks. This bold move by Mack and Renault to distribute Class 6 and Class 7 medium-duty diesel trucks in the U.S. and Canada will assure deeper penetration of the total truck market. A long-time leader in heavy-duty diesel trucks in the U.S. market, Mack has also gained a commanding share of exports in this field.

These three major parts of Signal, together with a group of smaller investments ranging from real estate to broadcasting, have produced rapid and sustained growth. Return on equity has more than doubled in the last three years, reaching 18.4% in 1978.

The growth continues. Sales and earnings for the first nine months of 1979 were the highest in the entire 57-year history of The Signal Companies.

To ensure future internal growth, Signal spent a total of $210 million in research and development in 1978, of which $102 million was customer-funded. Capital expenditures were $97.4 million. At the same time, our conservative financial posture gives us the flexibility to take advantage of external investment opportunities which may arise.

For a copy of our annual report write: The Signal Companies, 9665 Wilshire Boulevard, Beverly Hills, California 90212. Ticker symbol: SGN.

© The Signal Companies, Inc. 1979

The Signal Companies
Worth watching

UOP Inc. • The Garrett Corporation • Mack Trucks, Inc. • Signal Landmark Properties, Inc.

Job category	Number of persons
Officers of nonfinancial companies who participate in arranging the companies' access to new capital	172,030
Officers and partners or board members who establish general policies regarding trading or investment in corporate securities	83,850
Investment managers and their immediate superiors who make buy-sell decisions on corporate securities for privately held portfolios	51,970
Registered brokers, account executives, and other sales personnel and their immediate superiors who deal with the securities of specific corporations	50,040
Investment managers and their immediate superiors who make buy-sell decisions on securities for corporate institutional or tax-exempt portfolios	43,330
Corporate securities analysts and their immediate superiors	25,100
Officers who advise client corporations on their financing requirements and access to new capital	14,860
Officers who participate in underwriting or syndication of public offerings or in private placement of corporate equity or debt issues	10,920
Editors, authors, and writers of newsletters, reports, and articles on corporate securities and other aspects of corporate finance	8,710
Staff members of exchanges and federal and state regulatory authorities who exercise influence on the issuance or trading of corporate securities	540

Corporate Advertising and Acquisitions

There is a growing appreciation of the role that corporate advertising can play in successful mergers, acquisitions, and purchases of product lines or brands. Part of the selling price of a company or a product line is the reputation and goodwill enjoyed by that company, a fact long understood and recognized even by the courts. A good reputation has intrinsic value. While this reputation may be *built* on the good quality of products or services, *communication* of this quality enhances the reputation and hence the sales value. Just as product advertising enhances the value of an individual product or brand line that may be sold, corporate advertising can enhance the reputation and improve the value of the corporation itself. In effect, the corporation is the product being sold.

This relationship between corporate advertising and acquisitions can be understood by examining the effect the price-earnings ratio of a company can have on an acquisition and the effect corporate advertising can have on the price-earnings ratio. The fact is that if you want to acquire another company, it's a good idea to do it when your own P/E is high. Conversely, if you wish to avoid being gobbled up, remember that there is nothing more inviting than a low P/E.

Time quotes Donald J. Smalter and Roderic C. Lancey, who give the following example of the value of a high P/E in making an acquisition.[3]

Possible Transaction Affected by P/E: Company A to Purchase Company B

(Negotiated price: $202.5 million)

	Company A		Company B	
Sales ($ million)	$300		$100	
Earnings ($ million)	$ 25		$ 10	
Shares (millions)	10		2	
Earnings per share	$ 2.50		$ 5.00	
Stock price	$45	$54	$84	$100
Price-earnings ratio	18.0	21.6	16.8	20.0

Option 1:
Company A would issue 4,500,000 shares at $45 per share.
Composite earnings per share: $2.41 (35,000,000 divided by 14,500,000 shares).
Effect to stockholders: 3.6 percent dilution ($2.50 minus $2.41, or $0.09 divided by $2.50).

Option 2:
Company A would issue 3,750,000 shares at $54 per share.
Composite earnings per share: $2.54 (35,000,000 divided by 13,750,000 shares).
Effect to stockholders: 1.6 percent increase ($2.54 minus $2.50, or $0.04 divided by $2.50).
If price of Company B stock were $84, Company A would need to issue only 3,750,000 shares at $45 per share, increasing earnings by 1.6 percent.

You can see that Company A has sales of $300 million and earnings of $25 million, with 10 million shares outstanding. Earnings are $2.50 a share. Currently the stock is quoted at $45, giving Company A a price-earnings

[3]Reprinted by permission of the *Harvard Business Review*. Adopted from exhibit in "P/E Analysis in Acquisition Strategy," by Donald J. Smalter and Roderic C. Lancey (November–December 1966). Copyright © 1966 by the President and Fellows of Harvard College; all rights reserved.

ratio of 18 to 1. In contrast, Company B, just one-third of Company A's size, has $100 million in sales and earnings of $10 million, with 2 million shares outstanding. Its earnings per share are $5. The stock is quoted at $84, giving Company B a price-earnings ratio of 16.8 to 1.

If Company A buys Company B under these conditions at a $45 stock price, it could do so by trading 4,500,000 of its shares at $45. That's what the book value would be: the stock would equal the book value. Company A could then buy Company B.

The newly formed company, a combination of A and B, would have $400 million in sales, earnings of $35 million, and 14,500,000 shares outstanding (10 million shares plus the 4,500,000 that Company A had to float at $45 to buy Company B). Earnings per share would drop to $2.41. The shareholders in Company A would show a loss in earnings of 9 cents per share ($2.50–$2.41) as a result of this not very smart merger. Under these conditions, Company B would not do any better.

Smalter and Lancey go on to describe how the picture changes if there is a lift in the P/E of Company A. They assume that something exciting has happened, either a new product or some promising new situation, presumably communicated to the business community through corporate advertising and resulting in an improvement in the company's stock price from $45 to $54. This would be a very respectable 20 percent lift, but not an altogether unreasonable one. Company A, with the same sales and earnings, can now buy Company B, with the same sales and earnings, for only 3,750,000 shares of stock. Now the new company has combined sales of $400 million, earnings of $35 million, and 13,750,000 outstanding shares (10,000,000 plus the 3,750,000 shares paid for Company B). Earnings per share now come in at $2.54, representing a small but acceptable lift. Notice that while sales and earnings have remained the same, the share price and the resultant P/E have improved. Stockholders of Company B get an increase too, to $5.08 per share. So everyone has gained when the stock of Company A goes up. Of course, an exchange of stock follows essentially the same principle and works just as well.

There seems to be little argument that a high P/E is an advantage. The argument is whether corporate advertising can do anything about the P/E. The evidence presented in Chapter 9 seems convincing. In addition, Smalter and Lancey surveyed this question directly among 350 securities analysts and concluded that "much of the rating process is based on psychological reaction to future prospects and on subjective judgments." Many others have reached the same conclusion.

We have seen the somewhat unusual but very direct role that advertising played in one acquisition. This example demonstrates the street-level acceptance of corporate advertising as a means of improving the perception of a company to other businesses, would-be buyers, and merging partners. Following an acquisition made by one of our long-standing large clients, our account group had a first work session with the newly acquired company, now a division of its new parent, and reviewed the advertising that this company had been producing for the past 2 years. This was a middle-sized industrial company that had been quite active in promoting itself not only to its trade but to a somewhat broader business community as well. We asked the company's representatives why they had stopped most of this campaign, assuming that their answer would be related to the mechanics of the name change or a reevaluation of the line. Instead, we were surprised by the ad manager's candor. He had been with the company prior to the merger, and he said, "Well, we don't have to advertise anymore. That campaign did its job. The ads worked when they bought us. We weren't just trying to sell products; we were trying to sell ourselves. We made ourselves look a great deal bigger and more attractive through our advertising efforts, and that was the whole idea."

This puffing up like two birds confronting each other before squaring off is, we believe, a more frequent preacquisition phenomenon than might be expected. Clearly, it's not something that management likes to talk about, and if carried to extremes it can, of course, be viewed as fraud. It does, however, suggest the value of the contribution of a strong image in buying, selling, and trading in the business community.

A more subtle effect that corporate advertising may have during an acquisition is the broader familiarity of two parties with each other before and during the merger. On an individual basis the people of each corporation can have greater respect for their counterparts with a better knowledge of the background of the new members of the family.

The Future

As we go into the 1980s, we see a need for increasing the efficiency of reaching key financial segments. A combination of factors mentioned previously, including an increased number of worthwhile issues, fewer research facilities, and a growing demand for investment money, will make financial advertising as tough a competitive arena as any package-goods category in the advertising business.

I think the essence of the message that firms must communicate to the financial community in the future is the most basic one: their management's effectiveness. There's a growing search by investors for sound management and also a recognition that corporations vary greatly in effectiveness. The contest will come down to a basic street fight: "Our management is better than your management." And that's going to be a tough battle.

CHAPTER 6 CORPORATE ADVERTISING AND EMPLOYEES

Few if any corporate campaigns today have as their principal target either the company's own employees or prospective employees. During the shortage of engineers in 1960, such a target was not uncommon as a major objective in industrial corporate campaigns. Today if there are problems in this area, programs more specific than corporate advertising are directed toward them. Nevertheless, almost any corporate advertising campaign will have an important impact on employees, and if potential employees are included in the target audiences, the campaign can have a strong influence on them as well. An understanding of this relationship is important. Whether the corporate program has specific personnel objectives or not, its effect on employees should not be overlooked. Usually the programs exert a positive influence, but it is entirely possible that a corporate campaign which may accomplish its primary objectives with, say, the financial community may have a backlash effect on certain classes of employees. Care in the planning process can avoid such problems. Preliminary discussions with the personnel departments of various divisions and possibly a simple survey of employees are time well spent.

Effect on Existing Personnel

Employees' efficiency and productivity are, of course, dependent on their motivation, supervision, direction, education, and morale. These interrelated factors are influenced by countless elements in the employees' life. Some of these, among them genetic makeup, environmental background, and homelife, obviously are not under an employer's control. Other influences, such as working conditions, salary, supervision, and job training, are the customary controllable elements that an employer manipulates to get desired results. While corporate advertising is only one small element in this list of influences, it can have an important effect in a number of ways, principally in building pride and morale. It can influence the family and friends of employees and contribute to the employees' own understanding of their company.

Improving Morale

Personnel theory holds that employees prefer to work for and have greater confidence in large, stable, growing corporations. It goes on to suggest that morale is better when employees can take pride in the place where they work in the community. Now you can begin to see the role that corporate advertising may play. It should be a nice experience for an employee, when asked by a neighbor or a new acquaintance where he or she works, to be able to give the name of a company which is immediately recognized. So much the better if the reply is, "Oh yes, I've heard of them. They developed that new widget I've read about." Contrast that reaction with having to explain what the company does, what its role in the community is, what it is known for — all the things that the employee would feel constrained to cover in an effort to justify why he or she works for that company. An example is the wife who comments on an ad by her husband's company. Somehow anyone feels a little more important when his or her company is a little more important.

Educating Employees

In most instances, employees work in a well-defined but limited area of activity within a company. Very few jobs expose employees to the full scope of a company's operations. Corporate ads can broaden employees' knowledge and make them realize that they're an important part of a cohesive whole. Depending on the nature of the campaign, employees may learn a great deal about their company by following the company's ad campaign.

Career Opportunities

Corporate advertising may raise the sights of employees, stimulating them to consider advancing up through a company to other areas of activity. It can reassure them that there are indeed career opportunities in the company beyond their present, possibly narrow jobs. It may very well convince them that their future lies with the company and that they need not look elsewhere for job opportunities.

A very interesting attempt was made by *Time* magazine to place a dollar value on this aspect of corporate advertising. It demonstrated how corporate advertising could reduce recruitment and training expenditures by reducing turnover. The formula *Time* developed contains a number of unknowns and, at best, is a very rough guide. However, it demonstrates an impressive dollar-saving potential even when conservative values are assigned to the elements in the equation. *Time* confined its example to management personnel rather than production-line people. If you have the necessary information for your own company or care to make some guesses, the formula goes something like this:

1. Start with the cost of training a new employee for 1 year. (*Time* suggested a very low figure of $3000. Personally, I've heard estimates of over $20,000. Put in the number that feels right to you.)

2. Next take the total number of management people within the corporation. *Time* used its own organization as an example; when it did this, it had approximately 6000 management employees.

3. Know the yearly turnover of management people. Again from its own experience, *Time* cited a 15 percent yearly turnover, which in its case translated to 900 people a year. This was the number of people that *Time* had to replace each year just to maintain the existing number of personnel. Up to this point you've probably been dealing with fairly hard data: the number of employees, the yearly turnover, and even training costs are usually available.

4. Now for an estimate. Put down your guess for an answer to the questions, "What percentage of the employees who left might have been influenced either directly or indirectly through the opinions of spouses, brothers or sisters, or friends to have stayed with the corporation? What percentage might have stayed if they had felt that the corporation was well run and offered them a career opportunity?" Certainly a large percentage of the people who left probably could never have been persuaded to stay. Real job opportunities from other companies, offers of major salary increases, or even real negative problems with their existing company might all have been insurmountable obstacles. But there should still be some small percentage of employees who, if they had understood the corporation better, might have stayed. In *Time*'s own example it used the figure of 30 percent. These were the people that *Time* felt might have been persuaded to stay had they known more about the company and its opportunities. Personally, I think that number is high. Using *Time*'s figure and simple arithmetic would show savings of more than $800,000. Using a more conservative 10 percent figure still would provide savings of over $250,000.

Admittedly, all this figuring is tenuous. But by using it as a starting point, you may be able to develop an interesting estimate of cost savings — an unexpected dividend from a corporate advertising campaign.

Aligning Thinking on Company Policy

It's not unusual for employees to base their understanding of where their company is going and what its policies and directions are on the corporate advertising they see. Strategies, documents, and planning guides are essential in aligning middle management's thinking, but don't underestimate the effect that a well-written ad can have in this respect. An ad's appropriate illustration and concisely worded message, with all the emotion left in, can be a lot more forceful expression of a company's policy or corporate mission than a 30-page, closely typed white paper.

Don't depend on employees' accidentally finding ads in the magazines they read regularly or seeing the commercials shown with the TV programs they watch. Merchandise the advertising to your own employees. Facilities for doing this will vary with the company. You'll think of dozens of ways to take advantage of opportunities peculiar to your company, but here are some ideas to get you started:

- Present to key department heads or divisional executives concepts of the new campaign — live, in slides, or on film — explaining corporate objectives and how the program is calculated to meet them. Advance notice of the program is essential for later cooperation by subsidiaries and departments. If possible, convene a 1-day meeting at the executive offices, calling in necessary executives from around the country. If this isn't practical, you may find that you can tie the presentation in with an already-planned executive conference at which you can get time on the agenda. If these methods fail, consider putting the show on the road, possibly at regional meetings or one-night stands if the number of subsidiaries and branches is limited. Generally, if you give enough time to visiting the field and presenting the program, subsidiaries will respond by supporting it. On the other hand, if you spring a new campaign on subsidiaries and they see it for the first time by opening a magazine or turning on a TV set, you can expect very little support or even sympathy. The folks at the other company locations don't know why you're running such a campaign. They don't realize that they may be expected to support it locally, and they won't even be able to explain the program and answer questions from their employees, who may ask what the new ads are all about.
- Keynote the announcement of new campaigns in a brochure or folder which explains the purpose of the corporate program and interprets its value to employees. Examples of the opening ads can be included along

with photoboards of TV commercials. Inexpensive floppy records of radio commercials can be included. If all this sounds like too much money, reconsider. Small though it is, this may be your single most important audience. You can probably get some help from the magazines on your schedule. Most magazines have a merchandising fund that is customarily used by product advertisers to merchandise their advertising to wholesalers and the trade. Such merchandising credits are frequently untapped by corporate advertisers, but most publications are happy to see them used for merchandising the campaign and their publications to your own employees.

- Start regular ad mailings. These can take many forms. One consists of simple reprints with letters circulated on a regular basis or, better still, of reprints sent directly to employees' homes with personalized letters explaining the purpose of the program. Again, you can invite the publications in which you're buying space to participate in merchandising the ads by having them send copies of their magazines on a one-time basis to key personnel throughout the company. Usually, a customized bookmark will indicate your advertisement. It should be accompanied by a letter from the publication, which acts as a third-party endorsement of the campaign. Each participating magazine gets a chance to describe its audience and the importance of these people to your corporation. Such merchandising campaigns require planning and coordination, but they can be well worth the effort.

- Simplest of all is the bulletin board, and most companies have loads of boards in all plants and offices. Have someone post all new ads for you. And, just as important, have them taken down and replaced regularly. There's nothing worse than a ragged, old, dog-eared, yellowed message which shows that nobody cares. You may also want to explore having blowups of the ads made. These can be displayed quite spectacularly throughout a plant or office. Laminated counter cards are a good touch in reception rooms, and they stay cleaner and neater-looking longer than unlaminated ads.

- If your program is fast-moving, is subject to change, and has news value, by all means set up a special phone number that employees can call to hear the company's latest commercials or the newest wrinkles in the campaign. Inexpensive equipment can provide a recorded message which you can change as regularly as you want. The novelty itself will last for several months, although it is rarely sustained for a longer period.

- Consider showing commercials in company cafeterias or on closed-circuit facilities, which are becoming increasingly available in offices and plants throughout the country. If you have any ham in you at all, don't be afraid to go in front of a camera and make a video cassette presenting the commercials. A simple stand-up presentation of the objectives of the campaign is all that is required. If you're bashful, just do a voice-over while the cassette presents the objectives in title form. Either way is better than sending commercials out unexplained or leaving descriptions and explanations to the local audio-visual operator. Say it yourself on tape, and you'll know that the employees will have the message.

- If the campaign and the theme are suitable, you may have the basis for an internal promotion or contest, possibly tied in with specific employee objectives. And don't forget existing house organs' which are always hungry for material; to them the new program is news. They may well wish to carry local schedules so that employees can see commercials at home or look for ads in local newspapers. When employees are made to feel that they're inside and reasonably well informed, they are usually very supportive. When they are not supportive, it's usually because they have been left out from the beginning. In campaigns which feature the products or activities of particular subsidiaries, you will notice a tendency to favor these ads in local merchandising. In fact, subsidiaries frequently can use these ads as examples of the support that dealers and wholesalers receive from the corporation. Merchandising goes beyond their own employees to the subsidiaries' customers. While this development is to be applauded, care should be taken that subsidiaries don't ignore corporate advertising which depicts the activities and services of other subsidiaries. In many ways it is more important to merchandise these other sides of the total company. Rounding out a subsidiary's view of the total corporation should be viewed as an objective of any corporate merchandising program.

- When a corporate communications program has run for some time and has been successful in achieving its objectives, it is quite all right to be proud of it. A brochure describing the entire program and its results makes an excellent piece to send to employees and stockholders. There is little or no need to be secretive about your corporate successes, as there is with product advertising programs and their test results. Remember that corporate compaigns are not usually directly competitive. Sharing your successful ideas can only help raise the entire level of corporate communications. Again, several magazines, particularly the newsweeklies, are anxious for such case histories. Even when the histories have been sanitized, they are useful. Get in touch with the magazines and discuss your ideas; they'll be glad to listen.

Setting Standards For Employee Performance

If employees are featured in commercials or advertisements regardless of whether the campaign is corporate or product, the ads may serve to set standards of performance for the other employees. In effect, they act as subtle training films.

If you find a cigarette butt in an Avis car, complain. It's for our own good.

We need your help to get ahead.

Avis is only No. 2 in rent a cars. So we have to try harder.

Even if it's only a marked-up map in the glove compartment or you waited longer than you felt you should, please don't shrug it off.

Bug us.

Our people will understand. They've been briefed.

They know we can't afford to hand you anything less than a new car like a lively, super-torque Ford. And it's got to be immaculate, inside and out.

Otherwise, make a noise.

A Mr. Meadow of New York did.

He searched and came up with a gum wrapper.

AVIS

"If you find a cigarette butt in an Avis car, complain. It's for our own good."

One of the earliest ads from Avis's "We try harder" campaign (which began in the 1960s), it certainly cannot be classified as a corporate ad. It does illustrate, however, how a campaign can set the service standards of employees. Copies of ads from this campaign were enclosed with payroll checks as strong reminders of employees' performance obligations.

Companies engaged in businesses which bring employees into regular contact with customers frequently have very special training and morale problems. Advertising has often been used to deal with such problems. Recall how often the telephone operator was the heroine in old phone industry ads. She was portrayed as always helpful, always loyal. She stayed at her post in times of disaster. This voice-with-a-smile kind of advertising set corporate objectives for the phone companies as human organizations rather than as cold, impersonal utilities; it had huge internal benefits for the phone companies as well. Today telephone operators take pride in their jobs. They can identify with the heroine, whether she is being helpful in little matters or showing great resourcefulness in times of emergency.

One of the original objectives of the Avis campaign "We try harder" was to raise the standard of performance of attendants at the various Avis rental locations throughout the country. Standard levels varied tremendously with the ability of local ownership and management to motivate employees behind the counter, those who serviced the cars, and even the people in the parking lots. Recognizing the importance of service to business customers, the principal market for the industry, the ads focused on small but important service details.

One memorable ad example challenged business executives to complain if ashtrays weren't clean. The clear implication to employees of focusing on a small detail was that attention must also be paid to larger matters. By focusing on these standards of performance, the ads not only had a major effect on how customers perceived the company but, what was perhaps just as important, had an effect on employees and on the way in which they perceived themselves in their jobs with individual Avis outlets. The employees knew from the ads what was expected of them, and they learned very quickly that if they did not live up to the increased expectations of business executives, they would have to live with complaints from dissatisfied customers. In this way the ads became a powerful weapon for quality control.

You may add dimensions to this technique by using actual employees in ads and commercials. This has been the practice in the American Airlines campaign of several years, "Doing what we do best." The use of real people heightens employee identification with the campaign. If the campaign is well merchandised within the company, it may become a major factor in employees' performance. This merchandising can range from simple slogan buttons worn on uniforms to elaborate performance contests. The selection of employees for the ads and commercials may even be worked into the contest itself.

Incidentally, current union practices call for paying scale wages to employees used in such campaigns. Only employees who are shown actually performing their regular functions without benefit of script are excluded from this provision.

DOYLE DANE BERNBACH INC., ADVERTISING, 437 MADISON AVENUE, NEW YORK, N.Y. 10022

CLIENT: AMERICAN AIRLINES, INC.　　　PRODUCT: AMERICAN AIRLINES

TITLE: "I AM"　　　CODE NO: ARAC 5116　　LENGTH: 60 SECONDS

1. (MUSIC BUILDS UNDER THROUGHOUT) WHITEHEAD: I work for American Airlines.

2. and I've trained over 400 pilots.

3. They all thanked me. But I thank them too for giving me a chance to

4. WHITEHEAD AND JOHNSON: ...do what I do best.

5. JOHNSON: Even the little things, like serving coffee.

6. As long as I know it's the best cup of coffee I can make.

7. JOHNSON AND KOZIATEK: As long as I know how

8. KOZIATEK: to change an engine on our DC10's.

9. But I can also change an engine on the DC8. Now we don't even fly DC8's.

10. Airplanes aren't just my business..

11. KOZIATEK AND JENKINS: Airplanes are my life.

12. JENKINS: I've flown them all, from DC3's to 747's,

13. but if there's one thing I've learned from 30 years with American

14. it's that I don't fly airplanes. I fly people, and I remember that..

15. JENKINS AND RITTER: Every time someone

16. RITTER: calls to make a reservation. I'm doing what I do best and that's important.

17. Because the way people feel about American Airlines depends on the way they feel about me.

18. I am American Airlines.

19. CHORUS SINGS: (VO) We're American Airlines. Doing what we do best.

1ST AIR DATE:_____
PROGRAM:_____

TIME:_____
1ST AIR DATE ON:
ABC_____
CBS_____
NBC_____

AMERICAN AIRLINES

While American Airlines would be the last to categorize this commercial as corporate, the content certainly enhances the image of the corporation through vignettes of the airline's employees doing their jobs. What is being sold, of course, is service. And if that were all this commercial conveyed, it would be doing an excellent job. But it goes further. "People commercials," as commercials depicting employees are sometimes called, impart a sense of pride to other employees and set standards for appearance and attitude.

132

Planting seeds for the future.

With that provocative statement as its theme, Champion has launched a new corporate advertising program this fall. Those "seeds" are more than just seeds of trees, however; they're also seeds of *ideas* — ideas about what the

future may hold. It goes without saying that we're surrounded by advertising. From television screens, radios, magazines, newspapers, billboards, and countless other sources, we're bombarded by commercial messages. Advertising has grown into one of the primary channels of communication in our society.

Most of that commercial communication has, in the past, urged us to buy things. But within the last decade or so, the medium of advertising has come to be used more and more for purposes other than selling a product or service. At first called "institutional" advertising and now more popularly called "corporate" advertising, this new kind of advertising has something more on its mind than making a sale. What it hopes to do is tell the public about a company as a whole — its products, its financial performance, its position, what it stands for, its people — whatever the individual company believes is important for the public to know. The over-all objective is to create in the public's awareness a positive impression of a company. It was assumed that if the public knew you and thought well of you, it would help your company sell its products more easily, sell its stock to investors, boost employee moral, and help recruit new employees, and in general facilitate all its activities. In a word, it was assumed that it is a business *advantage* to be known, and a business *disadvantage* to be unknown. (Any of you — and there are

Once upon a time there was an Art Director. With blood and sweat, day and night, he labored to conceive a new idea. And behold, he found he had created a blue-blooded stallion, with flashing eyes, proudly-arched neck, powerful legs and a flowing tail. This was such a perfect animal, in short, that not even the ancient gods could have done better.

A conference was called to view the masterpiece.

The Sales Manager declared:
▸*He trots too lightly.*
There was a lot of talk and the stallion was given the feet of an elephant. Someone else piped up:
▸*I think his range of vision is too limited.*
There was more talk and the stallion wound up with a giraffe's neck. Finally the Boss remarked:
▸*He isn't fancy enough.*
They agreed, and gave the animal a peacock's tail. *And then everybody wondered why the idea didn't pull.*

probably many, many — who have had to explain that you *don't* work for a sparkplug company can especially appreciate one of the values of corporate advertising.)

That assumption — that corporate advertising really did help a company — has taken a long step toward becoming fact with the recent release

by David R. Brown

of the results of studies conducted by Yankelovich, Skelly and White, the national research firm.

The first study demonstrated that it was, indeed, a business advantage to be known and a business disadvantage to be unknown; and that corporate advertising was one effective way for a company to get better known. (The results in summary showed that corporations who advertise are 10 percent better known, 20 percent more familiar to the public, and enjoy a 33 percent better image than companies who don't advertise.)

The second study was much more ambitious. It was designed to find out *how* corporate advertising worked to a company's advantage. The study measured 64 major companies in a dozen industry groups. Through in-depth interviews with over 1500 Americans (carefully selected to be representative of business, professional, government, and financial decision-makers), the study attempted to discover what effects corporate advertising had on a variety of things: likelihood of buying one company's product over another's; likelihood of investing in a company's stock; likelihood of recommending employment with a company; likelihood of supporting a company in a dispute with government; and general overall image — good company, sound management, responsible, and so forth.

The results of this expanded study supported the conclusions of the

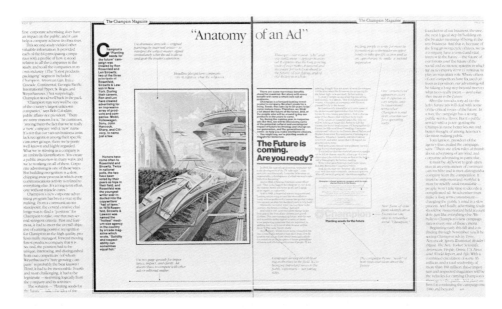

Effect on Recruitment

Finding people, just any people, is not difficult today. But finding good people can be difficult in many job categories in most industries. Some of the largest corporations view their long-range competitive success as directly related to their ability to employ the outstanding students from the outstanding business and technical schools. As they see it, the corporations that win the top 2 or 3 percent of the graduating classes will win the future. Corporate advertising can help, although it is certainly no substitute for recruitment advertising. Listings in help-wanted sections and display recruitment ads in newspapers and industry journals are still needed to fill difficult key positions.

Corporate advertising's role is less direct and less measurable but is nonetheless real in facilitating the job of recruitment. Really good people today have a choice of jobs. Whether they are just out of college, have a specialty sought after by many major corporations, or already have a job track record, the better people in the 1980s will probably have little difficulty in finding work with a company that appeals to them.

Good people are attracted to a company because they have heard good things about it in the marketplace or from their family or friends. Or they may be interested in the things in which they know the company is engaged. The knowledge that these job candidates have of a corporation is most likely very incomplete. If yours is a large multidivisional corporation, knowledge of it may be confined to a somewhat limited localized view. Your local branch office, in effect, often represents the entire company to the residents of a community. Job candidates may not realize the broad scope of your business. They may not realize that you have exactly the challenges that they are seeking. Advertising can round out a picture of your company, making it easier to be found or sought out. Advertising also ensures that the reception given your on-campus recruiters is positive.

If recruitment costs are a known factor in your company, you can once again try the formula worked out by *Time* magazine and mentioned earlier in this chapter. But again the outcome is dependent on your guesstimate. The results therefore may be shaky.

Whether you can place an exact dollar figure on the benefits to be derived from a corporate campaign or not, there is no doubt that benefits do exist and should not be overlooked in your corporate communications planning. Not to be overlooked is an overlay campaign in key recruitment areas. This entails determining which geographic areas form your principal pool for new employees. Such a pool may be a single school in a single city or an area of the country. By increasing the weight of the corporate advertising in this area, favoring the local media most apt to reach the target groups, awareness of the corporation and perception of it as a good place to work may be improved.

CHAPTER 7 CORPORATE ADVERTISING IN A RECESSION

At this writing we are at the start of one of the longest-heralded, most highly touted recessions in history. We are again entering one of those year-or-so-long dismal stages that have marred the tremendous economic progress achieved in the United States since World War II. During that 35-year period, broad economic measurements such as gross national product and personal income have enjoyed an average growth of approximately 7 percent a year. Inflation has reduced the real values, however, to a growth of less than 4 percent since 1950.

During this postwar period a number of studies on the effect of advertising or not advertising during recessions have been conducted. Traditionally, an advertiser's response to a recession has been to cut the ad budget on the basis of what appears to be sound reasoning:

1. People and businesses reduce buying during recessions, so advertising can also be reduced or discontinued.
2. Individual budgets can be reduced because competitors do the same thing.

Conversely, advertising men and women, particularly those with advertising agencies, have responded with equal knee-jerk predictability that a recession is no time to cut a budget. Their reasoning is that all affordable advertising dollars must be used to keep sales from sinking any lower.

Gradually, thanks to a number of research projects conducted during and after many of the six postwar recessions (and I assume after this one), a pattern of what really happens has begun to emerge. (The work done by the Cleveland agency Meldrum and Fewsmith, Inc., with the *American Business Press* is especially commendable.) I am happy to report that "us advertising guys" appear to be winning, although not for the reasons we have suspected. Unfortunately for our purpose, these studies do not differentiate between corporate advertising and other types of advertising and, in fact, lump them all together. Nevertheless, implications suggest to this writer that corporate advertising may be one of the sounder programs to retain during a recession. Of course, this may be considered heresy by many, particularly high-pressure sales managers, but a fuller understanding of the dynamics of recessions and what takes place is quite convincing.

Just What Is a Recession?

A technical recession begins when the inflationary growth is greater than the overall dollar growth in the economy and real growth comes to a halt. A number of technical recessions have occurred over the years. There were slowdown cycles in 1953–1954, 1957–1958, 1960–1961, 1969–1970, and 1973–1975. The explanations for these economic declines are not all the same. Traditionally, a slowdown follows a period of rapid expansion, according to a relatively normal cycle of adjustment, in which reduced production follows a period of expansion or overproduction.

Major events affect the cycle and can lend a specific character to a specific recession. They may be strikes, wars, international events, or energy shortages. Crop failures, though rarely considered today, are still a real possibility. Government action can be a significant influence and is expected to be a powerful controlling force in smoothing the peaks and valleys while correcting domestic conditions to minimize a recession's effect. Although no one appears to be willing to guarantee that there will never again be as complete a collapse as occurred in 1929, we do, indeed, seem to have entered a new era in which cycles are less severe and shorter-lived, but closer together. (The last point is perhaps a reflection of the general shortening of most cycles in today's society.)

Imperfect as the art of economic forecasting and control is, knowledge is improving, and the government's ability and willingness to minimize cyclical effects are encouraging. The United States government, however, has little or no control over nondomestic international developments, which may be expected to exert a dominant role in the future, particularly in the area of oil. Oil's escalating price and the resultant inflation and its ripple effect on our economy were seen dramatically in the 1973–1975 recession. That recession was preceded by sharp increases in the cost of crude oil, and by mid-1975 costs were actually 5 times those of mid-1973. The rise in the cost of this basic raw material, common to all industry including agriculture, sent out inflationary waves which affected all sectors of the economy. This same factor appears to have triggered the current (1980) recession.

The Psychology of Fear

Short, sharp downturns in the economy used to be called "panics" (think back to your history books). Deeper, prolonged economic slumps were weighted down still further with the term "depressions." The frame of mind characterized by these two terms frequently has resulted in action by individuals and companies that has only made matters worse. This action can range from jumping from a Wall Street window to postponing a badly needed capital improvement which could help alleviate a company's individual recession.

If we were to remove terms like "panic," "depression," and "recession," then strip away the psychological responses associated with them, and examine what actually takes place during these periods, we would be in a better position to react to facts rather than labels. Our judgments and decisions would be far more appropriate.

The image most people appear to carry of these downturns can be summed up as "A lot of people are out of work, and no one has any money to spend." To a large extent that image is based on the 1929–1932 Depression. It is a personal heritage in many people's memories of times when employment fell by 18 percent and the unemployed represented almost one-fourth of the nation's workforce. Let's examine the reality of the downturns that we've experienced since World War II and see whether these fears are founded in reality.

Customarily, our fears are fanned by the well-publicized *unemployment rate,* the percentage of the labor force out of work, which does rise sharply in a recession. What we rarely hear about is *total employment,* the number of people working. This figure has actually declined only slightly in modern recessions because it is offset in part by an increasing population. The following figures are those of the Department of Labor, Bureau of Labor Statistics, for total employment, seasonally adjusted (in thousands):

Recession	Start	End	Change (percent)
1948–1949	58,417	57,269	−2.0
1953–1954	61,397	59,908	−2.4
1957–1958	63,959	62,631	−2.1
1960–1961	65,959	65,588	−0.6
1969–1970	78,740	78,537	−0.3
1973–1975	85,578	84,180	−1.6

Even in the longest and deepest recession, that of 1973–1975, we can see that employment declined by less than 2 percent. The growing population is just one of the factors that compensate for some of the recessive elements. Unemployment benefits, of course, are another. Inflation, too, has an interesting effect. Inflation actually produces a consumer spending picture completely counter to our fears. We forget that even if the unemployment rate is 10 percent, 9 out of 10 people are still employed and that, because of unions and other resistive forces, salary levels tend to be stabilized or may, in fact, rise.

Consumer Spending during the Six Postwar Recessions (Billions of Dollars)*

1948–1949	1953–1954	1957–1958	1960–1961	1969–1970	1973–1975
+1.17	+1.34	+1.44	+0.97	+5.44	+12.44
$178 $180	$231 $234	$283 $287	$326 $329	$596 $628	$833 $936

*Personal consumption expenditures during the quarter when the economy peaked and bottomed.

The modern recession also appears to be of short duration. The average recession since World War II has lasted less than 1 year, as shown by the following figures from the National Bureau of Economic Research:

Duration of Postwar Recessions

Peak	Bottom	Number of months
November 1948	October 1949	11
July 1953	May 1954	10
August 1957	April 1958	8
April 1960	February 1961	10
December 1969	November 1970	11
November 1973	March 1975	16
		—
Average		11

What about Advertising during a Recession?

As you may have gathered by now, there is a real question of whether the almost knee-jerk response of cutting ad budgets during a recession is sound. At one time this response was almost universally accepted as a natural result of an economic downturn. The growing marketing sophistication in business today may account for the continued advertising pressure which was applied in the 1973–1975 period. An increasing number of companies recognize recessions as periods which offer an opportunity to increase their share of the market, if not actual sales levels.

United States Advertising Expenditures, 1947–1977 (in Millions of Dollars)

Year	Local	Percent versus year ago	National	Percent versus year ago	Total	Percent versus year ago	Recession periods
1947	1,760	+26.6	2,500	+28.2	4,260	+27.5	
1948	2,075	+17.9	2,795	+11.8	4,870	+14.3	} November 1948–
1949	2,220	+ 7.0	2,990	+ 7.0	5,210	+ 7.0	} October 1949
1950	2,440	+ 9.9	3,260	+ 9.0	5,700	+ 9.4	
1951	2,710	+11.1	3,710	+13.8	6,420	+12.6	
1952	3,040	+12.2	4,100	+10.5	7,140	+11.2	
1953	3,225	+ 6.1	4,515	+10.1	7,740	+ 8.4	} July 1953–May
1954	3,330	+ 3.3	4,820	+ 6.8	8,150	+ 5.3	} 1954
1955	3,770	+13.2	5,380	+11.6	9,150	+12.3	
1956	3,970	+ 5.3	5,940	+10.4	9,910	+ 8.3	
1957	4,020	+ 1.3	6,250	+ 5.2	10,270	+ 3.6	} August 1957–
1958	3,970	− 1.2	6,340	+ 1.4	10,310	+ .4	} April 1958
1959	4,415	+11.2	6,855	+ 8.1	11,270	+ 9.3	
1960	4,655	+ 5.4	7,305	+ 6.6	11,960	+ 6.1	} April 1960–
1961	4,545	− 2.4	7,315	+ .1	11,860	− .8	} February 1961
1962	4,735	+ 4.2	7,695	+ 5.2	12,430	+ 4.8	
1963	4,980	+ 5.2	8,120	+ 5.2	13,100	+ 5.4	
1964	5,430	+ 9.0	8,720	+ 7.4	14,150	+ 8.0	
1965	5,910	+ 8.8	9,340	+ 7.1	15,250	+ 7.8	
1966	6,480	+ 9.6	10,150	+ 8.7	16,630	+ 9.0	
1967	6,660	+ 2.8	10,210	+ .6	16,870	+ 1.4	
1968	7,290	+ 9.5	10,800	+ 5.8	18,090	+ 7.2	December 1969–
1969	8,020	+10.0	11,400	+ 5.6	19,420	+ 7.5	} November
1970	8,200	+ 2.2	11,350	+ .4	19,550	+ .7	} 1970
1971	8,965	+ 9.3	11,775	+ 3.7	20,740	+ 6.1	
1972	10,270	+14.6	13,030	+10.7	23,300	+12.3	
1973	11,345	+10.5	13,775	+ 5.7	25,120	+ 7.8	} November 1973–
1974	12,010	+ 5.9	14,730	+ 6.9	26,740	+ 6.4	} March 1975
1975	12,820	+ 6.7	15,410	+ 4.6	28,220	+ 5.6	
1976	15,135	+18.1	18,585	+20.6	33,720	+19.4	
1977	16,970	+12.1	21,090	+13.5	38,060	+12.9	

SOURCE: *Advertising Age.*

The ad record seems to bear out the contention that American business executives are learning to resist the temptation of cutting recession ad budgets. People do indeed buy during recessions, and while overall advertising volume may decrease somewhat during some recession periods, the reductions generally occur in specific areas. Perhaps most important, the advertisers who elect to continue their advertising pressure may be your competitors.

A number of studies which go back as far as the Depession of the 1930s have been conducted. Naturally, they vary in thoroughness and reliability. All, however, indicate virtually the same things, namely, that companies which maintain advertising programs during a recession recover more quickly from the effects of the recession and that these companies have shown the greatest sales and profit increases on long-term bases. It's not necessary to review all the extensive available literature, but the following examples will demonstate the conclusion:

1. During the 1940s a group of ninety-five companies of varying size and representing all industries reported on their recovery from the setback of 1937, a classic Depression year. Of these, forty-five did not cut advertising and their sales responded quickly after a temporary setback, while fifty firms did cut their budgets in 1938 and suffered accordingly. The accompanying table gives the ad budget and sales changes from the 1937 base.

	Companies that did not cut budgets		Companies that did cut budgets	
	Advertising (percent)	Sales (percent)	Advertising (percent)	Sales (percent)
1937	(100)	(100)	(100)	(100)
1938	+ 8.0	− 2.0	− 5.2	− 10.9
1939	+ 15.3	+ 9.0	+ 12.3	− 11.8
1940	+ 20.8	+ 19.7	+ 25.1	− 8.2

SOURCE: *Printer's Ink,* Aug. 28, 1958.

The conclusions drawn were: "Such a policy [of continued advertising increases] gives a company the impetus it needs to carry it through a recession" and "It strengthens the company firmly enough to guarantee its continued growth."

2. McCann-Erickson, Inc., performed an analysis of 64 of the 100 leading advertisers from 1948 to 1957, a decade that included the recessions of 1948–1949 and 1953–1954, when some advertisers held back on ad spending. The conclusion reached was that "all the companies surveyed showed some growth, but those that had advertised most aggressively showed proportionately larger sales volumes." Specifically the study noted that:

a. The [20] companies reporting highest sales volumes increased advertising by 197 percent and experienced a 113 percent rise in sales (over 10 years).

b. The [28] companies showing the slowest growth collectively increased advertising by about 155 percent, and their sales rose by 42 percent.[1]

3. The most extensive series of studies covering the entire postwar period has been conducted under the direction of J. Wesley Rosberg,

[1]*Printer's Ink,* Aug. 29, 1958.

senior vice president for administration of Meldrum and Fewsmith, Inc., conducted in cooperation with the *American Business Press*. There have now been four separate studies. The first, in 1958, examined the sales record of companies that advertised during the recessions and of those that did not. In 1970 the study was virtually repeated, covering the recession periods from 1958 to 1961. The third study was conducted in 1974, covering the recession year 1970. The study completed in 1979 covers the recession period 1973–1975. Substantially the same pattern of findings resulted from each of these four studies. To quote from the *American Business Press*, the latest report says:

> The findings of this latest study are equally consistent with those of the previous three: companies which do not cut advertising budgets in periods of recession post greater increases in sales and net income than companies which cut back their advertising dollars in times of economic down-turns.
>
> The findings of the six recession studies to date present formidable evidence that cutting advertising appropriations in times of economic down-turns can result in both immediate and long-term negative effect on sales and profits. Moreover, these studies have repeatably shown that maintaining or increasing advertising budget levels during recessionary periods may, in fact, be necessary in terms of protecting market position vis-à-vis "forward looking" competitors — those who consider advertising an integral component of the total marketing mix.[2]

4. The Laboratory of Advertising Performance (LAP), a division of McGraw-Hill Research, has reported on an advertising-sales analysis of 468 industrial companies for the 1974–1975 recession period.[3] Those companies which did not cut advertising in that period realized a higher sales growth both during the recession and for 3 years after it. Sales growth for companies which did not cut their 1974–1975 advertising expenditure averaged 12 percent higher during those years. In addition, by 1978 those companies which had not cut 1974–1975 advertising expenditure had sales 132 percent above their 1973 sales level, as compared with sales 79 percent over the 1973 level for companies which had cut advertising.

Among the 258 durable-goods manufacturers analyzed, those that had not cut advertising expenditure realized a 163 percent sales growth from 1973 to 1978, as compared with an 83 percent growth rate for those companies that had cut advertising. The most pronounced variance occurred in the machinery industries, with a 195 percent growth compared with 104 percent. For 210 nondurable companies, those that had not cut advertising experienced a 96 percent growth in sales from 1973 to

---

[2]*How Advertising in Recession Periods Affects Sales,* pamphlet, American Business Press, Inc., New York, 1979.

[3]LAP Report No. 5262, McGraw-Hill Publications Company, Economics Department, New York, 1980.

1978, as compared with 75 percent for companies that had cut advertising expenditure.

A statistical test was performed to measure the significance of these data. The results of the Wilcoxen-Mann-Whitney test support the view that measured differences in the sales performance of companies that cut their 1974–1975 advertising expenditure and those that did not. And while the data do not permit a statement of causality, their consistency underscores the common experience of the companies studied.

If we consider these historical events along with the many articles and case histories of companies' experience, we come to a general conclusion that's almost inescapable: *Maintaining an ad budget or increasing it to counter inflationary effects is one of the surest ways of recovering quickly after a recession.* If you accept this point, you may say: "But what about corporate advertising?" Or, "Advertising products during a recession may make sense, but why should we be putting money into corporate advertising when we need all the support sales can get?"

Much of the effect of advertising during a recession seems to be felt toward the end of the recession period, as the upturn begins. The actual dollar-of-sales return during a recession is not as impressive as the effect advertising has on making recovery strides following the recession. The operating principle appears to be one of using the recession period to gain a larger share of the market.

Marked by somewhat reduced competitive pressure, a recession is an opportunity to gain market share and/or *a greater share of the customers' mind.* It is this fact that lays the groundwork for capitalizing on improved conditions when they occur and for eliminating the need of rebuilding an eroded franchise. We saw the same effect work after wartime shortages, principally in World War II. Advertisers who continued to keep their message before the public with institutional advertising, as it was called in those days, rebounded most quickly following the war and showed the largest sales gains. Similarly, it is the longer-range effect of corporate advertising that is important. Corporate advertising improves the public's attitude toward a corporation, building acceptance for the days ahead when the public is again in a position to make purchases.

This is not said to minimize the tremendous pressure to cut that exists during a recession period to meet profit requirements. A recession is a painful time in which to invest in anything, and with something as intangible as corporate advertising the pressure to cut is almost irresistible. But this pressure does not change the reality that a recession is a good time to maintain one's franchise in the public's mind, using an otherwise fallow period to get ready for the growing season. Or, perhaps in an oversimplified way, it's like chumming until the fish start biting again. To simplify the argument even further, if people aren't going to be influenced by product ads to buy products, then why not position the same people for the inevitable upturn?

SECTION 3
THE HOW

This section assumes that you are already a competent general advertising practitioner. Though it is not a how-to of the basics, it's a how-to-go-about, using advertising tools in a somewhat specialized way to meet corporate advertising's somewhat specialized needs.

CHAPTER 8 APPLYING MARKETING DISCIPLINES TO CORPORATE ADVERTISING

Although corporate advertising has its own special needs, few advertisers or their agencies provide for them. These special needs are seldom understood by the majority of advertising people. No corporate advertising courses are available in colleges and universities. Because corporate advertising represents only a small percentage of all advertising, few people are exposed to enough of it in its various forms to become truly expert. Many agencies have never had a corporate account. When one comes in, it's handled with varying degrees of success, depending upon how successful that particular agency is in reinventing the various wheels that make the program go.

Other practitioners have grown up within the narrow environment of a corporate advertising department. They've developed great expertise regarding the company itself and its particular brand of corporate advertising, but they don't necessarily have the breadth of view to gain from other related advertising disciplines. Carried to an extreme, as in the case of in-house agencies, this inbreeding may result in a loss of perspective of what the campaign really is all about.

Programs produced in this manner can be quite polished while reflecting precisely what a corporation wishes to portray. However, they generally fall short in ability to communicate with current society. The objectivity of an outside group such as an agency is of even greater importance to corporate advertising than it is to product advertising.

The tendency of a corporate program to become a chief executive officer's ego trip offers a very tempting career path for in-house communication executives. Lost on this path, they find it virtually impossible to be objective.

Most frequently corporate campaigns are one-of-a-kind occurrences developed by inexperienced people because a particular need has arisen. Typically, someone within a corporation identifies a new problem. Wondering whether advertising might be used to help solve the problem, he or she turns to the advertising department, which may have been dealing in, say, the advertising of a company's electronic products to the industrial and scientific community or, perhaps, selling consumer products to the children's market. In either event, the ad department is pleased to have the chance to try something new and different, and it views the project as an opportunity for better exposure to top management.

The ad manager, in all likelihood, turns to his or her agency, outlines the problem, and asks if the agency thinks that advertising may offer a solution. And the agency, all too frequently, jumps at the opportunity to develop a program which may or may not do exactly what the situation calls for. If this procedure works, a new corporate program can actually get started, live, and prosper. Frequently, however, after a year or two the shortcomings in the program become obvious, and management simply decides that "corporate advertising just doesn't work for us."

Launching a new corporate campaign as an immediate, isolated problem solver, while sometimes necessary, can lead to presenting a disjointed view of a corporation to the public over a period of time. Many companies make a halfhearted attack on their corporate image problem, give the attempt up, and then start again 5 years later to present themselves in yet a different way. Over a period of time this process can destroy the outward appearance of a corporation.

The problem-response, problem-response approach is, at best, a quick cure and, in all likelihood, is out of step with the total communications picture being presented by the various divisions of the corporation as well as with its product advertising and publicity. What is needed is a way to synchronize all the corporation's channels so that they lead to a common goal.

Judging by the speeches and trade articles that have appeared in the last 2 years, it is clear that there's a growing sense of this need for greater organization in corporate advertising. The speeches and articles often attempt to lay down ground rules for tackling a corporate communications program on a more systematic basis. Undoubtedly, a greater number of proprietary approaches will be developed by agencies as part of their new-business efforts.

A very sound approach is simply to get down to the basic marketing principles which have been developed and sharpened over the years in product advertising and adapt them to the marketing of a corporation as though it itself were the product. If we take that as a starting point (which our agency did with one client who had a strong need and desire to bring together a total communications program), the result is something like the following eight-step program, which we developed. Such a program can have more or fewer than eight steps, depending on how you want to divide the individual processes, but in the end the logic of the order of activity outlined below should prevail.

147

Applying
Marketing
Disciplines
to Corporate
Advertising

Step 1: Fact-Finding

Few people will argue against the need for a sound base of information on the awareness and attitudes of the various publics important to a corporation. Studies conducted by individual divisions of the company on behalf of their own products and services may already exist. These can be helpful. Usually, however, because of their product and service orientation they're not totally adequate. Obviously, a broader, company-wide orientation is desirable. Furthermore, the work done by a given division will rarely be entirely compatible with that of the other divisions to give comparable data. It is usually necessary to design a new survey or even a number of surveys to meet a corporate need, although past work of the divisions may be very helpful in formulating the new study. A corporate awareness and attitude study is analogous to a segmentation or environmental study of the marketplace by product advertisers.

The study should be conducted among those publics that affect the corporation, which are likely to include key members of the financial community, stockholders, stock analysts, and brokers. The press may be a very important public to certain companies, while government officials may be the key to another company. Levels of trade within certain industries may be vital in their attitude and awareness of the corporation. The list of publics suggested in the matrix presented below is a good place to start. It's then necessary to determine from such a list which audiences are likely to affect the future of the company. Next a survey should be developed to learn these people's awareness of the corporation, their depth of knowledge about it, their attitudes, and the strengths and weaknesses of these attitudes concerning the company's activities, products, and services.

One of the publics frequently forgotten consists of the corporation's own employees. The attitudes they hold about the company, both the negatives and the positives, can later be very helpful in shaping strategy for the corporate campaign. Of course, a study of this type conducted by researchers and management consulting firms specializing in such work may far exceed the needs of simple corporate communications. A very sophisticated management tool, it can lead to the reshaping and restructuring of an entire organization.

At this stage it is necessary to take an inventory of the various company and divisional departments which regularly communicate to the various publics. Through internal questioning, you can itemize the divisions and departments and learn how they are communicating and with whom. (You'll probably be amazed to learn how many people are responsible for molding a company's image with the various publics.) Such communication goes far beyond the public relations group and the ad department. The entire sales force communicates with the industries with which you are concerned. The financial group certainly communicates with stockholders and may already have a financial relations department. The personnel department may have a community relations program or a house organ for employees. Each presents some face to a public. Total communications call for some mechanism to direct these channels of communication toward a unified, positive corporate image.

Step 2: Analysis

The surveys should reveal the health of the current corporate image. You will have some idea of what percentage of each public is aware of the company. More than that, you will learn how others perceive your company. Is the company old and stodgy? Does it have good management or bad? Is it thought of as honest and believable in its transactions? Frequently, correctable problems will quickly be apparent. Conferences with individual divisions should reveal how many of the reasons for the views held by the publics are based upon reality. Perhaps practices within the company are causing problems. Make no mistake, such an ambitious self-analysis will reveal warts and blemishes that should be removed. Total corporate communications can't cover up; they can only communicate reality. Attempts to communicate anything else will ultimately fail.

Divisional conferences may also reveal the need for further pinpoint studies to get a better understanding of the isolated problems.

In a large corporation with multiple divisions and departments, each communicating in a variety of ways with various publics, it's a good idea at this stage to develop an organization responsibility matrix to provide a visualization of who's doing what and where. Such a matrix can show at a glance what types of communication are being carried out and how they interrelate. Perhaps you will find that the publics important to the company are receiving virtually no communications while others are getting a variety of possibly conflicting messages from diverse departments and divisions. Until you attain a full understanding of how the various publics receive their impressions of the company, it's impossible to develop a total program implemented by the various divisions, all moving cooperatively in the same direction. In other words, until you know who's doing what to whom, the program can't be monitored, redirected, improved, or handled in any way.

A Corporation Matrix

149

Applying
Marketing
Disciplines
to Corporate
Advertising

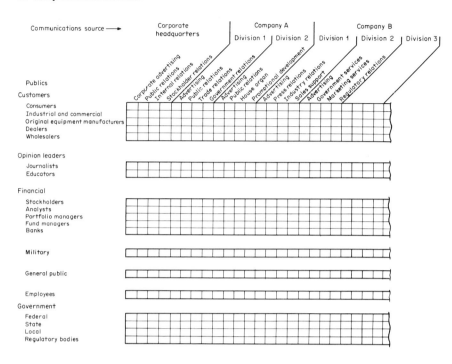

By using the accompanying simplified matrix, it is possible to find out who is communicating to the various publics of importance to the corporation. Redundancies, conflicts, and omissions will be revealed. Listed vertically are the various publics broken down into subgroups as required for individual corporate needs. Across the top are the individual companies and divisions broken down into the departments whose responsibility it is to communicate. The intersecting boxes may be marked with such information as channels of distribution used, frequency of communication, dollars spent on this communication, strategy employed, or even a thumbnail description of the image conveyed by such communication. In fact, anything that helps to give a better understanding of total communications for the entire corporation may be recorded in the boxes.

Step 3: The Need to Determine a Corporation's Own Corporate Mission

This step is every bit as important as fact-finding and, in fact, may be the first step, but it is likely to benefit from the data gained from the environmental and internal studies and from the analysis undertaken in Steps 1 and 2. The corporate mission is simply a statement of how the corporation sees itself, what it is, and what it wants to be. Clearly, it is the responsibility of the management of the corporation (likely of the CEO) to develop this succinct delineation of just what sets the company apart and the direction and aspirations that management has for near and long-range development. Such a statement must take into account what is known about the capabilities of the company, the background and direction in which it is moving (compared with the reality of the marketplace), and opinions held about the company. Simple as this step sounds, it is often a stumbling block. If management ignores the step at the planning stage or overlooks it entirely, it will set the stage for many problems later on.

All too many corporate programs are based on only a hazy concept of what the company is all about, and still fewer have any idea of the kind of company it should become. The step seems so obvious. After all, if you don't know where you're going, how are you going to get there? The CEO who has faced up to this seemingly obvious responsibility of deciding what the corporation should be can take pride in having made one of the greatest contributions possible to the company: the first step toward pointing all the company's activities in the same direction. Few things are more destructive to a company than the movement of the various divisions and departments in different directions. The CEO can be guided in the development of the corporate mission by the environmental studies, which can be the basis for far more than corporate communications. With them the CEO can check on what other steps must be employed to achieve corporate mission objectives. Some structural modifications may have to be made. Perhaps there are service standards that the public considers inadequate. These defects should be corrected. Perhaps the financial community feels that certain activities are a drag on the total corporation. The remedy might even be divestiture.

Using the package-goods analogy, the CEO may have to make changes in the product (corporation) before it can be promoted. Just as a segmentation study for a package-goods product may reveal an opportunity for greater acceptance with a change in color or taste or fragrance, so the corporate environmental study may reveal the need for changes in the corporation.

This is no area for a cover-up. What corrections are needed should be made or begun before an attempt is made to convey the reality of the company. No corporate campaign can succeed in portraying a company that doesn't exist in reality. Nothing will fall flatter than a campaign based upon the projection of a false image.

Step 4: Setting Objectives

Once the program has been soundly based on an understanding of the real environment and the corporate mission, it is possible to state the direction to be taken in objectives which later will be translated into advertising objectives and even into target-audience media objectives. These objectives should be specific, comprising not only the goals to be attained but quantification wherever possible. If the environmental studies have revealed a specific level of awareness in different publics, reasonable expectations for a percentage increase in this level should be established. Establishing such quantification before the program begins makes it far easier to read the results of later tracking studies. You are able to know not only where you are and where you are going but how rapidly you are making progress.

The objectives should also be specific as they relate to the various divisions and departments of the corporation. They should be firmly established by corporate management before the next step is taken.

151

Applying
Marketing
Disciplines
to Corporate
Advertising

Step 5: Planning

With clear objectives, planning of the corporate ad campaign can begin. Planning will be on a sound basis and should move much more quickly than the preceding steps. But it is in this planning stage that a new element should be added to enhance the program.

Each company or division of the corporation should be directed to submit its own plan showing the contribution that it can make to fulfill the corporate mission. Just as each division is given the bottom-line responsibility to deliver a margin of profit, so it should be given the responsibility to develop a plan which will bring it in line with overall corporate objectives and contribute to the well-being of the total corporation. This "invitation" to participate in the achievement of the corporate mission can be extended not only to the companies and divisions but to the departments within them as well, thus bringing to bear the combined communication forces of the corporation.

Implementation of this process need not be as difficult as it sounds. Those divisions and departments that customarily deal with the publics of concern to the corporation show up clearly on the matrix. Given the overall corporate objectives, these business areas are charged with developing their own programs, budgets, and timetables. Care must be taken, of course, to emphasize that their first priority will continue to be their own product advertising and communications. Clearly they are not expected suddenly to drop their line responsibility. In fact, there is no danger of a division being carried away as long as its profit responsibility exists.

It is surprising how few corporations ever consider this very simple step in their corporate communications programs. Few divisional executives have ever been asked what they are doing to help the total corporate image. In fact, it is disheartening to see how few companies bother to communicate to their divisions what top management is doing, let alone ask for assistance in helping to achieve corporate goals. If yours is one of the many companies that haven't tried this step, try it now. You may like it.

Step 6: Corporate Review

In addition to reviewing the corporate ad program developed for headquarters implementation, management should review all plans of the divisions along with their budgets and timetables, comparing divisional efforts with the variety of audiences. It is at this point that overlapping and omissions can be corrected. Using the matrix system is likely to show that several divisions are targeting their programs toward the same publics. Efficiencies and joint ventures may well come to light. It is also at this stage that budget control is exercised and priorities are established. Plans may call for research tracking by the divisions themselves to monitor progress of their programs, or the corporation may elect to conduct its own ongoing tracking, which would encompass the specific publics of a number of the divisions.

Step 7: Implementation

With corporate approval, the divisions and departments implement their own plans while corporate headquarters implements its corporate advertising and public relations efforts. A decent interval of time is allowed before the final step is taken.

Step 8: Tracking

The program is monitored by tracking studies conducted regularly at appropriate intervals. Depending upon the objectives, the time period may be as short as 3 months or as long as 2 years. The original environmental study is used as a base or bench mark. It may not be necessary to repeat the entire study: a simplified form may be sufficient. In this case, questioning is focused on areas related to the objectives of the program.

PLAN FOR CORPORATE COMMUNICATIONS

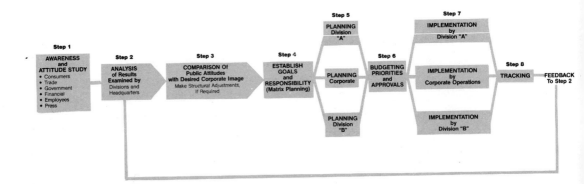

Not only do tracking studies serve as report cards for the entire program, they also are a source of feedback to be folded into the program as it continues. Thus, plans can be modified and changed as required. By putting the studies into regular continuing cycles, the findings can be refactored into the total program, making it self-renewing and self-correcting over a period of time. The CEO reexamines the corporate mission while the divisions reexamine their activities each time that a new tracking study is conducted. The accompanying chart illustrates the eight steps and the inherent feedback capability.

Is such a seemingly formalized eight-step program truly practical in the real world of business pressures, executive time constraints, and daily demands for expediency? The answer is that such a program is not only practical but essential for the very reasons of business pressure. Unless a corporate program is started on a sound basis, management must spend a great deal of time correcting it, fussing with it, and trying to make it work.

It's true that a crisis situation may demand the immediate launching of a program based on quick seat-of-the-pants judgments by the executive staff. Well and good; simply apply first aid with an interim program. But while management's attention is focused on that program, it should take the time to work toward the long-range goal of a more solidly based total corporate communications system. Nor is such a system necessarily formalized. Depending on the size of the corporation, it may be very close to procedures already in place.

153

Applying
Marketing
Disciplines
to Corporate
Advertising

CHAPTER 9 THE VARIOUS ROLES OF RESEARCH

Hardly any corporate advertising is conducted today as an act of faith. Advertising is being researched and studied as never before to prove and re-prove its effectiveness, to refine it, and to improve it. The *Public Relations Journal*'s annual study of November 1978 showed that 94 percent of respondent corporate advertisers had research-based measurement systems. The ANA's 1977 study indicated that 83 percent of corporate advertisers regularly or occasionally used research to track or predict the effectiveness of corporate advertising.

In some cases measurements may be executive security blankets, but even personal reasons for measurements can be sound and can have a legitimate place in business planning. Anyone who does not employ some form of research in a corporate communications program is extremely vulnerable (if a company's first duty is to survive as a company, an executive's first duty undoubtedly is to survive as an executive).

The major factor leading to the wide use of measurements of corporate programs is the obvious need to know what is happening. The immediate effect of a corporate program is usually far removed from normally available data, such as sales, profits, and market share, with which a company deals. As a result, without special tracking research there is a real lack of feedback.

It is fortunate that good research is fairly easy to undertake in this area, often for small expenditures. Frequently it is easier to find out whether a corporate advertising program is achieving its objectives than to determine whether product advertising is achieving its sales objectives. At first this statement may seem contrary to common sense, but when you think the matter through, it isn't.

Corporate goals are often stated in terms of increasing awareness levels and improved attitudes toward a corporation. These goals are easily measurable by quite ordinary research techniques. In determining whether product advertising is fulfilling its ultimate function of selling a product, a full-scale test-market situation is required to tell with any degree of accuracy whether the advertising will, in fact, move the product. Even then you're still faced with the problem of separating the effectiveness of the advertising from the other elements of the marketing mix. Corporate advertising's goals, however, usually include improving public awareness of the company or its products and services or the attitudes held about them.

It can be argued that corporate advertising goals should also be related to the end result, such as securing additional stockholders, attaining specific legislation, or raising the price-earnings ratio. If these objectives are indeed to be the measure of the success of an ad program, the situation becomes similar to that for product advertising. That is, advertising must be considered for what it is, namely, just one element in a total marketing mix to achieve end results. But usually a change in awareness or attitude is in itself an acceptable goal for corporate advertising.

Measuring the effectiveness of corporate advertising is just one of the types of research that should surround a corporate ad campaign. At least five categories of research may be involved. Depending on the situation, some categories can be eliminated, and some can be combined with others to reduce the number of research projects. Conversely, the number of research projects may be increased because of the complexity of the program. Let's start with the following five categories:

1. Environmental studies
2. Diagnostic studies of the corporation's strengths and weaknesses
3. Copy and ad development research
4. Bench-mark studies
5. Follow-up studies (tracking)

Environmental Studies

It is essential to understand the current climate and environment within which the corporation operates. This environment can be as broad as the total population with its multitude of social factors, changing trends, and public views on issues that relate to the company. Or it can be as narrow as current trends within the specific industry in which the corporation is engaged. Whatever the scope of the examination, a solid understanding of current events as they relate to the corporation is a must.

As obvious as this requirement seems, this is the most generally overlooked area of study in campaign development. The neglect of this area probably stems from the assumption that almost everyone stays current, reading newspapers and magazines and keeping abreast of what's going on in this country and in the particular industry. We know how our friends and neighbors feel about various subjects, and we have our own opinions. In our thinking we often project opinions to represent the climate for the entire United States, perhaps not consciously but unconsciously. Needless to say, these subjective assumptions can be far from accurate. There are a number of relatively inexpensive ways of gaining the kind of knowledge of the environment that is needed.

- **Existing studies:** Studies conducted by a corporation's subsidiaries or divisions which may have been oriented to product development may contain important environmental data. Many new-product programs employ segmentation studies to examine a field or an industry, consumer habits, usage trends, and changes in lifestyles. While this information may not have been developed with corporate needs in mind, it may provide useful knowledge. At the least, it may give clues to the direction that more specific research should take.

    If the timing is appropriate, it is sometimes possible to enlarge these studies to include specific information for corporate needs without detracting from the original divisional research intent.

- **Syndicated studies:** When broad, nationwide public information is required, there are a number of good multiclient syndicated studies that are conducted regularly. To name a few, there are Opinion Research Corporation's *Public Opinion Index*, the *Harris Perspective*, Cambridge Reports' *Quarterly Surveys*, and Yankelovich, Skelly and White's *Corporate Priorities*. The last-named firm also issues an ongoing tracking of the United States population's major sociological shifts called *Monitor Studies*. Any of these studies offers a broad view of the public's attitudes, interests, and opinions at a given point of time.

- **Industry sources:** More specific information is often available from industry sources. Your industry association can provide current information not only on industry statistics and trends but frequently on the attitudes of the public surrounding the industry, those groups with which it is most deeply involved. Thus, the brewing industry has an association which monitors the climate of legislation as well as a number of other subjects which are important to bottlers and brewers.

    Other sources not to be overlooked are trade and business magazines serving the industry in question. Although they vary tremendously from industry to industry in both availability and reliability, such publications are quick to share whatever information they have and can help direct you to other studies in the field.

- *Customer studies:* It may be necessary to mount your own survey if the available material is inappropriate or insufficient for your needs. If this is the case, you should consider combining it with some of the diagnostic work that may be necessary.

External diagnostic methods may range from fairly informal discussions with small groups of customers or stock analysts to more formal focus-group studies among many important publics to explore their reaction to proposed changes in the company's policies or products. Such sessions can be used to seek the unique characteristics of the company. Outsiders may see you in ways quite different from your preconceptions. Perhaps the financial community, the press, or major industrial buyers may be aware of things which are unnoticed by the company itself.

Characteristics uncovered in this way may be positive ones upon which to build, or they may be negative ones that should be eliminated or minimized. At this stage the exploration consists largely of searching for qualitative points of difference and of understanding the dynamics of the corporation's relationship to its environment. The process is a searching out of weaknesses and strengths. This stage is particularly appropriate to the refinement of long-range plans. It is a time at which the corporation decides where it wishes to be in 5 years. Most important, it is a time to establish the corporate mission. This is also a time to determine your company's true corporate identity and to commit adequate resources to attain its fulfillment.

Diagnostic Studies of the Corporation's Strengths and Weaknesses

Special studies may have to be devised to get at the root of the issues involved in the campaign's development. These studies can be considered diagnostic research. They fall into two categories: (1) surveys and studies among *outside* publics of importance to the corporation, such as customers, the press, financial groups, and legislators; and (2) the often-forgotten *internal* public, the company's employees. Analysis of both categories may be necessary to understand the dynamics of why the company is what it is.

Internal diagnostic work within a small company may be relatively simple. Interviews with a few selected executives may provide all you need to know to understand the various functions, service standards, product qualities, communication channels, and other workings of the company. In very large corporations with many subsidiaries and divisions the reality of what is happening within the corporation may be quite different from corporate management's view. What management thinks should be going on and what is actually going on are often distressingly different. An internal study of this sort may be nothing more than the running of available statistics (certain sales data, for example) in a way that's meaningful to the question at hand. Or it may require hiring an outside research or consultant firm to dig into the company's actual procedures and practices. A survey of the attitudes of employees toward the company may be particularly revealing, and it could be a diagnostic tool for many purposes other than corporate advertising.

Copy and Ad Development Research

Throughout the campaign development process, ideas and hypotheses may be examined for their advertising potential. This examination will extend from checking corporate positioning statements to on-air testing of finished commercials. Virtually any of the accepted techniques used for tests of product advertising copy may be employed for corporate ad development. It isn't necessary to chart new, unexplored research territory. Many research companies even provide normative data for copy testing.

There is no single system of copy testing which answers all the advertising questions that may arise. Any rigid reliance on a single score as a measure of effectiveness will at times be counterproductive, since specific measures can vary in importance with the problem or the situation. You must decide in advance what you expect from the copy test. Whatever provides the best estimate of the needed information may be selected from available services, or a custom-designed methodology may be required.

Obviously, the earlier an ad or a commercial is tested, the greater the opportunity to act on the results. While this procedure may result in the testing of ``rough executions,'' the trade-off may be worthwhile. Bear in mind that the degree of finish required varies with the intended execution. Whether you're considering a small specific study to determine comprehension or a full test-market operation to test the effect of an entire campaign, the overriding point to keep in mind is that the test must be designed in terms of how the results are to be utilized. The results should be an aid to good judgment, not a substitute for it.

Generally, you will find that preexposure-postexposure measurements are not especially relevant to corporate ad problems and that natural postexposure and forced postexposure copy-testing methods are more useful. Attempts to measure changes in attitudes just prior to and then following the exposure of either print or TV material (whether the same sample or matched samples are measured) may work in product ad tests, but they have not been successful in corporate ad measurements. The more natural the exposure, of course, the better. However, natural exposure usually implies that testing will be done late in the ad development process, usually after ads or commercials have been completed. More limited in validity but far more flexible are the forced exposure methods which may be applied at an early stage.

While we are not recommending any specific companies, by way of example Gallup & Robinson, Inc., is a strong practitioner of on-air natural exposure only. The firm has done considerable corporate advertising work in both the print and the television fields. Its magazine-impact research service is a syndicated multiclient service. This service consists primarily of a 24-hour–recall study among readers who are given the test issue of a specific magazine and asked to read it that evening at home. Ads are tested regularly in scheduled issues of ten magazines. Two of these, *Newsweek* and *Time*, are frequently used to test tipped-in advance proofs of ads. Regularly scheduled ads may also be tested. A telephone call-back on the following day measures the recall of the test ads. The proportion of proven readers who can recall and describe a particular ad accurately on the day following exposure provides a rating which is adjusted to compensate for the unit cost and readership level of the particular issue.

Palshaw Measurement, Inc., is another research organization that is very active in corporate ad measurements for both TV and print. Palshaw forces exposure through both special showings of commericals and direct presentation of ads in either finished or concept form. No attempt is made to simulate actual viewing or reading conditions. An advantage of this system is that it makes survey work practical among hard-to-reach special audiences. It is especially suitable for reaching professionals in the medical or pharmaceutical fields as well as the financial and business fields, making this system a useful corporate ad tool. Both Gallup & Robinson and Palshaw have developed special corporate norms.

Many other research firms such as A.S.I. Advertising, Inc., and Burke Marketing Research, Inc., have worked in the corporate field. You will need to secure a number of proposals before deciding which of the suggested methods is the most suitable for your own research needs.

Here are a few points to remember:

- Recall for TV commercials and recognition levels for magazines are helpful in determining whether anyone out there is paying attention, but they won't tell you whether the real message is getting through or whether it's the right message in the first place.

- The single most valuable characteristic of corporate advertising is *believability*. If your ad is poor or dull or fails in other ways, only money has been wasted. But if the ad is not believed, you've actually hurt your corporation. You may have spent ad dollars to help convince people that you're lying. Test for credibility by all means.

- Remember that when you test a group of ads, the best ad in the group may still be a terrible ad. It may just be the least bad ad in the group.

- Figure out in advance what will constitute ''good'' and ''bad''. A set of research figures with results somewhere in the middle of the scale may leave you as much in the dark as before. When possible, compare scores with known successes. If you work against norms, get an idea of what those norms are and what they are based on. Are the norms current, and are they truly comparable with your own situation?

If scores are adjusted to compensate for space unit costs, economics will favor less expensive units. Spreads and four-color units will be hard-pressed to justify their cost on this basis, but they still may be exactly the right units to use. If the product demands color or if the look and message of a major corporation must be conveyed, a four-color bleed spread may be the cheapest luxury.

Bench-Mark Studies

To find out what progress you have made you need to know two things: where you are going and where you are at the start. A bench-mark study provides the latter information. Ideally, the study should be conducted just prior to the start of the campaign. It should be designed to provide information related directly to the objectives of the campaign itself. Furthermore, it should be substantial enough to reveal differences between a variety of target audiences.

If more than one public is being addressed by a specific corporate program, each public should be surveyed. It may seem unnecessary to make this point, yet it is not uncommon for a national probability sample to be used to find awareness and attitudes among a general public when, in fact, the campaign is being targeted at a select socioeconomic group. If the objectives of the campaign are relatively simple, it may be adequate to buy participation in an ongoing syndicated survey. An example would be one of the studies of R. H. Bruskin and Associates, such as the AIM study, which is conducted monthly against a national general-public probability sample. It consists of corporate logos individually printed on playing cards. A deck of fifty-two such cards, representing the signatures of many American corporations, is given to a respondent to sort into two piles, familiar logos and unfamiliar ones. This is a simple but effective technique which can provide a basic though limited level of awareness in a national sample of 2500 households. Subsamples of specific audiences may also be purchased from Bruskin.

Other syndicated surveys are conducted among specific target groups. For example, Opinion Research Corporation conducts one survey among Washington, D.C., thought leaders. Participation is limited to subscribers to the broader ORC *Public Opinion Index*. In the spring and fall of each year, ORC interviews members of the legislative branch, executive departments, and regulatory agencies. It also samples nongovernmental participants in the lawmaking process such as officials of labor unions, leaders of public interest groups, and the Washington press corps. A limited number of questions of specific interest may be inserted for a fee.

ORC also conducts similar surveys in other fields. Its *Investment Community Survey* is a biannual evaluation of the attitudes of professional investment advisers toward leading American companies. The organization has been doing this work since 1959, and its trend data, which also are provided, are thus extremely useful. Multisponsor studies are conducted by ORC every 2 months among national cross sections of the adult public and teen-agers and quarterly among business executives. Every 2 years ORC also conducts shared-cost studies of the images of major United States corporations among the adult public and among some 200 members of the nation's media.

Whether bench marks can be established with a syndicated study or whether a specially designed study must be fielded, the study should seek to arrive at certain fundamental elements of the corporation's reputation, principally:

1. How well known is the company among groups of particular interest? This is the general-awareness level.

2. What is the knowledge held by the surveyed groups concerning the company's
    a. Products
    b. Reputation
    c. Service practices
    d. International activities
    e. Management
    f. Policies
    g. Advertising

3. How do respondents rate various qualities of the company and its products?

4. Ask comparative questions to add relevance to many of the statistics selected for comparison with other companies in the same industry (competitors included).

Development of this type of research is, of course, a highly developed science in its own right. An account executive or an ad director should not attempt to develop these questions or methods on his or her own but rather should seek the most professional counsel available.

Follow-Up Studies (Tracking)

This is your bottom line. Usually this procedure is a follow-up or a rerun of the major portions of the bench-mark study. If you conduct the study on a regular basis at about the same time each year, seasonal variations are eliminated. But you may wish to shorten or lengthen the time interval, depending upon whether a slow educational process or a relatively fast response is anticipated. (Watch your graphs if you chart irregular time periods; they can even fool chartists.) Take care that all changes in the implementation of a program in the target audience are reflected in the research-audience sample as well.

The findings are far more than a report card. What has been learned must be factored into your plans for the following year, when you will begin the process all over again. Certain goals may have been accomplished; others may be added to take their place.

CHAPTER 10 ATTAINABLE OBJECTIVES

One of the comedian Alan King's old routines includes this cynical bit on magazine ads, "Here's this big ad with a picture of a blast furnace by one of the big steel companies. Now, what do they expect me to do about that? Go out and buy an ingot of steel?"

The fact is that years ago many readers indeed were confused about what the advertiser was trying to sell in ads of this type. While the contemporary reader is likely to be more sophisticated and can see through to the *real* message in the corporate advertiser's ad, there are enough vague, seemingly aimless corporate ads in today's magazines for us to question just how well attuned to objectives much corporate advertising is. So while this is strictly primer stuff, it's necessary to state first that one basic rule for all advertising, corporate or product, is to *start with the problem, not the message.*

Even if there is disagreement on what to label corporate advertising, there is complete unanimity among contemporaries that before work on any corporate ad begins, there must be clear objectives. And the more specific and quantifiable the objectives, the better.

Ron Hoff, writing in a 1977 ad for Foote, Cone & Belding, stated it quite well:

> Corporate advertising with fuzzy objectives will get fuzzy results. Unless there is a way of measuring a campaign's effectiveness in specific terms, you'll never know whether you spend your money wisely or not. Example: "Improve our corporate image in the business community." Too vague. Unmeasurable in precise terms. Compare it with this: "Increase awareness of our international capabilities among major exporters by at least 20% during the first year of the campaign." By doing pre-and-post research, you'll know if your corporate campaign is working.[1]

[1] *The Wall Street Journal*, March 29, 1977.

While we're not at all certain that there is a perfect formula for arriving at the exact percentage of improvement (or of how Ron Hoff arrived at his 20 percent figure), there is no doubt that being as specific as possible in your objectives has definite advantages. These advantages go far beyond the ability to track and measure results quantitatively. Objectives can also:

1. Allow you to determine whether the project is worth consideration.

2. Make possible the means to evaluate the project and determine whether the money expended on it promises a worthwhile return.

3. Help make a reasonable media selection.

4. Suggest creative direction, or at least provide a check to deciding whether the creative approach is on the right track.

In 1979 *Business Week* came up with ninety-nine jobs that corporate advertising can do. Its list may stimulate some thinking of your own needs and goals:

achievements

1. Show your company's most glamorous or dramatic accomplishments in order to build acceptance of standard products.

acquisitions; mergers

2. Help build the company reputation to facilitate mergers and acquistions.

3. Promote your firm's new corporate strength or diversification achieved by acquisitions or mergers.

anniversaries

4. Make known your company anniversaries or other milestones as evidence of stability, reliability, and achievement.

associations

5. Demonstrate industry unity to customers, government, and critics.

6. Mount an association campaign when an individual corporate campaign is inappropriate or inadequate.

brand identification

7. Discourage substitution through strong brand identification.

business constituency

8. Build a business constituency — a body of business supporters — who will defend your company's stand in a political or social controversy.

business executives

9. Build a favorable company reputation among executives throughout the business world.

change

10. Promote your firm as being flexible and adaptable to changing conditions in its markets or the economy.

conservation

11. Explain how your company conserves or replaces the natural resources it uses.

consumerists

12. Show concern for and make contributions to legitimate consumerist activities.

crisis

13. Issue messages to restore confidence after a corporate crisis.

customers

14. Enhance dealers' or agents' standing with customers.

15. Introduce your company to newcomers in the marketplace.

16. Take a stand in behalf of a customer industry.

17. Suggest new, improved products to your customers.

customers' customers

18. Get manufacturers' customers to specify your company's components or materials.

19. Help sell your customers' products to *their* customers.

delivery

20. Promote your company's record of on-time delivery.

directorship

21. Launch a campaign to improve conditions, set standards, reform methods, defeat proposals, etc.

22. Show how your company has been a leader in its industry.

distribution

23. Make known how widely your products or services are distributed. List local representatives.

distributors; dealers

24. Explain your industrial advertising support to your distributors.

25. Give recognition to your top dealers.

26. Help dealers gain parts and repair business.

27. Promote the names of distributors and dealers.

28. Show dealers how you back them with consumer advertising.

diversification

29. Build a favorable image outside your present markets to facilitate diversification.

diversity

30. Show the diversity of your product line.

divisions; subsidiaries

31. Link corporate and divisional names or trademarks.

education

32. Demonstrate interest in education and culture.

employees

33. Promote the experience and ability of your company employees.

34. Demonstrate the loyalty of skilled employees.

35. Reach employees as well as outsiders with your company's management philosophy and plans.

energy

36. Show how your company helps develop new energy sources.

37. Show how your company is conserving energy.

engineering

38. Promote the engineering skills and facilities behind your company's products.

environment

39. Counteract any false or misleading charges of environmentalists.

40. Show how your company's activities protect or improve the environment.

finanical

41. Make your company name familiar to the financial community.

42. Encourage confidence in your firm's stability and growth by showing the diversity of its markets.

43. Tell the financial community about your company's capital investments.

funding

44. Create confidence and trust in financial circles to make funding easier and cheaper.

government; politics

45. Counteract adverse lobbying by pressure groups.

46. Explain the harmful effects of excessive taxation or regulation of your industry.

47. Explain to politicians and legislators your company's or industry's side in a political controversy.

48. Educate public officials and legislators on the profit requirements of your corporation or industry.

49. Create confidence in your company as a government contractor.

growth

50. Tell your market about new production records and the growing demand for products.

guarantee; warranty

51. Make known a guarantee or warranty.

innovations

52. Impress your market with past innovations and contributions to the industry.

international

53. Create familiarity and preference for your company in overseas markets.

54. Encourage investment in your company by overseas investors.

55. Show how foreign nations benefit from your company's activities.

investors

56. Convince investors that your company is a safe investment in economic downturns.

57. Convince investors that yours is a growth company.

58. Present your firm's financial record to investors.

59. Make your company's profitability known to investors.

jobbers

60. Establish jobbers as a source of supply.

labor

61. Promote your corporation's enlightened labor relations.

62. Show how your management's decisions have benefited customers, employees, and stockholders.

media

63. Counteract a bad press by making your company's story clearer to media executives, editors, and the general public.

64. Develop positive media attitudes toward your company to encourage fair treatment.

name change

65. Familiarize your markets with a change of company name.

opinion leaders

66. Influence opinion leaders to accept your corporation's viewpoint.

opinion; policy; philosophy

67. Try to win over activists or critics to a corporate view by clarifying misconceptions.

68. Explain policies that might affect the goodwill or reception met by salespeople.

69. Reach your entire market with a special corporate announcement or message.

packaging

70. Show the advantages of your packaging and shipping methods.

patent rights

71. Protect patent rights.

plant communities

72. Show how your company helps plant communities.

problem solving

73. Promote your corporation's problem-solving abilities to attract new customers.

product line

74. Build up secondary items by promoting the entire product line.

75. Connect a new product to a well-established product line.

product service

76. Make known your service facilities and record.

production capacity

77. Make your firm's production capacity known to attract new business.

progress

78. Show how your company has progressed and share its plans for the future.

quality

79. Demonstrate the quality control practiced by your company.

recruitment

80. Publicize your employment policies and benefits and other advantages of employment.

reliability

81. Show how your company's products are tested before delivery.

research

82. Discuss the achievements and developments of your research laboratory.

83. Explain how your company funds or supports research by industry and institutions.

84. Offer research facilities and cooperation to others.

sales staff

85. Build up salespeople as experts in their fields.

86. Create a favorable image of your sales representatives.

87. Give recognition to your top salespeople.

88. Introduce your salespeople in print.

service

89. Emphasize your company's excellence in servicing customers before and after purchases.

size

90. Show how your company's large size is beneficial to customers and society.

91. Show how your company's small size affords greater flexibility and individualized customer service.

social responsibility

92. Demonstrate your firm's sense of responsibility to society.

students

93. Establish a corporate reputation with business students, your customers of tomorrow.

testing

94. Demonstrate how your testing facilities assure superior product performance.

trademark

95. Build and protect your company trademark.

96. Introduce a new trademark.

97. Secure the use of your company's trademark by fabricators.

union officials

98. Gain the respect and trust of union leaders by open discussion of mutual interests.

vertical integration

99. Explain how vertical integration provides superior products or services.

If that list is too long for you, try this one. It is culled from that list and from seemingly endless books, articles, speeches, promotion pieces, and meetings. The following ten jobs encompass the demands usually made of corporate advertising. Note that these are not specific objectives but rather general areas within which specific objectives can be constructed:

1. Build awareness of a corporation's identity.

2. Improve understanding of a company's area of business.

3. Overcome poor attitudes toward a company.

4. Explain corporate philosophy and policies.

5. Illustrate achievements.

6. Enhance a company's image as an investment.

7. Advocate social change useful to a corporation.

8. Secure support of useful legislation.

9. Provide a unified view of a corporation to its employees.

10. Aid in recruitment.

Although not listed above, there is little doubt that product sales can be positively influenced by corporate advertising (see Chapter 4). This is particularly true of big-ticket items for which the stature of a corporation can be a major influence on the buying decision. But to include product sales as a normal corporate advertising objective is to invite confusion. This is true because advertising dollars spent to benefit one product will almost certainly produce better sales for that product, whereas these dollars spent on corporate advertising will reach a more diffuse objective.

In spite of this situation, most companies consider that corporate advertising provides "a unified marketing support (i.e., umbrella) for their company's present and future products, services, or capabilities." This was determined in a 1979 survey by the Association of National Advertisers, which reported the corporate advertising practices of 173 major United States corporations with corporate programs. Provided also were six commonly used objectives. Each company was asked to describe the most important objective of its major campaign. The six objectives and the results are quoted here with the ANA's permission:

Objectives of Major Corporate Program
(Base: 173 users)

1. To improve the level of awareness of the company, the nature of its business interests, profitability, etc.

	Number of companies
Primary objective	83
Secondary objective A	14
Secondary objective B	13
Secondary objective C	3
Total mentions	113 (65 percent of respondents)

2. To enhance or maintain the company's reputation and goodwill.

	Number of companies
Primary objective	38
Secondary objective A	45
Secondary objective B	26
Secondary objective C	8
Total mentions	117 (68 percent of respondents)

3. To provide unified marketing support for the company's present and future products, services, or capabilities.

	Number of companies
Primary objective	35
Secondary objective A	46
Secondary objective B	16
Secondary objective C	7
Total mentions	104 (60 percent of respondents)

4. To inform or educate about subjects of importance to the company's future (e.g., economics, resource allocations, government policies, etc.).

	Number of companies
Primary objective	23
Secondary objective A	22
Secondary objective B	12
Secondary objective C	2
Total mentions	59 (34 percent of respondents)

5. To advocate specific actions or counter the advocacy of others on issues of importance to the company, its industry, or business in general.

	Number of companies
Primary objective	14
Secondary objective A	16
Secondary objective B	1
Secondary objective C	2
Total mentions	33 (19 percent of respondents)

6. To communicate the company's concern and record of achievement on social or environmental issues

	Number of companies
Most important objective	8
Secondary objective A	12
Secondary objective B	12
Secondary objective C	7
Total mentions	39 (22.5 percent of respondents)

The Corporate Mission

No matter which objective or combination of objectives is to be achieved by a corporate program, you will need to have the clearest possible idea of the essential character of the corporation. Know what the corporation is, what it stands for, and where it is going. This most primary of objectives, the corporation objective, has been frequently called the "corporate mission." It is analogous to the product-positioning statement in product advertising. A succinct statement is required to set and maintain all other objectives properly.

Determining this corporate mission cannot be delegated to an advertising agency. The agency may be asked to advise and discuss the mission with the client, but the task of making the final determination will fall to the top management of the corporation. Usually it falls to the chief executive officer, as it should.

The lack of a firm, clear, concise statement of the corporate mission, agreed to by the corporation principals, possibly the board of directors, causes most failures of corporate ad campaigns. Ironically, it is frequently the agency which gets the failing marks, but it is really the client who hasn't done the homework.

The Appropriate Audience

Once advertising objectives have been determined, it becomes possible to determine audience objectives not just for media planning purposes but for creative work as well. Usually the selection is fairly obvious, given the objectives, and will probably come from one or more areas in the following list. This list was compiled from a multitude of sources, and it appears to encompass those audiences most frequently selected for corporate advertising:

General Public

Financial

Stockholders
Brokers
Analysts
Portfolio managers
Fund managers
Banks

Stockholders and potential stockholders
Opinion leaders

Journalists
Authors
Educators

Employees and prospective employees

Federal
State
Local
Legislative
Regulatory

Customers

Consumers
Industrial and commercial
Original-equipment manufacturers
Government

Trade

Distributors
Wholesalers
Dealers

Many of these audiences are relatively small, discrete segments that are readily reachable by specific media. Even a modest budget may be very effective.

A number of these audiences constitute a considerable public in their own right. In its corporate advertising workshop *Time* magazine has compiled statistics which demonstrate how quickly these individual publics can turn into major audience segments, as shown in the following tables.

Government and Administration

Audience	Number
White House	300
Congress and staffs	3,300
Registered lobbyists	15,000
Lawyers (in government)	48,900
State administrators	117,000
Accountants (in government)	120,500
Local administrators	152,200
Federal administrators	246,500
Total	703,700
All state employees	766,000
All local employees	1,569,900
All Federal employees	2,279,300
Total	4,615,200

SOURCE: *Bureau of Labor Statistics; Congressional Directory.*

The business community, comprising managers, administrators, and professional and technical people, numbers more than 23 million.

Business Community

Audience	Number
Officers and directors of 2400 largest United States corporations	30,000
Certified public accountants	180,000
Lawyers (American Bar Association)	237,000
Officers and directors, 34,600 additional United States corporations	360,000
Other managers and administrators with individual incomes of $25,000 or more (1976)	1,339,000
Other professional and technical people with individual incomes of $25,000 or more (1976)	1,305,000
Total	3,451,000
Total target groups	
All managers and administrators	9,488,000
All professional and technical people	13,540,000
Total	23,028,000

SOURCE: *Consumer Income Reports*, U.S. Bureau of the Census, March 1977; Dun & Bradstreet, *Million Market Directory*, 1978; *Standard & Poor's Register*, 1978.

Time also categorizes a large segment of the population, numbering more than 20,000, as belonging to various public action groups: the shakers and movers.

Public Action Groups

Audience	Number
College administrators	50,200
Editors and reporters	156,000
Elementary and secondary school administrators	209,400
Clergy	245,000
Consumer action groups	275,100
Environmental protection groups	412,300
Public affairs groups (citizen, economic, tax, state, urban rights)	598,300
Political action groups	506,000
Major political parties (active members)	1,843,100
Total target groups	
College graduates (one or more activities such as voting)	11,286,000
Other college graduates	10,174,000

SOURCE: Bureau of Labor Statistics; *Encyclopedia of Associations*, 1978; W. R. Simmons and Associates, *Selected Markets and the Media Reaching Them*, 1978–1979.

If there are multiple objectives and audiences for a corporate campaign, as there frequently are, the combined audiences can quickly add up. When you consider that these bankers, investors, analysts, employees, and educators all have wives and friends who influence them, the total number of people of importance to reach grows to an unknowable size.

We do know that very often it's more dollar-efficient to reach a total audience than to reach individual smaller, more specific target groups. So it is often well to consider taking the giant step of going to more general publications as well as to the broadcast media when the sum total of the individual audiences begins to reach boxcar-like numbers.

In line with this theory, a new philosophy espoused by the *Reader's Digest* began to evolve in the late 1970s. Although the magazine might be expected to have a natural bias, its philosophy is equally applicable to other mass media, including television. In 1978 the *Digest* pointed out that today there is a need to go directly to the people. It calls this ``Corporate Advertising Goes Public'' or ``How to Close the GAP'' (GAP stands for the great American public). This GAP needs to be told about the positive role which business plays in strengthening the national economy, cleaning up the environment, holding down prices, rebuilding the cities, and training and hiring minority workers — all the good things which companies often do and about which the great American public doesn't know or is underinformed.

Reader's Digest points out that the attitude and opinions of the public about a company can affect the public's reactions to it and its products or services:

- Because the masses react not only as prospective customers but also as employees, distributors, educators, and investors and, increasingly, as voters.

- Because schoolteachers, librarians, engineers, farmers, press operators, bank tellers, and computer programmers are all influential parts of today's new corporate public.

- Because in this era of consumerism and antibusiness attitudes, government restrictions grow out of public pressures.

- Because the same people who are increasingly concerned about the natural environment constitute an increasingly important part of your business environment.

According to the *Digest,* some years ago, most corporate messages consisted of one business executive talking to another in the trade press. Perhaps, for a rather narrowly defined financial campaign this tactic may still be appropriate. But the more objectives are broadened to improve the image of the company and the more the message involves public issues, the greater is the need to reach downward toward the grass roots.

The implication is that today we have very few statesmen, legislators, or commissioners who actually *lead* the public. Instead, we have opinion leaders who are opinion *followers.* Too often the people are surveyed and their opinions learned, and then the politicians rush to the front to lead them in the direction in which they are already headed. This may be a nasty thought, but it is a provocative one to deal with in the 1980s.

Much advocacy or issue advertising does appear in the *Reader's Digest* and, we think, rightly so. If the need is a broad one, skip the specialized media and get right to the masses, who indeed are more influential today than ever before. Whether the *Digest*'s philosophy is correct or not, the fact remains that a corporation may look more important in a major medium.

Of the many corporate audiences, the most sought after continues to be the business community. In the valuable 1979 ANA study on trends in the way companies are using corporate advertising, we find that the total business community and the investor and financial community combine to lead, with more than 50 percent of the survey respondents naming one of these communities as the most important audience. As shown in the following table, another 62 percent name one of them as the most important secondary target.

Target Audiences for Corporate Advertising

Community	Primary target	Secondary target
The entire population (adults over 18)	29	17
Large segments of the general population	44	8
Limited segments of the public	22	37
Activists and government segments	16	50
Total business community	68	54
Investor and financial community	46	59
Employees and plant communities	11	53

The table actually understates the activity directed toward the investor and financial community as well as toward the business audience. The ANA survey further asked respondents whether they had any separate smaller corporate campaign or effort directed toward other target groups. Of 157 replying, 42 reported that they did. Of the 42, the campaigns of 18 were addressed to limited business segments such as customers and chief executive officers, and those of 13 were directed toward the investor and financial community.

In dealing with the business audience, keep in mind that there's a surprisingly high rate of turnover among top executives in major companies. By "turnover" we mean changes in key slots in management levels of organizations, whether they are caused by replacement through advancement, firing, hiring, or the creation of new jobs or titles. Studies conducted by *Time* show that 70 percent of top management is turned over within a 5-year period. One study, conducted among thirty-seven large companies between 1968 and 1973, showed a national turnover rate of 73 percent. There is no reason to believe that these figures are much improved going into the 1980s. This circumstance strongly suggests, of course, the need for continuity in any program to reach out to the new influences among a given target audience. The best advice is to regard the audience as a truly moving target.

Almost inevitably, we should see a trend in the early 1980s toward greater segmentation of corporate programs and toward smaller, more specific programs with limited objectives and target audiences. This trend is in line with the steadily escalating costs among larger magazines and the broadcast media along with the growing segmentation of magazines offering audiences with varying interests and lifestyles.

An example of how segmentation applies is shown in the case of the *American Druggist*. This publication studied its subscribers' stock ownership during the period from 1969 through 1974 and found that the percentage of pharmacists owning stock whose holdings included the stock of drug companies remained constant at 41.3 percent during this erratic stock period. And, most important, during the same period pharmacists increased their personal ownership in drug company stocks. In other words, druggists chose to concentrate their investment dollars to a greater degree in the industry with which they were most familiar. In 1974 a total of 18.9 percent reported that at least half of their stock was in drug companies, compared with 16.3 percent in 1969.

Mark J. Appleman, editor and publisher of *The Corporate Shareholder*, has made the same observation. He states:

> Shareholder studies conducted by corporations in different industries indicate that investors tend to buy stocks in companies about which they have some personal knowledge. Naturally enough, they feel more secure holding shares in an industry with which they are familiar, especially if they are in a position to follow developments closely and to react quickly to evolving trends or even trade scuttlebutt.
>
> What's more, these studies show, a company's customers, suppliers, employees, and others associated with the industry, including competitors, tend to be loyal, long-term owners. Even in down markets, when the general pattern is to liquidate stockholding, the record indicates that these owners increase their portfolio concentration in industry issues.[2]

There would appear to be little reason to believe that pharmacists are different from other professionals in their stock-purchasing habits. Thus, a suggested area for further study lies in exploring the stock ownership of people in other industries. An analysis of the electrical products, communications, mining, automotive, construction, and food-processing industries likely will show similar concentrations of stock ownership among professionals. This, in turn, suggests cultivation of these audiences with appropriate advertising in the industries' own publications. While some people in these industry audiences would be constrained from owning

---

[2] *The Corporate Shareholder*, Corporate Shareholder Press, New York.

certain stocks because of a conflict-of-interest problem, the majority would not be in a sensitive position vis-à-vis a particular company's issue.

Other examples of an expected trend toward segmentation of corporate advertising can be cited in the more sophisticated use of psychographics in determining which audiences are the most predisposed to accept a corporate message. It's a generally conceded fact that much corporate advertising of the past consisted actually of business executives talking to themselves. In other words, issues were being taken up before the wrong public. Let's draw an analogy. Making an impassioned plea for the Democratic party at its own national convention may make an orator feel good, but everyone there is already convinced. So what's been accomplished?

Recognizing this fact, many corporations have added to their media list other media whose demographics consist largely of people on the other side of the issue in question. Clearly there is as great an opportunity to err in this position as there is in the opposite one. Or, to follow the analogy, an impassioned plea for the Democratic party at a Republican national convention is not apt to get you very far either. What's needed is to put your message before as large a group as possible of open-minded, uncommitted, or so-called independent people. Finding them efficiently is one more challenge of the 1980s.

CHAPTER 11 BUDGETING

In reviewing our files on budgeting, I find a wealth of material with provocative and promising titles: "A New Tool for Setting Advertising Budgets," "How Many Ad Dollars Are Enough?," "Budgeting for Growth and Profit," "Budgeting in Accordance with Need," "Margin Analysis — A New Approach to Budget Control," "Taking the Guesswork Out of Budgeting."

At first I was hopeful. I thought that we might have overlooked some exciting new method that would make the whole process of budget establishment more businesslike. It may be that the state of the art of budget determination as we go into the 1980s is about where it was 20 years ago, at least as it applies to corporate advertising budgets. Budgeting still comes down simply to putting a price tag on achieving agreed-to corporate objectives. You will recognize this procedure as the old "task method" or "task-objective method." If you handle the task method correctly and start from scratch each year, reexamining the problems and costing out the solutions again, the process deserves the title "zero-based budgeting."

The inability to relate corporate advertising to sales spares it from many of the machinations that product budgeting has been experiencing in recent years. Quantitatively oriented persons who are still searching for a formula to predict the intersection of marginal costs and marginal revenue that will help them attain a so-called optimum spending level must first succeed in the product advertising category before such methods can survive the added complex of variables of corporate programs.

Personally, I will keep my eye on what Procter & Gamble Co. is doing, and if it can find a way to solve the problem in the product advertising category, I'll begin to consider abandoning the old task method. Not that the task method is without complexities: carried out correctly with alternative plans and high-low budget levels evaluated, it can be quite precise.

The task-objective method is preferred because it is keyed to specific objectives. Management can then decide whether those objectives are worth achieving at the particular price. Frequently, the first answer may be "No." In that case, the objectives themselves, not just the plans for achieving them, should be reexamined. Perhaps the corporation is trying to accomplish too much at one time or with too many audiences. Whatever you do, don't be talked into living with unattainable objectives in an undernourished program. It's much better to cut goals down to size, achieve them, and proceed to higher things later on.

Factors Affecting Budgeting

Let's examine some of the factors that affect advertising budgets and see how these considerations are either irrelevant or take on new meaning in corporate advertising budgeting.

Competitive Expenditures   The first questions posed in product advertising frequently are "What is the competition doing?" and "How much is it spending?" In some highly developed package-goods categories in which the competition's share of advertising is known, you can virtually predict your share of market by how much you intend to spend. Corporate advertising is not competitive in this sense. True, companies are all in the same marketplace looking for employees, financing, new stockholders, and other corporate aims. There is, however, value in examining the corporate advertising expenditures of similar corporations if such figures are available. In addition to giving you a feel for what's happening, these figures indicate the noise level to which your target audiences are exposed and may give you a better idea of the kind of level you must achieve to be heard.

Advertising As a Percentage of Sales   Because corporate advertising is not intended to be directly related to sales, this kind of relationship is probably not worth examining and, in fact, may lead you into problem areas. So many decisions at the top-management level boil down to where money should be put for the best return that this kind of ratio (corporate advertising expenditures to sales) may turn up, but it serves no useful function at the planning level. It may, in fact, serve to perpetuate inappropriate budgets that were wrong in the first place. Further, it neglects to take into account the elasticity of needs from year to year.

Conforming to an Industry Norm   This consideration probably combines the worst features of those discussed above. It involves determining what the competition is doing and then adjusting your budget upward or downward according to your sales levels compared with the norm for your industry. If the problems with this method aren't immediately apparent, the insufficiency of comparative data alone makes it impractical in most cases.

Finding the Funds   Establishing a budget is one thing, but the allocation of corporate advertising expense within the corporation can be tricky. In some companies allocation is simply a matter of setting funds aside as corporate overhead. But in many companies, especially the larger, more complex ones, the money must be drawn from separate operating divisions, each of which has its own bottom-line profit responsibility. Most frequently the allocation is made on a sales-volume basis; the larger the subsidiary's sales, the greater its contribution to the corporate fund. This appears to work about as well as any method of prorating costs, although allocation by overhead and a flat, uniform tax have also been tried. The least successful method is probably to prorate costs on the basis of profits, which blatantly penalizes the more successful divisions. The other approaches to allocation have worked with varying success.

An added consideration arises when a corporation's holdings include a utility. Depending on the state in which the utility operates, the local rate commission may or may not allow the utility's contribution to the corporate advertising budget as a justifiable advertising expense. If the commission does allow the expenditure as part of the utility's rate base, the company is, in fact, allowed to make a profit on the expenditure. Obviously, this is an excellent arrangement from the company's point of view. If, however, the commission disallows the advertising expenditure, it disappears from the rate base. On the surface this is not an altogether unreasonable position. It appears simply to restore advertising costs to the tax and cost status achieved by nonutilities. In practice, however, it probably increases utility users' costs by limiting one of the corporation's important management tools for lowering borrowing costs, an important factor for money-intensive utilities. (See Chapter 5, "Corporate Advertising to the Financial Community.") The problem arises when a state commission that has allowed the expenditure suddenly reverses itself. The corporate reaction, unfortunately, is frequently to kill the campaign.

Whatever type of expense allocation is used, it will in effect be a form of "taxation" that the divisions will feel entitles them to representation and a say in corporate advertising. This representation can destroy a corporate program. Unless strong central control of the program is maintained, it is likely to degenerate into a broad, multiproduct program which can easily be diverted from its target objectives.

The Accounting Trap   In reality, advertising is a form of investment in which money spent today will build future benefits. This is true of corporate advertising even more than it is of product advertising.

The Internal Revenue Service unfortunately doesn't see things that way, and accountants therefore treat advertising as part of the company's budget. They must deal with advertising in exactly the same way as any other raw material, such as steel or electricity, which is bought and used in the process of doing business. Don't you look at advertising that way? The fact is that a campaign should yield benefits over a long period of time, and from a planning viewpoint budgeting should consider advertising's long-term effects even if accountants cannot.

What to Do Until the Budget Grows

Given ambitious management and an imaginative advertising group, there is never enough money in a budget of any size to do all the things you would like to do. And, of course, some budgets are so anemic that it may seem hopeless to try to do anything worthwhile at all. Here are some thoughts that may be helpful.

If you're going to do it at all, do it well. That aphorism may sound as if it came from one of Aesop's fables, but it's one of the soundest generalities you can follow. It can apply at many levels, from the development of campaign objectives right down to the final media selection. You can make great gains by applying this rule from the beginning. It is most important to limit your ambition when objectives are being set. Select only goals judged to be the most important to accomplish, and direct your resources toward accomplishing them well before going on to secondary objectives.

Saving money at the ad production stage is another matter. If such saving affects the look of the material, this may be the worst place to economize. The image of your corporation should be substantial and evidence every sign of quality, style, and good taste. A cheap look may be appropriate for the ad for a bargain-basement sale, subtly conveying the advertiser's low prices and lack of regard for fancy advertising. But such a cheap look is totally inappropriate for a corporate image. This doesn't mean that the ads must adopt every production luxury available. A black-and-white ad can look as rich as a full-color advertisement if it is done correctly. If there are photographs, make sure they're good ones. Frequently, however, an all-type message presented with good type design may do just as well. Money saved wisely on production is better spent in media. Here the temptation may be to stretch the budget by running very small space advertisements. Examine such a decision carefully. Depending on the objectives and the campaign needs, it may be the right choice, but often you are better served by using larger space units which convey a look of importance and speak of a corporation that is serious about its ad message. If prestige is important, remember that it's very hard to achieve it in fractional space. If your message is of an announcement nature, you are almost surely better off by taking larger space units, running them less frequently, and adding the look of importance to your message. Keep in mind that it is a big, indifferent world out there and that no matter how persistent your whispers are, they may not attract as much notice as one good shout.

Your major economies will be achieved by the skill with which you select media. Once again, whatever medium you select, use it adequately and fully before going on to the next medium so that you're not running a little bit here and a little bit there. It's easy enough to find broad-reach publications that will cover the audiences in which you're interested. The skill and hard work will be applied in narrowing your audience objectives. Concentrate on reaching these objectives as efficiently as possible, with a minimum of waste on audiences of little or no interest.

Perhaps your company is one with largely local or regional interests, in which case it will be fairly simple to find economies by using local and regional media. The business pages of newspapers and news and business shows on radio and television come immediately to mind. You may also wish to consider regional editions of magazines. There is a premium for this selectivity, but it may facilitate your entry into an otherwise unaffordable environment. In recent years there has been great growth in the availability of regional and sectional buys, which can be obtained either by zip code or by other breakdowns, depending on the particular publication. Coverage of some of the newsweeklies, for example, can be as specific as individual cities.

If you can't narrow your target audience through regional means and are faced with a national program, special demographic magazine editions may be of service. Several publications offer editions for specific target audiences. Examples are *Time* B and *Newsweek*'s executive edition, which deliver business executives.

If your audience objectives can be defined narrowly enough and you can locate an appropriate list, do not overlook direct mail. Infrequently used as a corporate medium except for stockholders' reports, direct mail is nevertheless a perfectly suitable avenue to reach well-defined groups. Dun & Bradstreet's lists broken down by standard industrial classification (SIC) categories may be an excellent place to begin the development of such a direct-mail program. Lists are also available through list houses, or they may be purchased from publications that make available to advertisers their subscriber lists, broken down demographically as commercial lists. Obviously, any direct-mail material must have an appearance that preserves it from the junk-mail stigma. This does not necessarily make the material expensive. For certain purposes, a well-written letter may be the best device to send. As you wrestle with the problems of a limited budget, you'll find that imagination and innovation are the best tools; and they are fun to use.

A last note on budgeting viewed from the agency side: the economics of corporate advertising are somewhat different from the economics of most advertising. Frequently, campaign objectives can be met with relatively small appropriations addressed to key target audiences. While several giant corporations whose names are household words spend many millions of dollars on corporate advertising, most companies have corporate campaigns of less than $1 million — many of them, much less.

On the other hand, the workload in creating corporate advertising is frequently heavier than that for other types of advertising. Generally more mature people within the agency are needed to deal with the client's top management, which should be guiding and directing the program. The creative work also requires a high degree of business sense and acumen, which can be provided only by senior writers. This is no area for juniors to dabble in, although unfortunately there is some tendency to treat corporate advertising like trade advertising and/or put a junior team on the project. This approach is generally self-correcting because the discontented client either protests or transfers the program to another agency.

The combination of relatively small budgets and relatively heavy internal agency servicing costs makes it difficult to maintain an agency profit under the conventional 15 percent commission system. In view of the possible benefits from a well-founded corporate campaign, a client should consider a supplementary fee to assure the use of top talent in the advertising development and execution.

Many corporate programs do, in fact, represent very profitable business under the conventional 15 percent system. But if this does not appear to be the case, the issue should be addressed openly by client and agency, which both stand to gain by a successful campaign and lose by an inadequate one.

CHAPTER 12 CORPORATE ADVERTISING AND THE CREATIVE PROCESS

This chapter takes guts. So does good corporate advertising.

First, it takes courage to decide what kind of corporation you are and what kind you want to be. Then it takes courage to strip away nonessentials that get in the way of this basic corporate mission and face the issues of your real subject. It takes courage to allocate enough funds to do the job right instead of diverting them to shorter-term benefits and seemingly safer product ad budgets. Finally, it takes courage to be yourself, unique, to stand up before the public and especially before your peers, the rest of American business, and say, "This is us. This is an expression of what our company is and what we stand for." With the need for all that courage, is it any wonder that so much of the advertising we saw in the 1970s was so bland, so seemingly safe? The companies seemed to be copying each other. And this kind of advertising is still being produced. To prove this point, just browse through a newsweekly and see for yourself.

Another explanation for the mediocrity of corporate advertising is that it is more difficult than other kinds of advertising. Yet it seems deceptively simple. After all, doesn't the chief executive officer know just what should be said?

Start with one basic given. You are dealing with one of the *dullest* subjects on earth. Usually no one who doesn't work for the particular company cares. Basically, you are in a position of trying to tell the public all the things which you would love to have them know about your corporation but about which they don't give a damn. See for yourself.

Here is a checklist suggested by the *Financial Times* in 1975 in a promotion piece on corporate advertising. It admits that "it is not an exhaustive list and none of the messages may fit your own situation, but it does show the scope of information which corporate advertising can communicate — and it may act as a useful prompt."[1]

Messages to customers

Size of corporation.
Diversity of product ranges.
New-product research and development.
Problem-solving skills.
Experience and ability of employees.
Vertical integration.
Delivery record.
Continuity of customer relations before and after sales.
Cooperation of suppliers, bankers, and workforce.
Internationalism.
Successful contracts completed for other customers and in other overseas markets.
Product quality control.

Messages to the financial community

How you are using investment money now.
How you would use additional investment in the future.
Messages to restore confidence after a crisis.
The role of good management in turning situations around.
Spread of interest which creates stability during economic cycles.
Short-term messages at times of take-overs.
All forms of financial statements.

Messages to government

Your organization should not be nationalized.
It is an essential part of the nation's economy.
Your profits generate taxation and hence are a contribution to the economy.
Your dividends ensure future investment.
Reequipment is producing high productivity.
High productivity is producing higher earnings.
You serve the communities in which you are located.
You reduce your dependence on imports.
You do not waste scarce resources.
You are a large employer of labor.

[1]Financial Times Ltd., Bracken House, Cannon Street, London, had the courage to compile this suggested list.

Messages to unions and employees

You are a good employer.
It is in your interest and theirs to work together.
Wages and productivity are linked.
Full information about the status of the company.

Messages to the media and the general public

Growth of the organization over the years.
Different companies in the group.
Contribution to exports.
Explanation of profits.
Protection of the environment.
Social responsibility.
Contribution to the community at local levels.

Now can you picture any reader being anxious to read up on those subjects? Admittedly, this list was prepared by a non-United States publication, but with the possible exception (and I underscore possible) of the one listed as "Your organization should not be nationalized" these are all subjects with which an American manufacturer may very well wish to deal. Frequently, the problem can be stated in two words. "Who cares?" There's a very real need to convey thoughts which are of vital importance to the corporation — things which, if known by the proper publics, could be of even greater importance but about which people apparently care very little.

A variety of devices is commonly employed with varying degrees of success to add borrowed interest to the real, but frequently dull, subject of corporate advertising. Following are a few of the more common devices with comments:

1. Feature Company Products

Products that are of benefit to the reader may be used as the apparent subject while the ad itself pursues a different objective. For example, an ad discussing the reliability of one of your popularly known and reliable products is probably a better way to get across your quality control story than an ad which bluntly presents that story. An ad showing a new product is a more convincing argument for your research and development program than one which simply states that you are on the "leading edge of technology." There is, of course, a trap in this approach. The subject matter should be selected with the objective of corporate advertising in mind and not under the pressure of a divisional president or product manager who would like "free advertising" for a particular product. Frequently, the better ad subjects are among the lesser-known unadvertised products and perhaps even among the unprofitable ones. Why? Because there is still news value in these products.

2. Relate Your Corporation to the Future

The product or service you select need not even exist. It need only be honestly presented as being on the drawing board. But obvious caution is needed in the selection of subjects. If the subject is not sufficiently unusual, it's ho-hum. And if it's too far out, the reaction is "Who are they kidding?" Future products are favorites of the airframe industry, in which prototype designs serve the further purpose of stimulating interest in more advanced products.

3. Use a Spokesperson

In the mid-1970s the celebrity spokesperson seemed to be a ready-made solution for many product campaigns. The competition for celebrities drove their prices out of sight. A $500,000 price tag was not unusual. Corporate advertising had its share of spokespersons as well: E. G. Marshall for Rockwell International, Bob Hope for Texaco, Perry Como for GTE, and Bill Cosby for the Ford Motor Company. The company spokesperson is still a viable technique, but the advertiser had better be prepared for a long, hard search for the right celebrity in addition to accepting a high price tag. Matching a compatible personality and image with the one you wish to portray for the corporation can be very time-consuming. On the other hand, the rewards are great when the right match is made, particularly for a corporation with extremely diverse features. A good spokesperson can unify these elements and convey a single identity. The risk involved if the celebrity becomes a target of controversy is real but infrequent. A morals clause in the talent contract protects the advertiser from the more serious problems.

4. Feature Employees

You needn't go the celebrity route to add the human element. Your own employees may be excellent representatives of the corporation. Scientists, engineers, or employees from almost any job category may provide an opportunity to portray the corporation through its people. It is easier for an audience to relate to people than to a corporation. But be prepared to lose a few employees if they become too famous in their roles and are picked off by the competition. This is usually more of an inconvenience than a hardship and should not stand in the way of using this technique if it seems appropriate.

5. Relate to a Public Issue

The corporate message may be an integral part of an ad that appears to concern a public issue. Or the message may be implicit within the issue itself. This is a device often used by oil companies in their need to assume good-guy status in the face of the oil industry's size, huge economic responsibility, price increases, scarcities, and frequently poor press. These problems led oil companies to such devices as early as 1962, when Mobil Corporation began an extensive campaign of giving automotive safety tips. A more recent example is the Shell Oil Company's program ``Come to Shell for Answers,'' begun in 1977. Howard W. Judson, Shell's consumer relations manager, says: ``Let's face it. In recent times business has been viewed as being slow to respond to consumer expectations, and regulations and legislation have forced action in areas from automobile safety and economy. . . . Small wonder that the public feels that business on its own volition will not make the changes they see.''[2]

Accordingly, Shell's approach to issue advertising is first to build a platform of credibility by proving in the marketplace its sensitivity and responsiveness to consumer expectations. The company hopes that this step in itself will rebuild favorable attitudes among those it serves. Abraham Lincoln reminded us: ``With public sentiment on its side, everything succeeds. With public sentiment against it, nothing succeeds.''

Judson's description of Shell's campaign as issue advertising is interesting. Of course, in and of itself this portion of the campaign does not deal with any issues; rather, to use an old-fashioned term, it is ``goodwill advertising.'' Judson goes on to say: ``Once we have built this platform, we are confident that then, and only then, will we be able to address specific issues through advertising in a meaningful and credible fashion.'' We hope he is right.

6. "You Don't Know Us, But You Know Our Customers"

This classic approach is used by manufacturers of ``hidden'' products, makers of components which find their way into other everyday products used in the home but which lose their identity in the manufacturing process. The success or failure of the approach depends on whether there is sufficient interest in the end product.

If there is genuinely interesting news in the relationship, this approach can work, but more often than not it doesn't. The fact that your company makes, say, the nuts and bolts used in lift trucks that a famous consumer company employs can rarely be made exciting or seem important to most

[2]Speech given at the ANA Corporate Workshop, New York, Nov. 29, 1977.

readers. Even the fact that your hidden product is part of a very sophisticated, technologically demanding end product is usually ho-hum; so the hoped-for quality-reliability rub-off rarely occurs.

If, on the other hand, as a reader you discover that some major component of one of the products with which you are very familiar is actually made by another company that perhaps makes this component for most of the industry, the fact can be very interesting. It can also be very dangerous to advertise the fact without prior discussion with your original-equipment manufacturer (OEM) customers. Briggs & Stratton Corp. makes the most vital components of most lawn mowers, for example, but it wisely doesn't preempt this story. Customers have been known to become very upset when they see their own reputation as a manufacturer eroded by the announcement that major components are actually produced by some other industry supplier.

A variation of this strategy is the featuring of components which are made for the military. "We make the nail that went in the shoe that went on the horse that the rider rode who saved the war." Clearance in this area, of course, is even more important. It's no longer just a business risk, but a legal one, if the components are used in a sensitive military area.

The nature of the corporation's products will determine whether this strategy has merit. Before embarking on it, make sure that the ads will actually fulfill the objectives of the program. It is doubtful that they will. Frequently, this kind of ad is simply an exercise in trying to tell the world that you exist. If that is all your objective is, maybe it's all right, but it is loose as objectives go, particularly if the program results in ads that few people will read.

7. "Look What We're Doing for Humanity"

This approach still has its adherents, although it is past its peak of popularity, probably because of the overly stretched credulity of the public. If a product or service is directly related to human benefit or health for the aged or for children, it can be a winner in attention, readership, and goodwill. The closer it is to the personal experience of the individual the better: a new device in the health-care field described as a cost-cutting product for hospitals may be all right, but obviously the advertiser is much better off by relating the product to a human benefit such as a lower hospital bill.

8. Relate Your Corporation to News

All advertising should be current and in step with the news environment of the day, but beyond this criterion there are news events that may relate specifically to some corporate or major product feature. Make no mistake about it: news is of universal interest. The way in which the General Telephone Company rallied to restore communications after the Johnstown flood made a powerful statement about its repair capabilities in an interesting way. The flood was news. Without the news, the corporation's ability to marshal human resources from all over the United States as part of an overall reliability message would have been pretty dull.

But watch out for the bandwagon effect of a news story. This effect probably reached its low point when astronauts first walked on the moon and *The New York Times* carried no fewer than thirty-eight advertisements claiming active and major participation in the event. The total effect became rather silly for a few days as various corporations hung in undignified positions from the bandwagon.

Perhaps the biggest corporate winner in the moon-walk corporate orgy was Volkswagen, which had had absolutely nothing to do with this tremendous American achievement. Its attractive photograph of the model of the LEM with the headline "It's ugly, but it gets you there" became an instant classic. The same advertiser greeted a water shortage in New York with the suggestion "Save water. Drive a Volkswagen." While these two VW examples may, strictly speaking, be product ads rather than corporate ads, they serve as examples not only of how news may be used but of the need for creativity to make it work.

There are no formulas to assure great advertising. There are certain essential steps of fact-finding, analysis, and interpretation which must come first. There is the need to know, which research can help fill and which interviews with a company's CEO, middle management and factory management, and employees on the line can also help satisfy. But when all the work has been done, an alert, sensitive, creative team must take the facts and relate them in a fresh way to corporate needs and to public interests. (If you hope to find out how to do this in this chapter, I'm sorry. You will be disappointed, nor are you likely to find it in any other book.)

Effective corporate advertising results from the very same disciplines that produce good product advertising, but to a greater degree and with fewer guideposts. Relating corporate advertising to ongoing news stories, such as the economy, an energy shortage, or even wars and food shortages, in which corporate needs mesh with any type of newsworthy situation, can be relatively easy to factor into a corporate creative platform.

Beyond this there are news breaks which may offer fine opportunities to gain attention. To take advantage of these breaks, you need good internal communications. Within the company and the agency there should be a prearranged team and procedure, complete with home phone numbers, as good standard procedure. The hotter the news, the sooner the ad runs. Such prearrangements must include coordination with the public relations department, because the interpretation of the relationship of the news to the corporation falls within its functional area.

9. Look Important

The natural reaction to a paucity of reader interest is the use of large space units. Full-page ads are almost the minimum size. Spreads are very common, and four-color units are a reasonably certain way to attain greater impact and visibility. For obvious reasons very few fractional pages are successfully employed. This situation may not do much for your cost per thousand, but it does maximize the number of readers. Dominant units do something else which may be even more important. Dominance adds a look of importance to the subject matter and subtly says: "We thought enough to make an all-out effort to tell you this message about our corporation." And it also implies the size and stature of the corporation itself.

10. Fit the Medium to the Message (and Vice Versa)

While it would be difficult to attribute the increased use of television for corporate advertising to the dryness of the same ad subject matter in print, there is no doubt that TV offers opportunities to dramatize and capture interest which print does not. Without getting into a media debate, we can state that it is harder to ignore a TV set than to turn a page.

11. The Right Tone of Voice

But whatever the medium and whatever the space, as we have said, there are no formulas to assure great advertising. In October 1977, David Ogilvy, founder of Ogilvy & Mather, in his first public address on the subject of corporate advertising before the Dallas Advertising League, had this advice to give about the subject:

> Corporate advertising should be plain-spoken, candid, adult, intelligent, and specific. It should avoid preachment and self-congratulation. It should be rooted in products, or services, or policies. . . . It should be interesting instead of boring. You cannot bore people into admiring a company.
> Creative genius is required to "penetrate the filter of indifference" with which people regard most corporations. If nobody reads your corporate advertising advertisements, which is usually the case, nothing happens. You cannot save souls in an empty church.
> Corporate advertising should avoid the verbal and visual clichés of Madison Avenue. It should use the quiet graphics and speak the language of editors — not ad men.

Certainly, this is sound advice for corporate advertising. In fact, it's especially good basic advice for copywriters of almost any type of advertising. Being candid, adult, and intelligent as well as plain-spoken can rarely get a copywriter into trouble. And who wants to indulge in the verbal and visual clichés of Madison Avenue? The advice brings up a point that is especially important to corporate advertising, namely, a tone of voice. This tone or point of view should be consistent in any given corporate campaign. It shouldn't wander. Ideally, it should be the tone of voice of the true personality of the corporation. It should sound like the corporation as an individual (which, in fact, a corporation legally is).

Thus the solidity of an investment house can come through if that is the desired tone of voice. The fatherly protectivism of a holding company can have a sound of its own. The young, aggressive new company in a hot industry can have a brashness in its tone of voice that might ill fit an old-line oil company.

Ads and commercials, after all, should have the character of the corporation — the real corporation. There may be a temptation to change this character to a seemingly more desirable posture before the public. That's a dangerous venture because you are dealing with the element of truth and the truth will out. There are very real limits to how far you can stray from the real personality and tone of voice.

To cite a personal experience, in an all-out effort to break through the public's indifference to one client's very involved corporate message, we resorted to animated commercials. They did almost everything we wanted them to. They enabled us to convey a large number of products and services quickly, associating the corporate name closely to the products and giving an image of a young, aggressive corporation with great warmth. In tests these commercials also did very well. They broke through clutter, they were memorable, and they made the point we were trying to make. People loved them. And, at first, so did the client, who felt that they were innovative and daring. But in the course of a few weeks, as divisional managers were heard from, the real truth began to surface. As one outspoken manager summed it up, "I'm embarrassed by the ads. My wife said she didn't know I worked for a company like that. That advertising is just not us."

12. Most of All

If you think that up to now I've been laying down rules, maybe you're right. Just remember, "Rules are what the artist breaks; the memorable never emerged from a formula." My boss said that. He also laid down some very solid rules of his own about advertising in general. They are especially true of creating corporate advertising in the 1980s:

> Can creativity in advertising survive the mounting problems we face?
> Inflation, shortages, economic crises, battered consumers, threatening
> governmental bureaucracies, restrictions on what we can say, parity

products, an overwhelming clutter of messages to try to break through. "Creativity may have been all right for relatively good times," they say. "Tough times call for tough responses," they say. "Creativity is dead; positioning is everything." Or "Creating is dead; the 'hard sell' is everything."

Incredible.

What is the use of saying all the right things if nobody is going to listen to you? What is the use of being perfectly positioned if nobody will ever notice you because a dull, boring statement of your position never pierced through to the consumer's attention? The most criminal waste of money in business today is that spent on advertising that never gets looked at. And fully 85 percent of all advertising is ignored. Yes, we are getting boring in our communications to the consumer with real business-like efficiency. We are searching for *what* to say and forgetting that *how* we say it is the insurance that makes everything pay off.

The tougher the times, the more important creativity in advertising becomes.

It's the fastest, most economical way to cut through to the minds and hearts of the consumer.

If you can make fewer claims today, then you'd better care terribly about how you make them.

If what you have to say isn't that different, say it differently.

If the whole world hasn't been waiting for your message, make them awfully glad they heard it anyway.

Creativity is not, and never was meant to be, a substitute for another part of the advertising process. It is not blowing smoke rings and getting vibes. It is not *instead* of research, it is not *instead* of strategy, it is not *instead* of positioning. It comes *after* all of those things. And it is not *instead* of anything except dullness, lack of personality, not being noticed.

The fact is that after you have produced the best product, packaged it brilliantly, priced it right, distributed it magnificently, and positioned it to best meet the needs of the consumer, you will have sinfully wasted all these great skills if the consumer doesn't hear what you're trying to tell him. And his attention — because of the glut of messages bombarding him — is harder to get than ever before in the history of mankind.

To get attention for your product is not in the province of research, or marketing, or positioning. It's the job of communications, and here we plunge into the mysterious world of creativity, of art rather than science, subtle and ever changing. What was effective one day, for that very reason will not be effective the next.

There is no single method or formula that could possibly endure in the creation of effective advertising. Working from a method or formula is guaranteed to do the same thing to the effectiveness of an idea that time does to a loaf of bread. Only the new, only the fresh can continue to provide interest and excitement.

And that's why nobody worth a dash of creative salt has ever been able to predict what creativity in advertising will bring next year, or the year after.

But I will happily and confidently predict that next year and the year after and every year after that will bring forth more creativity in effective advertising, will prove its increasing importance in breaking through to the consumer.

And that people who have the talent to communicate in a fresh and exciting way will continue to be sought after by agencies (even the so-called big, stuffy ones).

Every client gives you his business for the purpose of selling his product. If you put enough time and dollars behind almost *any* message, it may eventually get through. And if the product has merit, and the basic strategy is sound, eventually even a dull or a shrill message will sell.

But who has that much time and money?

It is so much more *economical* to find the freshest, most appealing way of saying the thing that your research and marketing and positioning have told you must be said. And then to breathe life into your idea with the right execution.

How do you storyboard a smile? Yet the quality of that smile may make the difference between a commercial that works and one that doesn't work. How do you get its subtle nuances, its sadness or its happiness, its wistfulness or its bitterness? Yet the execution of that smile can either make people believe you and be with you, or not believe you and be against you. An idea can turn to dust or to magic, depending on the talent that rubs against it.

We *are* in tough times. We are engulfed in problems and restrictions and limitations that are true and real and now.

What's needed most now is the kind of creativity that can still make people laugh, cry, believe, and buy.

One last quotation from my boss: "To keep your ads fresh you've got to keep yourself fresh. Live in the current idiom and you will create it. If you follow and enjoy and are excited by the new trails in art, in writing, in industry, in personal relationships . . . whatever you do will naturally be of today."

Yes, when your boss is Bill Bernbach, this chapter takes a lot of guts.

CHAPTER 13 CORPORATE ADVERTISING AND THE LAW

This chapter is not a do-it-yourself legal kit. If you try to use it that way and go to jail, don't blame me. Today, as in most other advertising agencies, our legal counsel and the client's legal department both pass on the acceptability and the possible risks involved in any campaign under consideration. Such a procedure is really a must for any advertiser and its agency in today's environment. Having made that point, I still think a short discussion of the general law which surrounds corporate advertising, as one layman to another, may be of some assistance.

We start with a view that corporate advertising must meet the same legal ground rules that product advertising meets. Every claim and every fact used in an ad must have a source and be subject to validation. This validation may include library material, test results, or expert testimony in technical areas. The documentation is then submitted to the legal departments of the agency and the client. It is maintained in a file associated with the individual ad, where it is available for future reference. In addition, care is taken to be sure that the corporate ad's subject matter has not led us into a violation of special industry codes. These codes can be either governmental regulations or self-regulatory industry guidelines; it's important that they not be overlooked. Obviously, just because it's a corporate ad, it is not excused from meeting special industry rules such as those that drug manufacturers must follow or that the liquor industry uses. Even the toy industry's guidelines would apply if the subject matter and media placed the ad in this area of special concern. Corporate advertising probably requires more alertness than product advertising does in this respect because the subject matter frequently varies a great deal from ad to ad. This is especially true when a corporation has many products in many companies and the campaign features a variety of these products over the course of time. The quickest way to check and familiarize yourself with those special trade practices is to speak to someone in the industry, probably someone within the company who deals with them on an everyday basis. Thus, you can find out that it is necessary to add disclaimers concerning optional extras on cars and appliances and to measure television sets diagonally. The list of potential problems is seemingly endless. The regulations are seemingly countless.

Ads to the Financial Community

One area in particular requires special attention in corporate advertising. It is of particular concern when you are addressing the financial community. The ads must not be of a type that can be construed as ``touting the stock.'' They must not have information that can be interpreted by the Securities and Exchange Commission (SEC) as being a direct effort to influence the price of a company's securities. This is, of course, particularly vital during periods of registration. Typical of what to avoid in advertising during this period would be:

1. Estimates or projections of future earnings or trends in earnings

2. Predictions of increased revenues, sales, or earnings as a result of specific research or development work in products or services

3. Estimates of future sales and revenues or trends in specific industries or product lines in which the company is engaged, whether they are given in dollars, units, percentages, or even generalized terms

At this point it's important to reiterate that we are talking here only of corporate advertising as defined in Section 1, not financial advertising or, perhaps more properly, securities advertising in which a prospectus is offered. Nor are we talking of advertising presented by financial institutions such as banks. Nor are we discussing investment opportunities such as condominiums and land offerings, which all have their own legal restrictions.

Your legal counsel may differ with these ground rules. There is nothing official about them. That is the problem.

The SEC doesn't seem anxious to lay down a clear-cut set of rules. We thought at one time that the rules would be made clear. In the early 1970s there was some celebration over what appeared to be the SEC's statement by Allen B. Levinson, then Director of the Commission's Division of Corporate Finance, who stated:

> As a matter of policy, we encourage the flow of factual information to shareholders and the investing public. When companies are in registration, they continue to respond to legitimate inquiries for factual information about the company's financial condition.
>
> As to the point of a company initiating publicity or advertising which is not designed to facilitate the offering of securities in a proposed public offering, there appears to be no objection if such material has been previously published and disseminated in the company's annual report, and does not contain projections or opinions bearing on the value of the company's securities, and does not include statements which would be deemed to be puffing. The staff stands ready to assist issuers and their representatives in resolving questions in this area.[1]

While this statement led to a greater dialogue in the business and financial community, with informative ads appearing on a regular basis, it in no way eliminated the SEC's authority to decide when advertising during the registration period was in violation. Nor does the SEC today show any inclination to clear up this ambiguous state. Any clarification will, in fact, reduce its present power. We see more and more advertisers pressing the limits of corporate puffing during registration, and as of this writing we see very little in the way of SEC efforts to change the trend. Nevertheless, advertisers must continue to work in semidarkness, knowing that they can be called to account by the SEC at any time.

Advocacy Advertising

Corporate advertising to the financial community isn't the only area where we operate under the ''lore'' as much as under the law. Corporate advertising that is involved with sensitive public issues (or advocacy advertising) requires care as well.

As stated earlier, we consider that corporate advertising requires the same documentation of facts and statements that is required by product advertising. It's interesting to recall that in the late 1970s, as a result of statements by then chairman of the Federal Trade Commission (FTC), Lewis Engman, there was speculation that, on the basis of the First Amendment, corporate advertising might be immune to FTC regulation. Early in 1975 Engman had indicated that image advertising, as he called it, was not being scrutinized and that it was unlikely that a government agency would question information in image ads, on the theory that such questioning might interfere with First Amendment guarantees of free speech.

[1]Quoted in an editorial by E. M. Manning, publisher, *Finance Magazine*, March 1972.

Taken out of context, this statement was made shortly after a statement by the staff of the FTC on proposed enforcement policy regarding corporate image advertising. The Commission said:

> We propose that the Commission proceed against unfair or deceptive corporate image advertising in situations where the dominant appeal and likely effect of the advertising is commercial. Under Section 5 of the Federal Trade Commission Act, the question in each instance will be whether the dominant appeal and likely effect of an advertisement relates to consumer and business purchases, investment decisions, and employee recruitment or morale rather than to the formation of public opinion about or action on a public issue.
>
> Based upon our examination of corporate image advertising, we anticipate that the application of this standard will often require a careful analysis of the particular advertisement in question. Claims in certain corporate image advertisements may arguably be capable of eliciting both commercial responses and political ones — for example, claims which describe corporate behavior that is itself the subject of public controversy.[2]

We must wait and see just how this approach will actually be applied. It remains to be seen whether an ad that basically concerns a public issue, and therefore should logically be immune under the First Amendment, loses its immunity if it includes commercial corporate implications. Clearly, the reverse will not be true; that is, the simple addition of a public issue to an otherwise corporate ad will not gain immunity for the entire ad.

There is, in fact, a specter of a legislative backlash against corporate advertising as a result of some of the more outspoken advocacy advertisers' discussion of pet political issues. At this time such a specter appears unlikely, particularly after such court rulings as the Supreme Court's decision in the Massachusetts case of the *First National Bank of Boston v. Bellotti,* in which the Court struck down a Massachusetts law prohibiting corporations from spending money to influence valid issues that do not materially affect their business; but the possibility of additional restrictive legislation certainly cannot be ruled out. More likely is the adoption of more subtle restrictive measures, such as the very real likelihood that the Internal Revenue Service will disallow the writing off of ad expenditures when the intent is to change public opinion on legislative matters. Taxation in this area may very well have the ability to destroy or, at least, to inhibit greatly public issue advocacy advertising or the inclusion of public opinion issues in corporate advertising.

A very real uncharted swamp exists in this legal area, and it is one for which no federal agency including the Federal Communications Commission (FCC) seems willing to provide a map. Representative Benjamin

[2]Statement of proposed enforcement policy by staff of the Federal Trade Commission regarding corporate image advertising, Dec. 4, 1974, p. 21.

THE DOORS OF INJUSTICE

SENECA FALLS, New York—In 1976, an ex-policeman disappeared while fishing on Seneca Lake in Upstate New York. Two men were arrested and accused of his murder, even though the body was never found.

Carol Ritter, court reporter for Gannett Rochester Newspapers, went to cover the pretrial hearing for the accused.

When she arrived at the courtroom, Ritter and other reporters were barred from the hearing on the pretext that the accused would not be able to get a fair trial if the pretrial hearing was covered by the press.

The Gannett Rochester Newspapers strongly disagreed and challenged the judge's right to close the doors of justice to the people, including the press. They took that challenge to the Supreme Court of the United States.

Gannett believes no judge should have the right to shut the people and their free press out of such pretrial hearings, where an overwhelming majority of criminal prosecutions are resolved.

Can you imagine up to 90 percent of all court cases being settled in secret? Gannett could not. But on July 2, 1979, the Supreme Court ruled it could happen.

Gannett protests vigorously this abridgment of the First Amendment. Not only has the Court limited journalists' access to gathering and reporting the news for the public, but it has also trampled on the people's freedom to know, the cornerstone of our rights as a free people in a free society.

The freedoms of the First Amendment must be cherished, not shackled.

At Gannett, we have a commitment to freedom in every business we're in, whether it's newspaper, TV, radio, outdoor advertising or public opinion research.

And so from Burlington to Boise, from Fort Myers to Fort Wayne, every Gannett newspaper, every TV and radio station is free to express its own opinions, free to serve the best interests of its own community in its own way.

Gannett

A World of Different Voices
Where Freedom Speaks

GANNETT

"The Doors of Injustice"

A strong believer in advocacy advertising, the Gannett Company, with major interests in newspaper, broadcast, and outdoor advertising, has a tremendous stake in the protection of the First Amendment. To quote Allen H. Neuharth, chairman and president of Gannett, "In our advertising campaign, we hope to accomplish several goals. Naturally, we hope to make people more aware of Gannett. We hope to make all our audience more aware of all our commitments to freedom to journalistic excellence in the community service. Our commitments to freedom include our commitment to the First Amendment and to all of our rights and responsibilities under it. . . . Through strong, forceful corporate advertising, we believe we can express our opinion on the issues that matter to us and journalism professionals; inform our readers, viewers, and listeners what the ideals and aims of Gannett are; and let our employees know where their employer stands, and inform all of our commitment to editorial and business excellence, and to freedom." Gannett surveys the public's reaction to its advertising and reports that it's been very positive.

Rosenthal (Democrat of New York), chairman of the Subcommittee on Consumer Affairs, has been a particularly aggressive attacker of advocacy advertising. He conducted a survey of 467 of the *Fortune* 500 industries and 200 trade associations as well as labor unions and charities, questioning them about their grass-roots activities, which of course included lobbying as well as corporate advertising. Rosenthal concluded that corporations are improperly writing off at least $100 million a year. This "scandalously high figure," to quote *Fortune's* reporting, "came as a surprise, not only to businessmen but also to some of their frequent opponents in public interest groups. It seemed improbably high considering that Mobil Oil, the champ of advocacy advertisers, spent only $3.2 million on grass-roots lobbying last year and deducted none of it."[3]

The estimate does not seem so high, however, once you consider Rosenthal's definitions: "attempts to influence" (anything that could conceivably come before Congress) "the general public or segments thereof" (everybody). With definitions like these, it will be virtually impossible to separate corporate advertising from product advertising or anything else.

If your corporate client is interested in advocacy and the use of television at the same time, you will rapidly learn about the "fairness doctrine." You'll also probably wonder how the doctrine got its name. To the advertiser, it certainly appears to be anything but fair. The fairness doctrine is akin to the equal-time doctrine of the Communications Act, which requires that broadcasters give legally qualified candidates equal time. If one candidate is permitted use of a station's facilities, other legally qualified candidates must be granted the same privilege. The exceptions are newscasts, interviews, news documentaries, and spot coverage of bona fide news events. The fairness doctrine deals with issues rather than people. Required by law to operate in the public interest, a broadcast licensee must afford reasonable opportunity for the discussion of conflicting views on issues of public importance. Both these doctrines are confined to broadcasting, presumably because while almost anyone can either start a newspaper or is free to print and distribute his or her points of view, there is a technical limitation to the number of available broadcast channels. Broadcast operators are licensed, and licensees are required to operate stations in the public interest.

Both doctrines are clearly designed to bring a balanced point of view to the public. Perhaps, to a degree they do. However, the fairness doctrine also serves to limit greatly the amount of controversial material which can be aired. Broadcasters shy away from the great debates, recognizing that in the demand for equal time they stand to lose valuable air time. They are never sure just what the degree of jeopardy is, since it depends on how many people clamor for their side of an issue to be heard. This is one of

[3] *Fortune,* Aug. 28, 1978, p. 63.

Can a corporation speak its mind in public?

Not long ago, the Supreme Court ruled that corporations are entitled to the right of free speech.

However, when Kaiser Aluminum & Chemical Corporation tried to exercise this right recently, it was denied by the three major television networks.

Our idea was to produce three commercials drawing attention to issues we felt were of major concern to the people of America. One was about energy. The others dealt with free enterprise, and governmental red tape. (The commercials are shown below). We believed at the time that we were exercising our right to speak our mind. We were willing to pay for the air time to run these commercials. And we clearly identified these messages as opinions of our company.

But when we submitted them to the networks, the commercials were rejected. The networks said they would refuse to air them. Not because they were untrue, misleading, or in any way inaccurate. But simply because they were controversial or not acceptable material.

One network cited the "Fairness Doctrine" as a reason for rejecting the commercials. This doctrine was formulated by the Federal Communications Commission (FCC) to insure that a fair balance of opinion is presented on television. We believe, too, that television should present a fair balance of opinion. Even ours.

There is no doubt that television is one of the most powerful media in operation today. And we believe that access to this medium must be kept free and open.

If you believe a free exchange of ideas is as important now as it's ever been, write your elected representatives or write us at Kaiser Aluminum, Room #776 KB, 300 Lakeside Drive, Oakland, California 94643. Let your voice be heard.

Announcer
Is free enterprise an endangered species? How much government regulation is enough? Is business bad just because it's big? Or does a country like ours require a diversity of business — both big and small?
Will excessive control over big business lead to control over all our business?
The answers are up to you.
Whatever your views let your elected representatives know.
People, one by one, need to speak up now. You can help keep free enterprise free.
A message from Kaiser Aluminum.
One person can make a difference.

Announcer
Some people are calling the energy crisis a hoax. Others say that at the rate we're using our oil reserves we'll be down to our last drop in our children's lifetime.
Whoever's right, one thing is clear. America needs an energy plan for the future *now*. One that uses all resources available from coal and nuclear power to solar.
But we're only going to get it if people, one by one, demand it.
Whatever your views, let your elected representatives know now.
There's not much we can do when the light goes out.
A message from Kaiser Aluminum.
One person can make a difference.

Official Voices (Overlapping)
Applications should be filled out in triplicate...
Forms should be returned by the 19th or penalty charges...
The Bureau requires all permits to...
The Department must be notified...
Send one copy to...

Announcer
It's red tape. In 1977, America spent $100 billion on federal paperwork alone. And in the end we *all* pay for it.
But if people, one by one, start speaking out, we can begin untangling America's knottiest problem.
A message from Kaiser Aluminum.
One person can make a difference.

KAISER ALUMINUM & CHEMICAL CORPORATION

KAISER ALUMINUM & CHEMICAL CORPORATION

"Can a corporation speak its mind in public?"

The Kaiser Aluminum & Chemical Corporation tackling the issue of issue advertising. The commercials were rejected by all three major commercial networks. At least one network cited the "fairness doctrine" as a reason. The commercials ranged in subject from free enterprise as an endangered species to the need for an energy plan and to a general plea for less paperwork and red tape in government. It's hard to believe that these subjects are so controversial that their broadcast would have resulted in demands for equal time, but under today's rules the networks are judge and jury.

The ad drew a heavy response from readers: nearly 2000 letters. Of these 96 percent were strongly supportive of the messages expressed, according to information from William H. Griffith, Kaiser's director of corporate advertising. This ad may have given the corporation as much publicity as the commercials would have done. It's an excellent example of how silly the "fairness" situation has become in the 1980s.

those cases in which the results are not always what the law intended. Stations and networks don't welcome problems of this sort. When confronted with a controversial commercial, they may simply avoid the issue by stipulating that their acceptance policy covers only products and services and that commercials on any issues are unacceptable even in cases like the one in which, in 1979, Mobil offered to pay, in addition to its own commercial time, the air costs for equal time devoted to opposing views.

This is the arena as we enter the 1980s. There is a somewhat confused legal climate which suggests that our agency's current position of requiring that strict documentation of factual claims and statements be applied with the same vigor to corporate advertising as it is to product advertising is a good one. The same care is needed in public issue or advocacy advertising, as it overlaps and melds with other corporate advertising, to make certain that we do not abuse this area, which presently enjoys at least the residual remains of First Amendment immunity. We can look toward debate and possibly growing restriction in the area of advocacy advertising in direct relation to the number of false and misleading ads by misguided advertisers. Please don't make the situation worse.

CHAPTER 14 CORPORATE MEDIA (PRINT)

"There is no such thing as a bad medium, just bad media buys." While that Pollyanna view may not be strictly accurate, it makes the important point that the burden is on the *selection,* not on the medium itself. I am sure that somewhere there may be stations, newspapers, or souvenir journals that are downright rotten for any advertiser, but they are rare. And you won't read about them in this book. Almost any medium can have a legitimate place on someone's schedule, depending on media objectives and audience requirements and, realistically though unfortunately, on political expediencies.

Changes have been more radical in the media selection process in most large agencies than in any of the other major agencies' functions in the last 15 years. Research directors may argue that the computer has also made possible tremendous strides in their area. They are right, but much of this research data is now part of the flood of information available for media use. The changes that the computer has brought about in media work have added dimensions of quantitative sophistication previously unavailable in the analysis of comparative and alternative media approaches.

Most of this growing sophistication would appear, on the surface at least, to have been overlooked by corporate advertisers in their media selection. Whether this is, in fact, the case or whether it just seems to be so from outward appearances is difficult to determine. I suspect, however, that many corporate schedules are the result of intuition without much benefit from modern media selection techniques.

To understand this situation, let's first review the standard process of media selection employed today by major agencies on behalf of national products. To state the matter in a highly oversimplified way, media planning is considered an extension of market planning. Generally, it involves a definition of marketing requirements and a translation of these requirements into media specifications that can be acted upon. You might view the development of the media plan essentially as an evaluation of alternatives. Such an approach requires extensive manipulation of data on the costs, characteristics, and dimensions of each medium down to its demographics and regional variations. Today it is possible to make this evaluation far more thoroughly than in precomputer days.

The media selection process can be broken down into two basic steps. First, it is necessary to examine the general media alternatives available in order to isolate those media areas which are most appropriate within the creative and marketing guidelines. In other words, you must determine in advance whether a product and its selling message require the action and demonstration offered by television, a long exposition better suited to print, or a high-frequency reminder calling for outdoor advertising. Essentially, the media planner at this stage is broadly determining strategy: the areas in which planning development and refinement will take place.

The second phase is the development of specific media. This phase gets down to tactics: the selection and use of specific publications and broadcasting stations. It recognizes budget limitations, regional needs, day parts, seasonal timing, and possibly requirements for copy length. The media planner, knowing the target audience and probably the primary and secondary audiences as well (this information has been determined from market research), examines the various media in terms of their ability to deliver an audience by sex, age, income, family size, education, marital status, and employment. A few other demographic breakdowns pertinent to the particular product or class of product may also be considered.

Once the basic media mix and the target audience are known and the vast amounts of data on the audience of the media are available, all the basic ingredients are ready for the computer to analyze. Various attainable reach and frequency levels can be determined by an almost endless shuffling of specific buys within the basic framework.

Quantitative versus Qualitative Selection

Note that in this very simplified model little attention has been given to individual stations or to the editorial content of publications. Media differences and characteristics have been explored largely on the basis of a station's or a publication's audience demographics generated by whatever editorial means have been used. The medium is viewed primarily as a vehicle to carry the advertisement physically into the home or into the hands of the subscriber or viewer.

The tendency to analyze and codify statistical data has increased in recent years. The growing use of the computer has made available vast amounts of information for analysis which with its sheer bulk often outweighs the relatively small amount of editorial subjectivity involved in the selection of a specific medium. Certainly in good media planning, particularly in the early stages of media analysis, editorial judgment is employed. A very clear example is found with the corporations which have a policy of not supporting sex or violence on television. This policy is automatically factored in to avoid such programming when media selections are made.

Nevertheless, the media buying process today is a far cry from that of the good old days, when media selection depended almost exclusively on a well-worn Audit Bureau of Circulations statement and a media buyer's judgment of the various publishers' and stations' editorial philosophies and formats. If a publication seemed to feel right, its cost and rate structure would be examined along with its circulation. (The pass-along audience was unknown or perhaps merely conjectured.) Also factored in would be whatever information the publication might be able to offer about its readership. Such information would come from separate studies conducted by magazines, which were always favorable. Some audience data might consist simply of extrapolations from what was known of a magazine's editorial content and the type of people whom it would logically attract.

It is my guess that most corporate advertising is still being selected by this old method, largely because the pitfalls of the strictly analytical approach are so obvious. Instinctively many old-line corporate advertisers appear possibly to recognize this media-numbers-game pitfall. They prefer to rely on what is largely their own subjective evaluation of the media and their own reading and watching preferences, plus those of their friends, peers, and relatives. Smaller corporate advertisers particularly appear to take the "safe" course of running their corporate ads in media where they see a heavy placement of the corporate ads of other advertisers.

While this seat-of-the-pants type of media selection might be condemned out of hand as being very naïve, it does have certain advantages over the extreme opposite approach of letting a buy be dictated strictly by statistics of audience efficiencies. To give an overdrawn example of the danger, let's say that you are seeking a young, aggressive, on-the-move urban audience, perhaps for recruitment purposes. Perhaps statistically *Hustler* magazine may be (I don't say it is) the most efficient deliverer of such a target group. I'll let you explain that selection to your chief executive officer while I solicit the account. Maybe that's a silly example, but it makes the point that the environment of the medium is far more important in corporate advertising than in product advertising.

It must be clear by now that a way should be found to select corporate media which combine the best of the demographic-analytical world while retaining an effective editorial evaluation. We need a method which will allow the addition of certain publications which are editorially right although possibly somewhat weak in cost efficiency and a system which can eliminate even a powerhouse efficiency buy if its editorial environment is viewed as inappropriate.

The solution to this problem exists. It takes a lot of work, but it is really very simple. Both methods are used. In brief, certain guideposts screen out from statistical evaluation the more obviously inappropriate media. This screening is done at the same stage that creative and marketing guidelines are first examined in order to isolate the general areas of media to be considered. All editorially marginal media should be examined statistically. They can be eliminated later if they are in a close statistical race. Simmons Market Research Bureau (SMRB) data are assembled according to the demographics and characteristics which are judged to represent the primary target audience as they apply to print media. These characteristics may be such factors as people who

- Currently owned commodities, warrants, calls, or options.
- Currently owned securities with a market value of $50,000 or more.
- Personally made three or more stock transactions in the past 12 months.
- Wrote to the editor of a magazine or newspaper.
- Addressed a public audience.
- Took part in some civic issue.
- Were involved in four to six public activities.
- Wrote to an elected official.
- Wrote something that had been published.
- Actively worked for a political party.

The list can go on. SMRB data include other characteristics which can be used to examine qualitatively the makeup of a medium's audience. You may decide to select one or two key qualitative points, or very possibly you may wish to list a number of them and give them various weights of importance. Out of this process will come a numerical weighted list, with a number or an index for each publication under consideration to represent its relative weakness or strength in delivering an audience with the characteristics that you have determined are important for your target. The number, of course, will be an artificial one. At this stage it will be related not to costs but rather only to the publication's standing compared with that of other publications. Generally, slavish adherence to numerical ranking is a mistake.

Statistical error in this type of work is so likely that it is wiser to break the magazines into the natural groups that will appear to form. You will find that half a dozen or so magazines will be grouped together. They should be judged as more or less equal, and from them you may make your selection. In actual practice, a number of selections will appear to offer promise. Lay out comparative schedules for these different selections or groupings. You then return to the real numbers world by applying an actual dollar cost to these hypothetical schedules, which can then be compared for their true dollar cost and their actual dollar efficiency, as expressed in cost per thousand.

The resulting alternative schedules, which by this time comprise only publications editorially acceptable as corporate environments, can then be judged with the reasonable assurance that you not only are making a decision with the best quantitative cost and efficiency data but are doing so among schedules which have been chosen through the selection of media with strong qualitative credentials. You are, in effect, following a formula which starts with judgment, proceeds to statistics, goes back to judgment, adds more statistical evaluation, and then returns to judgment once again. It's difficult to beat this combination. Whatever you do, follow this rule: do all your numbers homework, but also let your judgment have free rein.

A detailed examination of specific media is beyond the scope of this book, but each major medium has intrinsic qualities which take on new meaning when it is evaluated for corporate advertising use. Let's examine the various forms of print first.

Magazines

Magazines continue to hold the lead in corporate advertising expenditures. In fact, the most recent figures in the *Public Relations Journal*'s continuing study of corporate ad expenditures show that consumer magazines are increasing this lead. They showed a 16.2 percent increase in 1978 over 1977. Expenditures for network television increased by 10.4 percent in the same period. However, when you consider the relative cost of network TV versus many of the principal magazines which carry heavy corporate ad schedules, it seems inevitable that sometime in the 1980s network television will outstrip magazines as the principal dollar beneficiary of corporate advertising. If spot television is included, total TV is already the largest carrier of corporate messages.

While TV may dominate in dollars, a far larger number of corporate advertisers use magazines than use television. *Business Week,* which tracks corporate advertising very carefully, calculates that in 1977 a total of 637 print campaigns were carried by itself and five competitive magazines. (More than half of these campaigns, or 360, were carried in *Business Week* itself. The next nearest competitor, *Forbes,* carried 278 individual corporate advertising campaigns.) *Business Week* points out that in 1977 corporate advertisers purchased 6425 pages in Publishers Information Bureau–measured magazines. More than 60 percent (3951 pages) was in general business and news magazines.

Business magazines and newsweeklies have long dominated the corporate scene as appropriate showplaces. *Business Week, Time, Newsweek,* and *U.S. News & World Report* are the leaders. If you add to these *Forbes, Fortune,* and *Dun's Review,* the top management of American business has been covered, and then some. But business executives, if they are your target, have many other dimensions besides their business side. They may read *Audubon Magazine* because they are birders or *Natural History* because they are conservation and nature buffs. Or they may stay current in the sports world by reading *Sports Illustrated.* Perhaps as blacks, they follow *Ebony* and *Black Enterprise.* Or, if their education was in engineering, they may read *Scientific American* as a hobby outlet as much as for business reasons. The point is that magazines constitute a highly selective medium. If you can identify the characteristic of a target audience, you can probably find a selective magazine to reach it.

Editorial formats and magazine distribution methods select target audiences with great accuracy. Among the hundreds of magazines currently being published, you're virtually sure to find ones which will reach with efficiency just the audience you are looking for.

The popularity of magazines as a corporate vehicle is based on a number of other factors as well:

1. Magazines are available for any pocketbook. Many of the 637 corporate advertisers are small. An advertiser may select one or two relatively inexpensive publications and, given appropriate frequency, do an important job against a particular audience. As its advertising budget grows, it can extend its audience reach simply by adding other magazines. Or the advertiser may move up to a larger-circulation magazine which includes much of the audience of the smaller publication.

2. Magazines provide a natural environmental backdrop for corporate advertising. Editorially, many are in the corporation's corner.

3. Today magazines are very flexible in their ability to offer regional and demographic selectivity as well as copy split-run possibilities. The newsweeklies have carried this specificity to awesome extremes. *U.S. News & World Report* and *Newsweek,* in addition to offering geographic splits by region, state, or major city, individually or grouped in a variety of ways, offer special high-level executive editions which are sent only to subscribers who are in key top positions in American business. Magazines seem to have discovered a new version of the injunction to divide and conquer, each one providing a division of circulation unheard of only a few years ago. *Time,* for example, can offer 400 possible splits and combinations to advertisers making their buys. It has eight regional editions, 152 spot-market editions, state editions, and primary and supplemental spot markets — markets enough to satisfy even the most esoteric geographic interests. Of possibly greater importance to most corporate advertisers are *Time's* demographic editions. Among them is *Time* Z, or ZIP, which is the magazine's ultrahigh demographic edition that concentrates national circulation in the highest-income zip-code areas in the 158 major markets. Others are *Time* B, a national edition that is circulated to business executives; and *Time* T, a national edition that is directed to the top management of companies in the United States. Two other editions, usually of less interest to corporate advertisers, are *Time* D, which goes to doctors; and *Time* E, which stands for "elite," a combination of *Time* top management and *Time* doctors. Be prepared to spend ample time with each publication's representative in selecting the buy that best suits your demographic and regional needs. This procedure can take time and effort, but it can be worth it.

4. Magazines also offer a readership pace which is compatible with most corporate advertising. An extended-copy message, which corporate advertising frequently requires, fits well into most magazine formats. Time constraints are not a problem.

5. Magazines provide the possibility for color and imaginative space units. These units may range from Gulf & Western Industries' dramatic presentation of its entire annual report in *Time* in early 1979 to multiple fractional-page units depicting a variety of corporate activities grouped or scattered throughout a publication but unified visually.

6. Many magazines are extremely helpful to corporate advertisers. Their personnel understand corporate advertising's peculiar needs and provide much of the background and service information lacking in the other media. An example is the yearly list of corporate advertisers in the major news and business magazines that *Business Week* offers.

Newspapers

Daily and even weekly newspapers have a place in corporate advertising, although they are not usually considered a primary corporate advertising vehicle. Their principal strength is in their regional selectivity and in their short closing dates and news environment. Certain papers, of course, stand out as frequent carriers of corporate messages. *The New York Times* and the *Los Angeles Times,* with their strength in two major cities, and the *Washington Post,* with its influence on government leaders, come first to mind. On a national level, *The Wall Street Journal* is virtually in a class by itself as a major carrier of corporate messages.

Newspapers throughout the country can serve as valuable corporate vehicles for a number of reasons:

1. Newspapers have the highest flexibility, with short closing dates making possible tactical announcements that can be timed to match public relations activities and news breaks.

2. Newspapers may be used to augment national programs in certain key cities. Their regional flexibility is superior to that of most magazines.

3. Newspapers generally provide higher penetration of individual city areas, particularly for an upscale audience, than any other single medium. They can carry long, involved messages — a fact particularly useful in advocacy advertising geared to labor problems or other business and community exchanges which require long expository messages.

4. Newspapers provide a news and editorial environment which is usually very appropriate and compatible with corporate messages.

Outdoor Advertising

Although few people would consider outdoor advertising a principal medium for a corporate message, it is estimated that just under $1 million a year is placed by corporations with nonproduct or service-type announcements. The limitations are at once apparent. They include the required brevity of the message, the general nature of the audience, the unpopularity of the medium among many vocal environmental groups, and the relatively long production time required.

Before I'm struck down by the ghost of the old National Outdoor Advertising Bureau, let me say that outdoor advertising too is an underused medium for corporate messages, provided the messages are of a certain type. An example would be the imaginative use of outdoor ads to encourage the recycling of aluminum or glass containers. The message must be relatively simple and the target audience broad to make the buy practical, but the outdoor advantages are obvious. They include regional market selectivity where recycling plants are available and ability to provide a reminder message with great economy, to name two.

Direct Mail

One of the most rapidly expanding ad forms today is the disciplined area called "direct marketing." It encompasses mail-order and direct-response marketing activities utilizing virtually all media. The medium most readily associated with direct response is, of course, direct mail. Maligned as junk mail and frequently viewed as below the dignity of corporate programs, it nevertheless is a valuable component that should be given greater consideration in corporate communication planning if for no other reason than that most corporations are already engaged in at least one form of direct mail as it relates to their corporate communications. That, of course, is the mailing of annual reports and stockholder notices. Communication with stockholders is an excellent example of the kind of thing direct mail can do best. As a medium, it has the advantage of being able to pinpoint a target group with great precision. Depending on your ability to target a specific group and secure a suitable list, it can be an effective and efficient medium. Although the cost per delivered message is high, because direct mail is so selective and controllable, it is often very inexpensive.

Needless to say, it's essential to convey a feeling of good taste, corporate solidity, and even dignity when direct mail is used to be sure that the pieces are not considered junk mail. Sometimes this approach may lead to expensive pieces, but remember that a plain, well-written business letter may be exactly the right thing to send. Such a letter often conveys precisely the right tone of voice for a corporate message and still is not very expensive.

Lists of many groups of interest to corporate advertisers are available: brokers, stock analysts, editors, government officials, and business executives classified by various SIC listings. In addition to lists from Dun & Bradstreet and list specialists, the circulation lists of many trade magazines are available to advertisers for a fee. The opportunity for a coordinated magazine and direct-mail program can be attractive.

Life can be cozy

Gas saving device.

at 55°

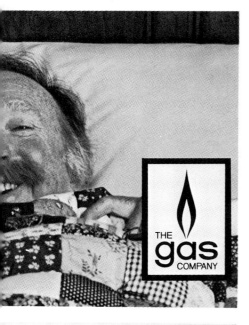

Two examples of the rare use of outdoor ads for corporate purposes: "Gas saving device" and "Life can be cozy at 55°." The Southern California Gas Company used outdoor posters from the late 1960s until 1972 in its traditional competitive battle with electricity. The marketing environment for the gas company changed dramatically in the early 1970s, when suppliers informed the company that future supplies of natural gas would not be available. As the actual delivery of gas to Southern California began to decline and the Arab oil embargo struck, the company was no longer in a position to market its product competitively. In fact, as it put it, it began its "de-marketing" program. No longer selling the product, it was selling energy conservation.

By 1977 these conditions had gelled to a point at which a special outdoor campaign seemed appropriate. The message was quite simple: use less gas. The means by which the public could achieve this saving were easy to convey: take shorter showers, don't waste hot water, lower thermostats, wear a sweater, turn down heat, etc. All these steps could be shown effectively in outdoor advertising. The problem was less one of education and more one of reminding the public of the gas-saving techniques that it already knew. The reminder, higher frequency, and the effectiveness of outdoor ads in the Southern California area made the choice of this medium a natural. The results were good as the conservation movement caught hold. Just as important to the client, the campaign was not a detriment to the helpful, professional image that the gas company had traditionally owned. There were virtually no complaints about the use of outdoor boards on environmental grounds, and the positive response to the advertising itself was quite high.

Designers of Destiny.
Vol. I

"A federal city magnificent enough
to grace a great nation."

That's what L'Enfant, a French engineer who served in the Continental Army during the Revolutionary War, proposed to create. George Washington, who had selected the site for the new Capital, appointed him to lay out the new town.

L'Enfant, one of the imaginative people in history whose objectives included planning for the future, applied the criteria of orderly growth to his plans.

Alas, when it came to implementing his plan—the actual construction—it was anything but orderly. Local landowners had agreed to sell the land for buildings for well below the market value, and to contribute the land needed for streets and avenues. That was before they saw the full sweep of L'Enfant's plans. These called for streets that were 110 feet wide, avenues that measured 160 feet across, and one grand 400-foot-wide avenue that was a mile long. The landowners balked.

Within a year, Washington was forced to dismiss L'Enfant. Shrunken plans went into effect, but they were never completed because…

CONGOLEUM

Charles Hanson of Hanson, Fassler, Gilliland, Inc., provided this capsule case history of a successful direct-mail program for Congoleum Corporation. The campaign won the Direct Mail Gold Echo Award for 1979 in the corporate category at the Direct Mail/ Marketing Association. As he describes it, the product being promoted was Congoleum Corporation itself, a diversified company with interests in floor covering, shipbuilding, and the automotive aftermarket field. The basic objective was to build a share of the minds of financial, governmental, and business leaders and to convince these leaders that Congoleum was preparing to prosper in the years ahead.

A customer list of 5,000 security analysts, banker, portfolio managers, investment counselors, business editors, writers, government officials, and key customers was developed name by name. This was the target market. Three mailings were made about 2 weeks apart in the spring of 1978. They were timed to correspond with the appearance of the company's annual report, calculated at a moment when interest in the company would be at its peak. No attempt was made to stimulate response through offers or even through reply cards because quality of the response was far more important than quantity. A buried offer was made in the covering letter of an unfolded paper printed version of the vellum insert in each piece. The cumulative response was 15 percent, exclusive of a number of telephone calls. Since that time the program has become ongoing with two other three-mailing sequences of a similar nature repeated in 1979. My thanks for this case history to the client, Ralph Rainor, vice president of Congoleum Corporation; the agency, Hanson, Fassler, Gilliland, Inc., in Northfield, Illinois; and the printer, S. D. Scott Printing Company, in New York.

Congoleum's criteria for corporate growth.

Business criteria:

1. Each operating unit must possess at least one of the following: technological advantage, proprietary product, market dominance, or high capital cost of entry—for a competitive advantage that enables it to enjoy a high return on capital employed.

2. Internal and external expansion must build on existing corporate strengths—and determined by an analysis of all aspects of the business to evaluate the strongest growth/opportunity areas.

3. Each operating unit must have management depth—to assure the long-term growth and stability desired by investors.

4. Each operating unit must participate in growing markets—to achieve shares of markets that will grow in the future.

5. Each operating unit must generate in excess of 15% of total corporate sales—to assure an efficient span of control by the executive management of the operating unit and to allow careful monitoring of all operations by top management of the Company.

6. Each operating unit must be national, or preferably, international in scope—to avoid the limitations of a regional economy, and to achieve stable earnings growth as well as longer product cycles.

7. The Company as a whole must achieve an overall stability in earnings growth—to serve the investor's best interests.

Excellence... since 1911! This Congoleum gold seal guarantee, as in this vintage Congoleum ad, has been symbolizing our promise of excellence since 1911.

Financial criteria:

1. Congoleum Corporation must achieve a 12% after-tax return on invested capital—to assure a healthy balance sheet and to position itself to take advantage of future opportunities.

2. Company must achieve a 13% annual growth in earnings—to protect the Company's capital base against continued inflation and, at the same time, attract investors.

3. Congoleum must generate a self-sustaining cash flow—to provide internally generated funds for expansion and maintain a strong balance sheet, thus avoiding dilution of shareholders' equity.

4. Congoleum's long-term debt must equal 30% of its total capital; total debt, including short-term debt, must not exceed 40% of its total capital—to avoid the risk associated with a continuing, highly leveraged position, and to be in a position, short-term, to take advantage of unexpected high-reward opportunities.

Congoleum

Kinder

"Trinity Harbor," a cushioned vinyl by Congoleum, turns the flooring into a room highlight.

The guided missile frigate, Oliver Hazard Perry, is the lead ship in what is expected to become the largest class of destroyer-type vessels in the modern Navy.

CHAPTER 15 MEDIA CONSIDERATIONS (BROADCAST)

Television

Just as product advertisers had discovered the magic that television brought to their advertising in the 1950s, so corporate advertisers began to discover television's force for themselves in the 1970s. A Television Bureau of Advertising workshop session on corporate advertising in 1976 saw blue-chip corporate advertiser after advertiser get up and testify to the effects they had seen from the switch to television as a major corporate medium. Union Carbide Corp., Manufacturers Hanover Trust Co., TRW, Textron, International Telephone and Telegraph Corporation, Rockwell International Corp., United States Steel Corp., Transamerica Corp., Occidental Life Insurance Co., and Trans International Airlines Corp. all gave their support to the medium. These were in addition to old-line TV corporate advertisers such as Mobil Corporation, Xerox Corp., and General Motors Corp.

Since 1971 television (spot and network combined) has accounted for more than half of all corporate expenditures according to one measurement. This growing acceptance of television as a corporate medium developed in the face of three formidable traditional obstacles. The first is television's cost in absolute dollars. For the advertising to be heard and seen on a national scale, the budget must be in seven figures. The next is TV's time limitation, a real handicap for many corporate messages, which frequently are more complex than product stories. Lastly, television's codes prohibit any form of issue or advocacy advertising. This third point has probably kept TV's corporate growth from being a complete runaway, perhaps to even double its current level. This is not an unreasonable estimate when you consider that the target audience for most issue advertising is the general American public. There are few demographic requirements beyond the ability and potential to speak up and perhaps to vote. TV's proven ability to move the general public on issues would have made it especially attractive for public causes.

Overcoming these three formidable drawbacks are a number of very positive advantages:

1. TV's well-recognized combination of sight and sound provides an in-home demonstration that comes closest to personal face-to-face communication.

2. TV provides immediacy. It can quickly generate reach and frequency at a rate unequaled by other media.

3. It's somewhat easier to capture and hold a viewer's attention than a reader's. As a more passive medium, TV makes possible the communication of thoughts and ideas which may not of themselves normally be of interest to viewers. In other words, while viewers might not go out of their way to read an ad on a particular subject, they might sit still and absorb some of the message from the screen.

4. A corporate advertiser using TV for the first time almost automatically gives the appearance of having stepped up to the level of an aggressive, on-the-move, ambitious company. The very fact of being able to afford the price of the medium is a subtle indication to the investment community that this is a prosperous corporation.

The television environment is certainly not an unmixed blessing. By and large, the clutter of low-end product commercials can detract from the setting for corporate commercials. The atmosphere provided by the late-night fringe and other cheaper time periods is inappropriate for most corporate messages. This circumstance is almost instinctively recognized by most corporate advertisers, who avoid such buys despite their attractive low cost and the efficiencies they sometimes provide in developing frequency of exposure, if not in total reach.

At the other end of the scale, there are shows which carry an aura of public concern, prestige, and good citizenship which, through association, enhance the corporate message. Prestigious regulars, such as ''Face the Nation,'' ''Meet the Press,'' and ''Issues and Answers'' are familiar examples — familiar, perhaps, more by reputation than by actual viewing habits. The unfortunate problem with shows of this type is their low audience ratings. Programs of the newer magazine-format type fare better in this regard. The well-established ''60 Minutes'' is a rare example of a show combining large upscale audiences and a prestigious environment. Unfor-

JUDY: I'm the school teacher who went on TV a few years ago to show you these binoculars.

To you, maybe they looked ugly -- but, with them, people who are blind at night...

from something called retinitis pigmentosa could see in the dark again.

But they _were_ bulky, and too expensive. Well, now there's a less expensive, pocket-size model.

And this, too, was created by the people of ITT...

with the Army Night Vision Laboratory and the Retinitis Pigmentosa Foundation.

In the dark, the world used to look like this to me.

But now — here's how it looks through one of these devices.

I can _see_ well enough to walk at night by myself...without anyone helping me.

ITT is selling this device at just what it costs to make. It's still not exactly cheap...

but, to someone who needs one, it could be priceless.

ITT

"Night Vision II"

ITT is a believer in coordinating print and television efforts to form a stronger message than either one would carry alone. This commercial complements and reinforces the print ad on a similar subject illustrated in Chapter 1.

DOYLE DANE BERNBACH INC., ADVERTISING, 437 MADISON AVENUE, NEW YORK, N.Y. 10022

CLIENT: GTE

PRODUCT: CORPORATE

TITLE: "FIBER OPTICS"

CODE NO: GTCP9471

LENGTH: 10 SECONDS

1. (OPEN ON WOMAN EXAMINING HAIR)

2. (SILENT)

3. (SHE LOOKS AT CAMERA) WOMAN: A new telephone cable fiber as thin as a human hair? Gee!

4. (DISSOLVE TO LOGO) ANNCR: (VO) No...GTE.

GTE

Somewhat unusual for its 10-second length, this is a shortened version of a 30-second corporate commercial. While it acts as a refresher and enhancer of the longer, fuller message, it also adds frequency of exposure at about half the cost of the 30-second commercial. This technique has been used increasingly in the face of increasing television rates. The television and print messages are coordinated as well.

tunately, all too often a large audience is achieved only with situation comedies and action shows, which often are coupled with some degree of sex or violence. This situation is of far greater concern to corporate advertisers, putting their corporations' reputation on the line through their sponsorship, than it is to product advertisers. The receipt of 100 negative letters regarding the sponsorship of a particular show might be an acceptable trade-off for audience goals and efficiencies for a product that's in a highly competitive battle with other heavy spenders in categories such as beer, analgesics, or soaps and cleansers. To a corporate advertiser, however, the same 100 letters would appear to be a hornet's nest. So regular large-audience shows suitable for corporate use can be difficult to come by.

Specials are an attractive vehicle for many corporate advertisers. Sponsorship or cosponsorship of a TV vehicle, especially one which has social merit, can provide a showplace. So a corporate advertiser can not only tell and retell the basic corporate message at each commercial break but go into a number of areas in some depth to give a more rounded view of the corporation as a whole. Specials may also be of the small-audience, prestigious type. Shows on science subjects, the arts, or social issues may require a relatively low dollar outlay, but their cost per thousand is likely to be high. Specials may range up to true spectaculars capable of delivering some of the largest audiences obtainable at an excellent cost per thousand.

With some specials there is an opportunity to develop a degree of sponsor identity. However, this is a declining programming philosophy that has largely disappeared from regular program sponsorship because of television's high cost. The "Bell Telephone Hour" and "Texaco Theatre" are simply budgetary dinosaurs. Even attempting to develop an identity with a series of related specials is a tremendously ambitious goal requiring large dollar commitments. Instead, there is a growing use of partial sponsorship and the acceptance of the fact of life that a show is merely a vehicle to reach a desired audience in a good environment rather than a corporate gift to the public which will be remembered and associated gratefully with the company by the audience. Once this fact has been accepted and programming, within the limits of good taste, is viewed simply as a means of attracting a specific type of audience, corporate advertisers suddenly have a far broader selection of programming from which to choose — programming with which they will not necessarily become associated but which will be surprisingly selective in view of the mass characteristics of television. Admittedly, preselecting programs is more difficult for the corporate advertiser trying to reach a select audience, but it can be done.

The greatest impediment is the difficulty in securing enough information on individual shows. It is virtually impossible to measure consistently and accurately the coverage of select upper-demographic viewers. The A.

TRW

"Earth Pictures"

For the ten years prior to 1974, TRW Inc. was exclusively a print advertiser. That year a new identity program using television and radio was begun in ten major markets where approximately half of all stockholders of common stocks are concentrated. Steven N. Bowen, TRW's director of corporate advertising and identity, summed up the need for the program as a recognition that the company had an identity void, its euphemism for "Nobody hates you. Nobody loves you. Nobody knows you." Its goal was to reach the shakers and movers of the financial community and acquaint them with TRW. A believer in research, TRW surveyed both the broadcast markets and a sampling of nonbroadcast markets. The view of TRW as an attractive personal investment increased to more than 60 percent from roughly 20 percent in September 1974. Meanwhile, in the control markets (those not carrying TRW commercials) the company's image remained virtually unchanged. Improvement has been seen in TRW's perception as a producer of high-quality products and a company with growth potential and technical capability.

By concentrating its broadcast activities in those key market areas, TRW achieved measurable improvement in a relatively short time. This is a good example of the use of spot TV'S and radio's local flexibility where a target audience can be isolated.

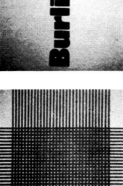

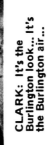

1. CLARK: It's the Burlington look.... It's the Burlington air...

2. ANNCR: (VO) Burlington house for carpets

3. for rugs, for lamps, for sheets

4. Burlington house ... all through the house.

BURLINGTON INDUSTRIES

In the 1960s, Burlington was primarily an ingredients manufacturer of textiles. The company wished to broaden its business to branded finished goods, such as Burlington hosiery, house draperies, carpets, etc. It knew that its awareness level among the general public was very low and that its name was more apt to bring to mind a railroad company than a firm in the textile business. Burlington began a long-term corporate campaign not only to improve the awareness level but to develop a strong association with textiles. This bold symbol, a stylized animation of the weaving process, came to life in television and served Burlington well to establish its reputation as a textile company. People's awareness of the company more than doubled and served as the base for the introduction of many new products in the housewares and domestic field.

C. Nielsen Company, sole supplier of audience data for individual programs, provides data for a limited number of broad demographic categories and several upper groups. Its method of data collection does not permit an accurate projection of very small groups. Nor is there sufficient interest by enough advertisers today in this form of data to justify financially Nielsen's providing it.

The A. C. Nielsen Company is a constant source of television data, but it is necessary to fit the corporate target audience into some kind of standard category in order to evaluate the merits and achievements of particular programs. There are available methods that provide indicators of upper-demographic viewing habits which can be used to increase the reliability of selecting programs with high-demographic audience appeal. The high cost of television makes accurate planning and execution in this area vital. As the size of the intended target audience diminishes, the importance of accurately defining this audience increases.

Syndicated research services such as TGI offer a partial solution to the problem of defining a target audience. While they are most commonly used to evaluate magazine audiences and to provide product consumption data, they also offer information on the television viewing habits and demographic characteristics of the American public. If you couple this information with computer access to the raw data, you can cross-reference areas of interest. This procedure can provide a good level of flexibility in answering specific questions.

The data can be broken down in far greater detail than regular demographic information. It's possible to tell if viewers are employed, whether they are employed by a business firm or in government, in education, in private practice, or in their own business, or whether they operate a farm. Also available are the type of business and an indication of the size of the firm. Both the household income and the respondents' income form part of the data. Of particular interest to the corporate advertiser are the activist habits of the audiences. They are interviewed to determine if they have ever

- Written to the editor of a magazine or newspaper.
- Written to or telephoned a radio or television station.
- Written to an elected official about some matter of public business.
- Addressed a public meeting.
- Taken an active part in some local civic issue.
- Actively worked for a political party or candidate.
- Engaged in fund raising.
- Belonged to any school or college board.
- Belonged to a hospital board.
- Belonged to a church board.

- Belonged to a business club.
- Belonged to a fraternal order.
- Belonged to a religious club.
- Belonged to a civic club.
- And so on.

It's also possible to learn whether the audience owns savings bonds, other governmental bonds, city or state bonds, shares of mutual funds, corporate bonds, and common or preferred stock in the company they work for or in other companies. You can add information on the number of stock transactions a given audience has engaged in during the past year and the current approximate market value of the stocks, which gives you a fair picture of its financial interests.

Caution must be observed in using such data for making specific decisions and recommendations. Remember that the data tend to be qualitative or indicative rather than quantitative like Nielsen's data. As questions become more specific or are applied to smaller and smaller groups of people, the number of responses decreases and the likelihood of statistical error rises. The key to using such data centers on questions that indicate rather than those that are overly specific; the target audience is then built selectively until it is at a level of known statistical reliability. The results of such studies are generally expressed in an index showing the target audience you have selected compared with ``all adult viewers.'' This is done to compare a variety of types of programming options. As a simple illustration using simple demographics, a typical target audience group for corporate advertising is frequently described as being upper-income, professional-managerial, college-educated, and consisting of heads of households with investments. Even though members of such an upscale group are relatively lighter viewers of television, they are selective in their watching and are reachable through such vehicles as late news and sports. Certain sports such as golf or tennis do better than, say, bowling in terms of the quality of audience. Golf will tend to attract higher-income viewers, while tennis will give a better index of the younger male audience. Within a single sport, such as basketball, college games will generally attract better-educated viewers. For such an audience, horse racing's major events generally show up very well while boxing does not. These generalities are not to be taken as recommendations: they are just examples of the kind of data which you can develop to meet your own specific target-audience characteristics.

Radio

Radio has not begun to reach its potential as a corporate advertising medium. When you consider that more than 72 million households have

230

OGILVY & MATHER INC.

2 EAST 48 STREET, NEW YORK 10017
MURRAY HILL 8-8100

Client: **SHELL OIL COMPANY**
Product: **CORPORATE**
Title: **"55/70"**
Commercial No.: **SECO 9043**
Date Approved: **6/19/79**

1. ANSWER:MAN: (OC) Can driving the speed limit really save gas? Watch!

2. Two cars. Same model. Both with two gallons of gas.

3. ANSWER MAN: (VO) One goes 70 miles an hour,

4. the other 55.

5. The faster car is out of gas.

6. The slower car goes one lap...

7. ... two laps...

8. ... three laps more. 25% better mileage.

9. ANSWER MAN: (OC) Learn how you can get the most out of gasoline in The Gasoline Book.

10. Free from Shell.

11. (SFX): Breakthrough.

12. Come to Shell for answers.

SHELL OIL COMPANY

Storyboard "55/70"

The corporate program for Shell Oil has strong public service overtones, building positive associations for an advertiser in a difficult industry today.

CORPORATE ADVERTISING: 1979-1980
TITLE: "GOTT"
RELEASE DATE: AUGUST 27, 1979

United States Steel

1. This ship is longer than the largest ocean liner.

2. It's U.S. Steel's new ore carrier, the Edwin H. Gott.

3. It transports iron ore.

4. ...to our steelmaking plants on the Great Lakes.

5. Our facilities require huge amounts of ore

6. ...And this ship will carry three million tons a year.

7. This is a major investment.

8. ...but we think of it as a thousand-foot vote of confidence in our future.

9. Confidence. At United States Steel, it's one of our strengths.

UNITED STATES STEEL CORP.

"Gott"

United States Steel uses spot television in combination with its print program. Harold O. Drosethes, director of advertising and sales promotion, states that its objective has been to emphasize to audiences of importance the "many strengths of United States Steel." Its messages have generally stressed United States Steel's growth in chemicals, its self-reliance in energy and mineral resources, its improved steelmaking technology, its research capabilities, and some of the achievements of its various divisions.

an average of six radios each (including car radios) and that there are 7626 radio stations in the United States, the fact that only about $1.2 million was spent for corporate messages on radio in 1978 is astounding. According to the *Public Relations Journal*, however, that is the correct figure, and it was down from $2.9 million in 1977. It would be a pity if this decline were part of a trend.

Nevertheless, with few exceptions, it's difficult to recall many corporate advertisers who have used much radio in recent years. The reason for this situation can only be surmised. Perhaps it is that the audience is so fractional that multiple-station buys are required to achieve adequate penetration. Or radio may not suit most corporate messages. It is true that radio is a particularly demanding medium for which to create. It requires an all-out effort to gain attention.

Radio's role as a background sound in the automobile and the home is commonplace. But while a partially heard and remembered jingle or product reminder message may afford adequate exposure for some products, it is certainly insufficient for the full attention required for most corporate stories. If we assume that this obstacle can be overcome creatively, there are a number of very good reasons for radio's inclusion in the corporate schedule:

1. Merely because it has been used so little for corporate messages, radio can make advertisers stand out as innovative and imaginative in their approach to communications, a fact that in and of itself can be important to many financial analysts.

2. Geographically, radio is highly flexible. It can give added weight in key markets or regions when this is desirable.

3. Radio's closing dates are comfortable. An ongoing buy can be interrupted quickly and easily with new copy for news breaks.

4. Production costs for the medium are relatively low. In certain cases, live announcers reading copy are the ideal device, but even full-production-value tapes cost only one-tenth as much as TV commercials.

If objectives are national, radio requires the use of a great number of stations to reach a large enough proportion of the general population to be meaningful. But when you are after a select audience, the very fractional nature of radio provides a selectivity of audience types that can be used to advantage to reach the varied targets typically sought in corporate campaigns.

First to come to mind is the traditional driving time, a standby to reach business people either in their cars in the morning or evening or early in the morning before they leave for work. Certain evening music shows can also have a high attraction for extremely loyal audiences that appreciate uninterrupted evening music. Good music has a special affinity to the upscale audience, not just to older people but increasingly to younger adults. Special sports and business news programs can also be useful vehicles.

Radio can be used tactically much as newspapers are used for local company or plant relations within a given community. Announcements concerning plant closings and unusual weather conditions or strikes can be handled with dispatch through this medium. A local events show can be an ideal medium for small or suburban towns, particularly if you desire a strong community presence for your local plant or branch office.

CHAPTER 16 DON'T BOTHER TO MAKE THESE MISTAKES

They've been made. Although you are going to make mistakes in developing any corporate program, you might as well be original and make new ones. Here are some mistakes you can avoid. A few are very obvious, but others may surprise you.

Mistake 1: Let Your Corporate Advertising and Product Advertising Each Stand on Its Own Feet Now there certainly can't be anything wrong with that recommendation. Certainly each type of advertising has its own objectives, and in companies in which product advertising is addressed to consumers for consumer products, separate treatments may well be the best course to follow. But if yours is an industrial company, there had better be someone in authority pulling the two programs together so that they do not work at cross-purposes. The major concern here is to be sure that both the corporate and the product advertising programs have a tone of voice sufficiently similar to appear to be coming from the same company. If your corporate advertising is attempting to convey an image of an aggressive, young growth company, the product advertising should do no less. Keep in mind that much industrial advertising is addressed to the same audience. Business executives form the same target but wear different hats when they read your corporate ads. The ads need not have a campaign look, but they should be compatible and whenever possible should provide a strong logo and name treatment. This approach will help both the products and the corporation.

Mistake 2: Do It Yourself   Set up an in-house facility to handle the corporate program on your own. Possibly, you've got a good writer in the public affairs department. Assign him or her to it. After all, who knows your company better than yourself? You don't want outsiders handling program for you.

Sometimes this approach works, but success is very, very rare. In-house agencies suffer from two major problems. The first is attracting, holding, and continuing to stimulate good talent, especially creative talent. After all, what writer or art director doesn't benefit from the stimulation of working on a variety of products and services and wouldn't prefer to take his or her chances in the riskier but more exciting agency field? Even more important in the case of corporate advertising is a house agency's lack of objectivity. A look at the sampling of corporate ads displayed in this book will illustrate how widespread the problem of ego-centered corporate advertising is. While the development of a corporate advertising program requires a good depth of knowledge of the company, it also requires an impartial viewpoint to sort this information and position it into an attractive package for the public.

If a move to in-house preparation is considered for economic reasons, make sure that a complete and objective cost analysis is carried out first. In-house advertising can be a great area for empire building, and empires cost a lot of money. The effort-income ratio in the preparation of corporate ad programs is usually relatively high. Even well-run agencies have difficulty in making a profit on the conventional 15 percent of most average-size corporate programs without a fee.

Mistake 3: Assign a Team of Hot Young Turks to the Account   You get a nice new account—not very large, but important and prestigious. The subject matter is dry. Maybe what it needs is an aggressive, young creative team to get into it. The team members will make a name for themselves. Let them work with the new M.B.A. account executive who has a good understanding of business and finance.

Boy, are you in trouble! (Nothing against the young, mind you. I enjoyed youth myself once.) But if there's any area where a few gray hairs or at least some very mature judgments matter, it's in the corporate area.

The first problem with this setup is that the agency team will, in all likelihood, be working with the older executives and principals of the client. There are some 35-year-old chief executive officers, but the median age is apt to be in the fifties. While there are often age gaps in client-agency relations, there is some merit in contemporaries teaming up to solve problems. They bring with them common knowledge in terminology and an easier compatibility. Far more important is the sensitivity which a mature team can bring to an understanding of the real corporation that exists behind the paper organization charts—the dynamics that form the corporation's true personality. Lastly, corporate advertising is rarely a place for the downright radical and brash. A young team is far more likely to come up with something that will look good in its book but not in the company boardroom.

Mistake 4: Move Immediately to Cancel Any Ads or Entire Programs That Draw Fire from Irate Customers, the Public, or the Press After all, if a campaign can't do anything else, at least it shouldn't get you into trouble. Right?

Wrong, on two counts. First, it's very unusual for any really outstanding advertising not to contain some seed of controversy. If the ad doesn't stir the emotions in some way, it's not doing its job. Ads that fail to stir emotions are usually flat and bland, and when you stir some emotions, you're going to get some letters. It doesn't take many letters to seem like a lot. If you sit at a desk where these letters come in, you know that a handful may resemble an avalanche. Maybe a dozen have been received. If those letters should go to particularly sensitive persons in a division or subsidiary not accustomed to this kind of mail, they will feel as though they are being flooded with thousands of letters. Look into the matter, and read the letters carefully. They certainly should not be ignored, but you will find that many are either unreasonable or unrealistic. Some, in fact, will be downright insane, perhaps even written in crayon.

Other letters, and these are usually very well written, may run to identical patterns, even using the same sentence structure. These probably won't give you many details about your supposed transgression but will instead express very strong views on some issue or subject, most notably objecting to advertising support of certain magazines or TV programming. In such cases you are probably dealing with an organized letter-writing campaign of some nature, undertaken by a group whose members have been prompted to act. Depending on the group and the issue, you may or may not wish to respond.

Many letters will be from lonely people whose real wish is just to communicate to someone on something. The issue is almost secondary.

One former client, a very sensitive, outgoing person, used to respond in a very personal and even emotional way to much of this correspondence. After a while, letter answering became his major morning activity. He discovered that he was writing to the same people again and again, in many cases carrying on extended dialogues on various subjects about policies, products, or social issues. Eventually he had to call a halt. As he said, "There's just no way to keep up with all those pen pals," which is exactly what many of them had become.

This is not to say that letters should be ignored. They must be read and evaluated on their own merits, but some of them need not be answered. Sometimes, however, letters will uncover flaws in an ad program; then the only response is to hold everything. Thank the writers and start over.

Mistake 5: Enlarge the Scope of the Corporate Communications Program   Do this through additional objectives or through special additional subprograms directed to target audiences in critical geographic regions or industry categories. Find the money by making adjustments in the basic program.

There is nothing wrong with expanding objectives or audiences, but the budget must be expanded along with the added responsibility or someone will be disappointed. It's generally far better to tune back objectives to meet a budget realistically than to try to do a great many different things with an inadequate appropriation. Remember one other thing about advertising appropriations: until someone finds a way of bringing inflation to a halt, you will be working with less money every year if all you do is hold the budget at last year's level. At the present pace of inflation we are estimating a 10 percent increase just to stay even in our 5-year planning, and that estimate may be low. The increase can be even higher in certain media. Have your agency do a 5- or 10-year history of your company's expenditures. Have it also factor in what inflation has done to diminish this budget in comparison with your base year. You will be startled to see how quickly you can fall behind and how much money it takes to catch up.

Mistake 6: Feature the CEO as Spokesperson in the Campaign   Actually this sometimes works very well, but most often it's a mistake for three reasons. First, creative work is limited to a setting, a style, and a tone that usually are very inhibiting. This approach can preclude happier, brighter situations which might be far more appropriate to the subject. Rather limiting, too, can be the personality and character of the CEO. Second, unless you are blessed with a corporate head who doubles as an actor, you must certainly keep the CEO out of commercials (talk about limiting!). The third reason for this being a mistake is difficulty in getting ads approved. The difficulty is not necessarily with the CEO, although that can be a problem, but rather with the engineer, lawyer, chemist, scientist, or sales manager — with anyone involved in approving the facts and details of the ads themselves. You may have gotten the original information on a new project from an engineer who has been happy to give you all the facts and is, in fact, flattered that his or her project can be the subject of an ad. Later, when you return to the same authority for final approval, you may discover that your authority has now become very coy about signing off on the ad. There's something about seeing his or her project discussed in an ad signed by the CEO that makes them wonder whether everything they've told you is as accurate as it might be. Too frequently, the result is long delays in approval as well as endless revisions.

Mistake 7: "We Ran the Ad Once, So We Need a New One"   Here's an area in which the corporate ego can lead to a poor decision. It is easy to get so deeply involved with an ad that when it is finally produced and run once, you feel as if the whole world has read it and knows every line. Nothing could be further from the truth. There is a very real need to repeat corporate ads more often than they are usually repeated. The product people know this very well. It is not unusual to see product ads run for a number of years. Commercials especially show a very high level of repetition before a wear-out factor enters in. Corporate management seems to tire of a corporate message very quickly, however, and so it is not unusual to see an ad run once in a number of magazines and then be dropped as the company goes on to something else.

Industrial advertising is somewhat better than corporate advertising in its ability to stick with an ad and repeat it. This commonsense approach, which reduces production costs and steps up efficiency, has been championed by *Business Week* for a number of years. The magazine has now completed four studies conducted in different ways by separate research organizations. The results of all the studies are remarkably consistent. They say: "It pays to repeat." While the studies were conducted with ads in both the corporate and the industrial categories, there is no reason to believe that corporate advertising would differ to any great extent in maintaining readership and interest through a number of insertions. The possible exception would be ads that are of immediate news interest and are keyed to fast-moving national events. Such subject matter could well dictate a short life for a given advertisement. A full copy of these research findings is available from *Business Week* or McGraw-Hill, Inc., under the title "How Repeat Advertisements Affect Readership." The basic conclusion is that an ad may be repeated at least four times before any appreciable change in noting or reading, one way or the other, is shown.

Mistake 8: Never Make a Change in Your Tracking Study

Certainly you need consistency in sampling techniques and questioning procedure. But there may be changes in data which you may not remember to allow for in subsequent studies. One example is your target audience. If you're still sampling $15,000-plus-a-year households as upscale, better look again. Inflation has changed your sample. Or your audience objective may have changed too. Perhaps a media shift has been made to put greater emphasis on a male or a female audience, and the sample selection has neglected to allow for this shift. A good rule to follow is this: whenever your objectives change, recheck all questions and sampling procedures for your tracking studies.

Mistake 9: You Have a Good Ad Manager, So Turn Your New Corporate Campaign Project Over to Him; Give Him Plenty of Time and Leave Him Alone to Come Up with a Way to Go

That sounds logical, but the mistake lies in leaving the manager alone. He needs all the attention the CEO can afford to give him, with time for discussion and meetings to determine what the corporate mission is and what the direction of the company should be. Corporate campaigns don't work up from the bottom; they come down from the top. Don't rely merely on input from middle management or division heads. You need their information, but the overall direction must come from the top.

Mistake 10: A New Year, a New Campaign Corporate advertising is frequently a slow starter. A soundly based campaign should have a life of several years. Perhaps with modifications and planned growth it can last for a decade or more. There is nothing magic about a 12-month calendar. January 1 does not have to usher in twelve new layouts. When a campaign is right, it can run on and on. When it is time for a change, the right time is now. Don't wait until the end of the year.

Mistake 11: You Know What You Want to Do, and You Know What You Want to Accomplish; So Go Ahead and Do It. What Are Tests Going to Show? They'll Just Slow You Down and Cost Money Sometimes you may have to adopt quick stopgap measures for a crisis situation, but your basic ongoing corporate program needs all the help it can get from all the information you can get.

Mistake 12: Surprise Your Employees with Your New Campaign. Let Them See It as the Rest of the Public Does When They Get to Open Their Magazines or When They Sit in Front of Their TV Sets What a terrible way to waste a good program! Merchandise the program to your people. It is a great chance for them to be on the inside track and be able to turn to their families and say, ''Yeah, I saw that commercial last week when they showed it to us at the plant.'' Merchandise the program to your employees just as you would product advertising to the trade. In fact, the ad campaign may be the best view of the company your employees will ever get. They may see the company as a whole and not just as the part they work in.

Mistake 13: Try the Program with a Little Money First; if It Seems to Work, Increase the Budget There is such a thing as an audible level. If you haven't the budget to reach this level with your audience, don't bother trying. A limited budget may limit your objectives or your target audience. But to the group you're addressing, do the job right.

Mistake 14: Let Your Agency Decide Your Corporate Mission That mistake is not even worth commenting on, but it happens all too often.

Mistake 15: Use Your Corporate Budget as a Dole. Run Some Special Supportive Ads Whenever a Division is in Trouble. A Little of the Budget Will Never Be Missed Realistically this may happen, but call the procedure what it is, or the corporate campaign will someday be damned for failing to deliver its objectives.

Mistake 16: Judge Your Results Strictly against the Awareness and Attitudes of Comparable Companies. In Effect, Compare Yourselves with Your Competition This can be very helpful. It certainly gives you a clue as to whether the first numbers in the bench-mark study are generally good or generally poor. The problem is: what is a comparable company? It's easy to find competitive, comparable products: a soap versus a soap, a toothpaste versus a toothpaste. But try comparing one conglomerate with another. Even if you can find relatively comparable companies of about the same size, more or less in the same industry, there will be enough substantial differences in the makeup of the corporations to account for wide variances in awareness and attitudes. For instance, one company may have a long list of consumer products carrying the corporate name. The advertising in back of these products is working toward the corporate image. Another company may also have consumer products, but these may be sold under separate brand names not readily associated with the parent company. Or one company may be a long-standing member of the community, while another may be a newcomer. In the first case, you'll have a solid, slow-moving base from which a corporate campaign will seem to move painfully slowly. In the case of the new company starting from near zero, the early recognition growth may seem meteoric by comparison.

Mistake 17: Leverage Advertising with the Media to Secure Editorial Support That's really a polite way of saying, "Use ads as a payoff to the media for running your public relations releases and giving you favorable editorial treatment." Discretion and good sense would probably dictate leaving this mistake out of the book entirely. Everyone knows that this practice is dishonest and is not used by reputable media or advertisers, or at least not by anybody *we* all know. On the other hand, just in case this topic needs airing, there are some very practical reasons for not engaging in this kind of media placement, reasons that go beyond the question of ethics and honesty. The overall disadvantages far outweigh any short-term tactical gains in individual "editorial opportunities."

Ad agencies are usually on the side of the angels in such cases. They hate to see media selections made for them by anybody, particularly choices which are contrary to normal media values. It's in their interest to fight this sort of thing because they will eventually have to account for the effectiveness of the campaign, including the media buy. Agencies generally know that a budget parceled out in small pieces, with an ad here and an ad there in different publications in return for editorial favors, adds up to a terrible waste. Publications that resort to this sort of thing are usually the weaker ones that find it a way to stay in business. Ergo, they're not going to perform as the best of advertising vehicles.

The *advertiser,* of course, takes a large risk with both the company's reputation and his or her own by adopting this kind of policy. The media world is small, and other people's morals are a great subject for gossip. The temptation for the advertiser is usually disguised with the rather honest feeling of a sense of obligation; or, particularly in local situations, there may be a feeling that support should be given to newspapers and stations which have been favorably disposed in their editorial handling of the company and its actions. Equally common is a desire to withhold ads from local media which may disagree editorially with a local company. Human reactions are too strong not to want to reward friends and punish enemies.

This reward-and-punish game is played by companies in local areas in which they have a strong community involvement, as utilities do. One way in which an advertiser can avoid playing favorites is to use virtually all the media in an area, giving a little bit to each with a more or less equal hand. This procedure can lead to frightful media buying as judged by advertising standards. As long as the public relations director is directly responsible for media choice, there is no way around this dilemma. The director will be faced with a constant series of Solomon-like decisions. The best solution may very well be to cop out, that is, to relegate media selection to the ad director or the agency which is charged with using the best media judgment and ignoring the possible public relations outcome. The director, of course, can still reserve his or her prerogatives and intervene in what are deemed the more glittering inequities.

The *media,* by and large, are to be congratulated for the tremendous job they do in isolating editorial activities from the advertising sales function. The integrity of the press is sacred to reporters and editors alike. Sales representatives who broadly hint at the consequences of nonsupport are usually bluffing. The problem sometimes arises at the upper levels, particularly in small operations when an economic pinch is being felt. But virtually all publishers recognize that they are on a downward spiral when their editorial content goes downhill with their readers and that selling out the integrity of their editors is probably the fastest way down.

An area to watch for abuse in the future is the magazine field. Publications have discovered the economics of building special-interest sections on specific subjects. These special-emphasis sections are frequently updates of the state of the art in various fields of interest to their regular readers, such as electronics, chemicals, materials, or classes of consumer products such as automobiles, stereo equipment, or even lawn mowers. The information for these sections has to come largely from the manufacturers. This may involve extensive interviewing of company personnel in laboratories, marketing, sales, or long-range planning, people who are normally far removed from the advertising scene. In their efforts to see that their company's products and services are given representation in the special section, the employees are frequently the first to suggest that a company run ads in the special section. This can put pressure on a corporate ad manager. Even more pressure results when these special ``advertorial'' sections are put together by industry specialists who may lack reporters' traditions of editorial independence. They may, on occasion, encourage a fear that the company will not be adequately represented if an ad is not forthcoming. Magazines that lose control of these special editorial services do themselves a disservice for their regular issues. Incidentally, this type of pressure is particularly troublesome to corporate advertising because the special issues, while possibly of great value for product and service advertising, are generally less attractive in meeting corporate objectives. This is true because the regular reader of the regular issue is sought rather than the specialist in a particular subject and the archival attractions of the insert are small.

Mistake 18: If You're an Industrial Agency, Treat Your Client's Corporate Advertising Like a Consumer Account If you're a large consumer agency, treat your client's corporate program as though it were just another trade campaign. By now you must know that corporate advertising is neither like a regular consumer program nor like a trade or industrial ad program. It's something else; it's something special. It's an extension of the corporation's personality, the business itself, not just one of its products. And it's an opportunity for everyone involved. For the company, it's a chance to get a dollar-for-dollar return equal to or better than that of product advertising. For account people, it's a chance to understand a client's business better and to work with the client at a level rarely enjoyed on product campaigns. For the copywriter, it's a challenge, but more than that, it's an opportunity for really fine creative writing. Generally, audiences are above average in intelligence, and the subject matter is mature. Honesty and candor are particularly effective. In fact, corporate advertising should be, and sometimes is, the area for some of the best writing in America today.

These are samples of some of the mistakes which seem to be made again and again by corporate advertisers, experienced companies as well as companies embarking for the first time on corporate ad programs. There are many more areas of error, but you're going to have to find them for yourself.

Good luck in the 1980s.

INDEX